Also by Randy Cohen

Diary of a Flying Man
Modest Proposals

PUBLISHED BY DOUBLEDAY
a division of Random House, Inc.
1540 Broadway, New York, New York 10036

DOUBLEDAY and the portrayal of an anchor with a dolphin are
trademarks of Doubleday, a division of Random House, Inc.

Much of this material appeared, in a slightly different form,
in the *New York Times Magazine.* "The Ethicist" and the l'il ethicist
cartoon figure are trademarks of The New York Times Company,
and are used with its permission.

Book design by Gretchen Achilles

Library of Congress Cataloging-in-Publication Data

Cohen, Randy.
The good, the bad & the difference: how to tell right from
wrong in everyday situations / Randy Cohen.
p.   cm.
1. Ethical problems.   2. Applied ethics.   I. Title: The good,
the bad and the difference.   II. Title.
BJ1031 .C57 2002
170—dc21   2001042084

ISBN 0-385-50273-7

April 2002

3   5   7   9   10   8   6   4   2

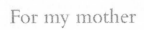
For my mother

CONTENTS

I wish the idea for an ethics column had been mine, but it wasn't, and to claim credit for it would set an odd tone for a book about ethics. The editors of the *New York Times Magazine* conceived the column and refined its format. And it is to them that I am most grateful.

Since the column began, I've worked closely with three editors, Ariel Kaminer, Hugo Lindgren, and Dean Robinson. Each has improved the column, and each, from time to time, has saved me from making a monkey out of myself. If, on occasion, I've still made a monkey out of myself, it was my own doing and not the fault of these excellent colleagues.

I particularly wish to thank Adam Moss, the magazine's head editor, for the opportunity to write the column, for the ideas he brought to it, and for his support and encouragement even when I wrote things that might have raised an eyebrow, and the blood pressure, of a less patient man.

I also received assistance from people outside the magazine. When a question pivots on a conflict between a personal belief and an official stricture, perhaps a matter of medical or legal ethics or religious precept, I must establish what the rule actually is. That's when I turn to various experts—a medical ethicist at the AMA, an orthodox rabbi, a lawyer in the state Attorney General's office. More people than I can name here have been generous with their time and knowledge. I can't imagine wandering into a moral thicket without such reliable guides.

I'd also like to acknowledge Frank Lynch, whose adroitly organized Samuel Johnson Web site <*http://www.samueljohnson.com/*> is a great place to track down an elusive bit of wisdom from the Great Cham. And I count myself lucky to work with my agent, David McCormick, who helped shape not just the sale but the book itself.

ACKNOWLEDGMENTS

Why Ethics, Why Now?

He that is most deficient in the duties of life makes some atonement for his faults if he warns others against his own failings, and hinders, by the salubrity of his admonitions, the contagion of his example.

SAMUEL JOHNSON: *RAMBLER* #14 (MAY 5, 1750)

Why Ethics, Why Me?

I am an accidental ethicist.

I do not have a doctorate in philosophy. I've not taught ethics at any university. I have no ethicist credentials. I am a writer whose essays and fiction have appeared in many magazines and several books. I've written for *Late Night with David Letterman* and other television shows. I studied music in college, attending graduate school as a composition student, a field for which I am singularly unsuited.

None of this deterred the editors of the *New York Times Magazine,* who, early in 1999, asked if I'd like to discuss a weekly feature to be called "The Ethicist." Note that this is the title of the column, not the profession of its author. The idea for the column, now carried by many newspapers, as "Everyday Ethics" originated at the magazine. I believe that when the editors were planning it, they discussed several people who might write it, some of whom were true professionals, university professors mostly. As I understand it, they concluded that, in a democracy, ethics ought not be a specialized field, but should comprise a set of questions every ordinary citizen can—must—address. I think I met their definition of an "ordinary citizen," and one who might make the discussion illuminating, the analysis thoughtful, and the prose lively. At least, that's what I try to do, and if I can present the questions in a way that lets the reader see them afresh, I'm pleased. (And I take some comfort in reminding myself that *Cat Fancy* magazine is not written by a cat.)

Several candidates were invited to audition for the job. We were each given the same three letters to respond to. Here is the first test letter:

> As I was dropping a memo on a colleague's desk, I glanced—inadvertently, I promise—at her computer screen and saw my name. She had written an e-mail to our boss deftly attributing the failure of a recent project to me. That was a rash overstatement, but how can I defend myself without acknowledging my inadvertent e-mail read?

It's a cunning problem, raising issues of privacy, deceit, and self-interest, all faced by a person who'd already acted imperfectly. I found it intriguing to try to devise an answer that could balance conflicting ethical principles and personal desires. (To see my reply, go to page 72.)

I would, of course, feel better about the job if I had a Ph.D. (And a nicer apartment. And one of those neat little sports cars. It may not be directly related to the work itself, but it couldn't hurt.) It is always better to know more. However, one function of such credentials is to help a prospective employer predict how well one will do in the job, much as the SATs are meant to assist college admissions officers by predicting how well a student will perform freshman year. Once one has been on the job for a couple of years, such credentials may no longer be germane. In fact, looked at with perhaps excessive generosity, there is an unexpected advantage to my lack of formal training. The reader must consider not my credentials but my argument, and be persuaded—or unpersuaded—by that. I can make no appeal to my own authority.

It is also true that ethics is not physics. While the latter has a body of knowledge and a methodology accepted by all practitioners, the former does not. Every physicist must know mathematics, general science, and the history of his own field. Every physicist must practice the scientific method. However, any discussion of ethics will come down to the values of the writer and how clearly and persuasively he can articulate those values and apply them to the particular scenario under discussion.

That is to say, ethics is an ideal subject for the general reader and the general writer, and perhaps that is what the *Times* editors concluded when assigning me the column.

Or perhaps there was some kind of clerical error.

Or perhaps writing for David Letterman is not such unlikely training for writing about ethics as it might first appear. A case could be made that *Late Night* was an essentially moral enterprise, one that encouraged its writers to subject their work to ethical scrutiny.

To begin with, *Late Night* was based on a coherent thesis: Your childhood has been bought and sold for profit, and as a consequence you grew up in a world of witless pop-culture junk. If the show was about anything, it was a critique of that culture, especially television. The show was built around a sense of right and wrong, and its mission was to articulate the difference between the two (sometimes through the use of glamorous actresses and trained circus animals).

This task was to be undertaken in honorable ways, governed by implicit guidelines for the writers. Most comedy attacks; the important question is whom do you attack and why? Dave intended the show to assail the wicked and powerful, not bully their victims. It was his policy that we attack someone only for what he does (e.g., his inept acting), not for what he is (a guy with a big hideous nose). That is, we are free to attack that which is volitional but not those things over which a person has no control.

If Dave, and the show, sometimes fell short, well, so do we all, but his moral intent was always present. Dave lived in a moral universe. He saw the show, and its staff, as subject to moral scrutiny. And while I can't really know the source of his values—he was my boss, not my pal—it seemed that he would have felt ashamed to do anything that would have disappointed his mother. Like most of us, he tried to live the values on which he was raised.

And so perhaps I am, despite myself, a highly trained, albeit inadvertent, ethicist, lucky enough to have an opportunity to see what ethical questions are on the minds of readers and to grapple with those fascinating problems. The column and the correspondence it generates have given me a vantage point from which to observe the moral landscape. This is how it looks from here.

What Ethics? The Most Frequently
Asked Ethical Question

That a newspaper feature about ethics has become popular is gratifying if somewhat mysterious. My first thought was that ethics is popular for the same reason antique furniture is popular: One sees so little of it. But as I continued in this work, it became apparent that those writing the letters had a sincere interest in the question of how to be good, not as an abstract matter, but in deciding how to respond to the conundrums of daily life.

The query I receive most often by far is "Do You Tell?" in all its variations—about the infidelity of a friend's spouse, the kickbacks extorted by a coworker, the shoplifting of a granny in a grocery store. These sort of Duty to Report questions are of continuing interest to my readers. They are tough questions, forcing one to find a balance between the socially beneficial effects of minding one's own business, so essential to a tolerant society, and the deleterious effects of ignoring wrongdoing, which can lead to a corrupt society indifferent to the suffering of others.

While laws vary—and I should say, not for the last time, that I am not a lawyer and do not purport to give legal advice—an ordinary civilian is seldom legally obliged to report a crime. Some professionals do have an affirmative duty to do so: Physicians are generally required to report a suspected case of child abuse, for example. But most people, in most places, have no such legal obligation.

The legal and the ethical are not necessarily synonymous—as I say, not for the last time—but the law is often worth noting as a guide to certain kinds of officially sanctioned behavior. And there are surely times when one has an ethical duty to call the cops—to avoid future wrongdoing, for example, particularly when it might lead to harm to another person. (If you saw someone heading for my house with a bomb, I hope you'd pick up the phone.)

Yet our culture seems ambivalent about this question. The whistle blower is a heroic figure, particularly in a David and Goliath story (particularly if David is Julia Roberts with her fabulous teeth and lingerie), the honest little guy takes on the big corporation. But much as we admire the whistle blower, we hate the squealer, the rat. "The Informer" is never a term of approbation, as Victor McLaglen discovered to his peril in John Ford's 1935 movie of that name. In part, this comes from a distrust of authority: We don't trust the cops; we'll settle this among ourselves. But it's more complicated than that.

These questions raise issues of loyalty, that dubious virtue. (Loyal to whom? Loyal to what?) We admire the courage of an undercover cop making war on the mob, but only as long as we see him as an outsider opposed to a despised group. We don't—*I* don't—admire the undercover FBI agent who "infiltrates" the civil rights movement.

And the cops (at least movie cops) certainly don't admire an undercover cop who is investigating them. In cop movies, no matter how pervasive the misdeeds in a corrupt precinct, no matter how sincere everyone's disdain for a crooked colleague, the Internal Affairs officer called in to investigate is treated with contempt; the blue wall of silence is sacrosanct. (Everybody was so mean to Al Pacino in *Serpico*.)

Perhaps the interest in these "Do You Tell?" questions reflects an admirable willingness on the part of my readers to grapple with tough questions. Or perhaps it is evidence of a nation that's grown too lazy to commit crimes of its own, instead wringing its hands over other people's chicanery. It's so much easier to watch than to do.

A pessimist would say we Americans have lost the gumption to get out there and have an affair or rob a convenience store. But I am not a pessimist. I know we are a vigorous people, and my mail confirms this, sometimes in frightening ways, via the next most common class of questions, rationalizations. Some people describe behavior they almost certainly know is wrong, hoping that I—or more precisely, the *New York Times*—will endorse their bad behavior, thereby absolving them. The typical letter begins, "I'm planning to get liquored up, steal a car, cram the trunk with illegal fireworks, and head for the beach at an excessive rate of speed and shoot a guy." Then come the mitigating details. "But lots of people do this, and I'm much more handsome than they are, plus I'm kind to animals and I really need the money, so isn't it okay?" Well, no. Still, it is a heartening trend. If more people would ask for the okay of the *Times* before doing wicked deeds, the world would be a tidier place. For one thing, that whole Watergate mess could have been avoided.

Ethics and the Just Society

The mail sent to "The Ethicist" offers an impressive picture of people sincerely struggling to be good. But if these letters exist in the foreground, they imply a background of action without inquiry. For every question posed, there are many more that are never asked at all. It would, of course, be impossible to pause and question the propriety of each of our actions. Such constant analysis would be immobilizing, or at least so time consuming that we'd never get out of the house, stuck by the closet door as we pondered the acceptability of leather shoes. Rather than subject every decision of daily life to moral scrutiny, most of us act as our culture directs, behaving no better and no worse than our neighbors. In his profound and moving book, *The Face of Battle,* the British military historian John Keegan considers the question of why, when faced with the horror and suffering of combat, most soldiers don't simply run away. He concludes that they are motivated not by high ideals of patriotism, not by ideology, not by anything one would identify as ethics. Keegan sees these soldiers standing fast so as not to be the least worthy among those assembled. And by that he does not mean the entire army, but those few men nearby. Keegan suggests that even under the most extreme and appalling conditions, most of us will behave about as well as our neighbors.

Something similar has been observed in the early careers of police officers. If a rookie cop is assigned to a corrupt station house, he stands a good chance of being corrupted himself. Put the same young officer in a clean station, and there's a very good chance he'll turn out to be an honest cop. His or her personal ethics hardly come into it.

In *Fast Food Nation,* his muckraking book on the fast food industry, Eric Schlosser makes a related observation. He reports that a high percentage of the robberies committed against McDonald's and similar joints are perpetrated by former employees. Schlosser attributes this to a reaction to low pay, poor working conditions, the lack of a chance to advance, and union busting. He sees these crimes not merely as the perfidy of a sociopath who works the deep fryer, but as a predictable response to a deplorable (i.e., unethical) work environment. Schlosser cites a study by Jerald Greenberg, professor of management at the University of Ohio, an expert on workplace crime, who reports that "when people are treated with dignity and respect, they're less likely to steal from their employer. 'It may be common sense,' Greenberg says, 'but it's obviously not common practice.' The same anger that causes most petty theft, the same desire to strike back at an employer perceived as unfair, can escalate to armed robbery."

This is not to depreciate individual virtue, but we are unlikely to understand any behavior if it is seen only as a matter of individual moral choice detached from any social context. And we are unlikely to significantly increase honorable behavior if we rely only on individual rectitude. There is a kind of ecology of ethics. No matter how much you hector them, most Spartans will act like Spartans; most Athenians will act Athenian.

Just as individual ethics can only be understood in relation to the society within which it is practiced, it is also true that individual ethical behavior is far likelier to flourish within a just society. Indeed, it might be argued that to lead an ethical life one must work to build a just society. That is, if most of us will behave about as well as our neighbors, it is incumbent on us to create a decent neighborhood. Every community is dynamic—Sparta or *Late Night*. We not only live in it, but by our actions we create it. And as important, our community exists not only in the world but in our minds. It forms our values even as we shape its structures.

Sadly, the very idea of civic life is increasingly out of favor, superseded by the values of the marketplace, privatized. The idea of public life is generous, encouraging you to see yourself as living among other people, and to identify yourself as one of those others, with common purpose and problems. The marketplace is where interests clash: The buyer's low price is the seller's lost profit. Privatization is a world of antagonists at worst, of autonomous, isolated figures at best. But in an age where all of our lives are interconnected—in our economy, our infrastructure, even in our health—this notion of the lone cowboy is a fantasy.

Civic life is a public park, paid for by all of us, enjoyed by all of us. Its ethical necessities demand that we act in ways that make other people's happiness part of its use. Private life is a walled pool in your backyard. You need consider no one else, you need compassion for no one else: You can fill it with piranha if you like.

My Ethics

When I respond to readers' queries, I work from this premise: Ethics is the rational determination of right conduct, an attempt to answer the question "How should I act now?" Ethics is not just knowing; it is doing. And so it is necessarily a civic virtue, concerned with how we are to live in society; it demands an understanding of how our actions affect other people. There can be solitary sin—you can sit at home alone and covet your neighbor's ox—but there is no solitary unethical behavior. If you want to be unethical, you've got to get up, get dressed, get out of the house, and actually try to con your neighbor out of his ox. That is, ethics isn't ethics until other people are involved.

In considering an ethical question, whether concerning the right conduct of an individual or the society within which we function, I refer to a set of principles I cherish as profoundly moral. This constellation of values includes honesty, kindness, compassion, generosity, fairness. I embrace actions that will increase the supply of human happiness, that will not contribute to human suffering, that are concordant with an egalitarian society, that will augment individual freedom, particularly freedom of thought and expression.

It can be difficult to satisfy any one of these principles without neglecting another. To answer an ethical question placed before me, I must mediate among them as if they were quarreling factions, each with its own demands. This is an approach to ethics that requires something like diplomacy among the competing principles. My challenge is to devise a course of action that best serves all of these clamoring constituencies. Is there such a course? What behavior comes closest? It is ethics as problem solving.

Other People's Ethics

There are, of course, other ways to make ethical choices. One such method, transparency, advises us to act as if everyone in the community could see what we were doing. In a letter he wrote at Monticello on

May 21, 1816, Thomas Jefferson recommended this to his young friend Francis Eppes:

> Never suffer a thought to be harbored in your mind which you would not avow openly. When tempted to do anything in secret ask yourself if you would do it in public. If you would not be sure it is wrong.

This approach, tenaciously adhered to, would no doubt eradicate much bad behavior (and many naked aerobic workouts, if one were literal about the phrase "see what we were doing"). A limitation of this method is its essential conservatism. It does not encourage a rational system of decision making; it demands only that we live according to the conventions of our society. If you were a Hun and you indulged your taste for slaughter on horseback, Attila would love you, and your Hun buddies would admire you, but a thousand years later, you'd come in for a lot of criticism from many Americans. There is nothing in this approach that would stimulate reforms in Hun culture.

A system more amenable to reform is that of the heroic model. When in a quandary, ask yourself this: What would Lincoln do? The benefit of this strategy is that it makes possible the transformation of society. Lincoln was able to issue the Emancipation Proclamation. The unfortunate thing about this system is that Lincoln is never around when you need him. Lacking his profound moral understanding, it is difficult to know just what he'd say about your perplexing circumstances. And even if death were no barrier to some kind of phone call, Lincoln doesn't drive stick, or trade stocks on-line, or for that matter, know how to use a telephone. Would he be able to apply his genius to your particular problem?

We see a vivid example of the heroic model—albeit a fictional one— in Atticus Finch, that magisterial figure of Harper Lee's *To Kill a Mocking Bird*. In the book, and even more so in the movie where Gregory Peck's very tone of voice radiates compassion and understanding, Atticus Finch is presented as a thoroughly admirable man. He is wise. He is good. He is kind. And if everyone acted like Atticus Finch, segregation would still be the law of the land. His ethical behavior is applied only to the most immediate personal exchanges, the narrowest social encounters. It provides him with no way to challenge the status quo. If an injustice is enshrined by custom, Finch accepts it. It is then called a way of life, and he treats it with the respect it requires to endure forever. Thus Finch might bravely represent the defendant at a trial steeped in racism, but he is unable to seek any real reform in the society that demanded this trial. We find in Atticus Finch the limitations of an ethics based on the heroic model, of transparency, and of an ethics divorced from politics.

Another ethical tool many people find helpful is the categorical imperative: Act as if everyone were to do as you do. It is, alas, not entirely reliable. If everyone followed your lead and went to the beach today, it would be pretty crowded. If everyone kissed your wife, you'd have to buy an enormous supply of Chap Stick. And yet kissing your wife, even at the beach, does seem a benign activity.

Some people employ the test of utilitarianism: Seek the greatest good for the greatest number. However, even if hanging an innocent guy in town square each day would deter crime, and thus do enormous good for the entire community, that hanged man is likely to object. People can be so selfish.

Unsurprisingly, the system of moral thought referred to by most of my correspondents is that of the religion in which they were raised, Christianity or Judaism more often than not. For many of these folks, there can be no ethical thought divorced from religion; the two are nearly synonymous. And while I was raised in an observant household (suburban Reform Judaism) and am undoubtedly affected by the experience, my approach to these questions is, at least overtly, resolutely secular.

Mafia Ethics

Unlike these ethical systems, some make distinctions not on what one does but on who one is. The most familiar version of a moral code based on the actor not the action is Mafia ethics. Or at least Mafia movie ethics. The code runs like this: It's okay to lie and cheat and kill those outside the family, those who threaten the family, but you must be honest to those in the family. It's not what you do; it's to whom you do it.

The most glorified and revered version of this system is nationalism. Thou shalt not kill, except the enemy. And while even war itself has, to some extent, been regulated by a code of conduct proscribing particular actions for all, such efforts cannot eradicate the us-vs.-them assumptions that underpin nationalism.

The pettiest version of this system is at play on many a TV talk show. I worked at one such place where a writer was called on the carpet by the show's host for "offending the child of a celebrity." It wasn't that the writer had done anything particularly unpleasant, it was whose feathers he ruffled. Here is an ethic where the determining factor is not what is done, but who is doing it. If you kill a guy, it's bad. If Barbra Streisand kills a guy, it's magnificent and—in a just universe—Oscar-worthy. Unless she kills Steven Spielberg, in which case it's an unimaginably painful moral crisis, an unanswerable ethical question, and any talk show staff member who tried to resolve it would probably burst into flames.

Such deference to an aristocracy is strikingly un-American, in principle if not in practice. Equal protection under the law is a cornerstone of our society. Our legal system is meant to enunciate acts not actors. Robbing a bank is illegal for everyone. It doesn't matter who the robber is. Similarly, one does not consider who is acted upon. It is just as wrong to rob your grouchy next-door neighbor who runs his power mower at six in the morning as it would be to rob that attractive and amusing Cameron Diaz. Ethics considers actions.

Of course, we do have a persistent aristocracy of money. The rich get to do much more under our legal system, not officially but in fact, if only because it is they who can afford better attorneys. If we are going to operate this way, let's at least create an aristocracy worth having, not rich layabouts, not pretty-boy actors, not the feckless children of genuinely accomplished parents. In Japan, an adroit practitioner of an important art or craft can be declared a Living National Treasure, the human embodiment of a valued cultural heritage. Surely we could try something like that here. What this would mean is James Brown gets to run his car over anyone he likes: The man recorded "Cold Sweat" and "Got the Feeling" and "Sex Machine." He'd get a free pass. And while there are certainly disadvantages to such a system—particularly to the person who finds himself beneath the wheels of James Brown's Cadillac—it represents a kind of moral progress from the current, nudge-and-wink system of a money aristocracy.

We are hardly the first culture to employ a two-tiered system. In ancient Mesopotamia, Babylon, Hammurabi's code made distinctions of social class and gender, writes Gerald LaRue in his essay "Ancient Ethics": "Personal injuries to members of the aristocracy called for the *lex talonis,* an eye for an eye. For injury to freemen and slaves, fines sufficed, and in the case of injury to a slave, the fine was paid to the master as recompense for damage to property." (*A Companion to Ethics.* Peter Singer, ed. p. 32)

William Bennett's Ethics

In "Responsibility," the third chapter of *The Book of Virtues,* perhaps the bestselling book of ethics of the past several decades, William Bennett takes another approach as he explicates The Three Little Kittens:

> Children should learn early the practical lesson that responsibility leads to reward, which leads to further responsibility. We must keep track of our mittens if we expect pie, and then we must wash them if we expect ever to have any more dessert.

By "practical" Bennett seems to mean "profitable"—not so much right behavior as behavior that will get those kittens what they want, and by dint of their own kittenish efforts. It is a curious notion of "virtue," although any kitten raised according to the stern precepts of this book will make an excellent employee someday. If I ran a mitten laundry, I'd hire that kitten.

It is interesting to read Bennett's book eight years after its enormously successful publication because in many ways, it is a precursor to "The Ethicist." Both *The Book of Virtues* and "The Ethicist" discuss the ethical implications of brief stories: the latter in the actual accounts readers send me, the former in the diverse moral tales Bennett has anthologized. Both apply to these particular examples general rules of conduct, and both reflect the very different values of their authors. In Bennett's case, the values are Victorian and the tone is cranky nostalgia. In just the first few pages, he mentions "time-honored tasks," material that schools, homes, and churches "once taught" and that "many no longer do." He wistfully invokes "a time—not so long ago."

Bennett admires his own courage as he knocks down modern straw men: "I know that some of these stories will strike some contemporary sensibilities as too simple, too corny, too old-fashioned." He sniffs at that newfangled soft target, television, asserting that "Nothing in recent years, on television or anywhere else, has improved on a good story that begins 'once upon a time . . .' " So much for all contemporary literature, drama, film, and some quite terrific stuff that's run on TV.

As Bennett notes, there are various lessons to be drawn from any story, and it is often interesting to see which one he emphasizes. For instance, to him John Henry is a story of courage and pride. But while it would have gladdened the heart of, say, Andrew Carnegie, if each of his employees had seen it that way—choosing in the face of dreadful working conditions not to petition for improvements, but to work harder, even to work themselves to death—the United Mine Workers, for example, might read this story differently.

But then, Bennett's heart is with the boss not the worker (unless the worker is working himself to death), with the general not the troops. In his chapter on courage, Bennett presents an excerpt from the last letter of Robert Scott, the British Antarctic explorer: "The causes of the disaster are due not to faulty organization, but to the misfortune in all risks which had to be undertaken." Scott led his party to ruin; every man on his push to the Pole died. (Amundsen's expedition not only beat Scott to the Pole, but every member survived.) That Scott possessed physical courage cannot be denied, but is this the lesson to draw from his story? Might one not learn about inept leadership, a cavalier attitude toward other people's lives, and a nearly criminal vanity?

One can't quite shake the feeling that Bennett is inviting us readers to think of ourselves as courageous people who'd do well in a crisis. Such a flattering image allows us to go about daily life less scrupulously than we perhaps should, like an out-of-shape boxer who ambles through the early rounds, confident that he can make it all good with a knock-out in the tenth. However, real virtue lies not in heroically saving poor orphans from burning buildings but in steadfastly working for a world where orphans are not poor and buildings have decent fire codes. *The B of V*'s hero is Horatio at the Bridge; "The E's" is Horatio at the Office Filling Out His Time Sheets Honestly Even When His Supervisor Is Not Around.

Citing only ten virtues, Bennett still finds room for Loyalty, that quality so prized by dog fanciers and Richard Nixon. And while Bennett mentions that one can be loyal not just to a person but to an ideal, his stories tend to celebrate personal loyalty—Castor and Pollux, Penelope and Odysseus, the Little Hit Man That Could Have (But Did Not) Rat Out His Capo (I may be misremembering that last one). And if loyalties occasionally clash, he is sanguine about how easily such conflicts can be resolved: "The times when one cannot stand both 'for God *and* for country' are rare indeed." This curious assertion would startle those Americans who opposed the Vietnam War, or the abolitionists in the early nineteenth century, or those fighting for women's suffrage in the early twentieth.

Of course, the virtues Bennett wishes to instill in the young are fine things. We all honor work and honesty, compassion and friendship. However, we do not all see virtue as an accretion of cowboy qualities, practiced by solitary and disconnected figures. For "The Ethicist" virtue resides in how we behave among others; it is a quality not just of individuals but of the societies they create. *The Book of Virtues* is the champion of individual rectitude. "The Ethicist" sees honorable behavior reflected in, affected by, and helping to bring about an honorable society. But I do want that pie, and so I will wash my mittens.

Law Book Ethics

Many ethical systems, both secular and sacred, delineate good conduct as a list of do's and don'ts. This sort of moral rule book is seen in most professional codes of conduct—medical ethics, legal ethics; even interior designers have a formal code. The rule of law is itself based on this approach. When it achieves nobility and grandeur, our legal system is not just the codification of self-interest, it is a guide to right conduct with a coherent moral base.

This approach, too, has its limitations. For one thing, it is impossible to stipulate every possible human action. If such a taxonomy of behavior attempts to regulate every conceivable interaction, it becomes unwieldy and overly specific. If it articulates more general laws, it can end up so vague as to become less a guide to good behavior than a stimulus to disputation.

Another limitation, the proscriptions are specific, the prescriptions are vague. Thou shalt not kill is about as clear as can be. However "love thy neighbor as thyself" is so vague as to be useless, ordering merely a general sense of: Be compassionate. We're provided with clear orders about how not to be bad, but we're given little specific information about how to be good. Neither law nor theology includes many injunctions as direct as this: Thou shalt mow thy neighbor's lawn if he's laid up with a bad back because he slipped a disc when he tried to move a piano himself because he was too cheap to call a real moving company.

Consider that most often invoked code of conduct, the Ten Commandments. Given the frequent call to post this list in the classroom, it is a curious guide to student behavior.

1. Thou shalt have no other gods before me.

2. Thou shalt not make unto thee any graven image.

3. Thou shalt not take the name of the Lord thy God in vain.

4. Remember the Sabbath day, to keep it holy.

5. Honor thy father and thy mother.

6. Thou shalt not kill.

7. Thou shalt not commit adultery.

8. Thou shalt not steal.

9. Thou shalt not bear false witness.

10. Thou shalt not covet.

The first four Commandments—40 percent of the list—consist of God talking about himself. (You'd think being God would give Him some confidence, but no; despite His widespread popularity—people do worship Him—He's as jittery and insecure as Marilyn Monroe.) Surprisingly, for a code so central to several monotheistic faiths, the first Commandment does not ban other gods, just assigns them a secondary rank: no other gods *before* Him. Surely this is, if not an invitation to, at least an acknowledgment of, polytheism. These are interesting strictures, but not all that useful to a student wondering if it's okay to download a prewritten essay from the Internet.

Number seven, "Thou shalt not commit adultery," presumably has little relevance in the third grade, what with so few of the kids being married.

Number ten, "Thou shalt not covet," is less a guide to behavior than a recommended attitude: Don't be jealous. Easy to say. Certainly a worthy goal. But can it be achieved as an act of will?

The fifth Commandment, honor your parents, if read to refer to all those in authority, does have something to say to a student: Treat your teachers with respect. As do numbers six, eight, and nine. "Thou shalt not kill." "Thou shalt not steal." "Thou shalt not bear false witness." Certainly these four precepts would be endorsed by most of us. Indeed, so broadly are they accepted that we hardly need a biblical injunction to embrace them. One wonders why there is such determination to see these ideas expressed as religious doctrine.

By articulating general ethical principles, the Commandments provide rather a meager guide to right behavior in school. What about treating your fellow students with civility? Valuing learning for its own sake? Being kind? Or these modest but nonetheless useful ideas: No hitting? Do your best? Seek the truth? Don't be a bully? Be kind to even the least popular kids? Easy on the sex and drugs until you get a little older? Don't make a big mess in the cafeteria for others to clean up?

Perhaps its enthusiasts wish to post the Ten Commandments on the classroom wall not for pedagogical but for symbolic purposes, as a statement of American values, much as we display the American flag and the image of George Washington; not to instruct but to declare. But that other American value, the separation of church and state, might encourage us to find a more secular expression of these ideals.

Relationships and Obligations

Regardless of what system of ethics one employs, it will be severely tested by the behavior of actual human beings, who seldom behave as systematically as the code by which one strives to assess them. For one thing, our sense of ethical obligation is very much affected by relationship of the people involved. You have a different set of responsibilities to your children than you do to your boss or to a customer in your shop or to a stranger on the street. These obligations are often unspoken, and hence we may not all agree what they are, leading to confusion and conflict. Further, these relationships, and their attendant obligations, are often multiple and hence contradictory: They overlap or clash. Your boss is also, to some degree, your friend. The shopkeeper's daughter goes to school with your son. In many situations, it is hard to know whether to kiss or to kick.

It is not the ethicist but the novelist who most skillfully limns the complex and subtle relationships and the unspoken obligations that bind people together. The ethicist is obliged to provide a concise and direct answer to the questions put to him, one that applies a broadly applicable principle. This means employing the approach of the lawyer, invoking the proper general rule—a rule that could be applied to every similar case—and so necessarily advising: You shouldn't shoot the guy. It would, however, be more congenial to me to employ the methods of the novelist, seeking not for the general but the particular. To do this, the column would have to be much longer, not so much for my answers, but so the questioner could present a more richly detailed picture of his situation. If I knew more about the complicated people involved, their long and tangled history, the mitigating circumstances and painful emotional blows, the financial pressures the cousin was under, the medical problems of the aunt, the romantic betrayal of the brother-in-law, the hundred ameliorating circumstances and exacerbating conditions, maybe the most honorable advice I could give would be: Shoot the guy. But you can't do that in four hundred words. That's why we read novels. And have gun control laws.

And so, considering one particular relationship, should you not have the same ethical obligations to any child you see on the street that you have toward your own? You have no more right to treat a strange child unkindly, but clearly you feel a more tender attachment to the child you know. Not necessarily a bad thing. You do indeed have a particular responsibility to that child. While it is fitting—indeed, inevitable—that you would feel a profound affection and sense of obligation to your own child, one must also deal honorably with strangers. One must be wary of an ethics that is based not on what we do but to whom we do it.

Is Ethics Etiquette? Is Ethics Politics?

Some forms of etiquette can be seen as ethics practiced on the small scale—in the number of people involved, in what's at stake. Much that is dismissed as mere etiquette does indeed have a moral foundation. (I take up this question more fully in the chapter "Social Life.") One way to understand right conduct is to imagine it on a continuum—etiquette, ethics, politics. And indeed, sometimes the column has been criticized for conflating ethics and politics. But I maintain that the difference between the two is artificial, if indeed there is a significant difference at all.

Sometimes, as with etiquette and ethics, the distinction is a matter of scale. If one guy robs you, it's ethics, but when 435 people rob you, it's politics—or the House of Representatives is in session. But surely the deliberations of that body are subject to an ethical analysis.

Politics can be a necessary expression of ethics: Often the only way to achieve an individual ethical goal is through group endeavor, i.e., politics.

Some political questions are not essentially ethical but a matter of two competing interests each with a morally legitimate claim. For instance, there is that cowboy movie classic: Should the land be used by the cattle herders or the sheep herders? There is a kind of partisan politics that an ethicist should, of course, eschew, no matter his personal feelings about cows. However, it is also his job to point out that the land belongs to the Navajo, and both the cattle and sheep herders should get permission before any grazing takes place. That is where what some call politics is quite properly a subject for ethical scrutiny.

An ethics that eschewed such nominally political questions would not be ethics at all, but mere rule following. It would be the ethics of the slave dealer, advocating that one always be honest about a slave's health and always pay his bills promptly. But surely any ethics worth discussing must condemn the slave trade absolutely, not quibble about its business practices.

Ethics and Incompetence

Much of the world's misery can be traced not to a lack of virtue but to a lack of ability—not wickedness but ineptitude. The transportation system that mires you in traffic for an hour while thousands of cars spew pollutants, the leaky pipe at the nuclear power plant, the witless sitcom are not the work of evil people but of maladroits. And this is a sad thing. To be a great villain requires intelligence and skill and clarity of vision, qualities in short supply. Shakespeare's Richard III was a man of magnificent towering wickedness; Captain Joseph Hazelwood, the skipper of the Exxon *Valdez,* was a doofus. Great evil is achieved by few, but bungling is accomplished by many. Fortunately, we live in a nation where one must not choose between these two qualities; indeed, we sometimes find both within a single person, often with a Washington address.

It is possible for ineptitude to become evil. When you realize that you are not likely to excel in a position of responsibility and seek it out of vanity, your fumbling is transmuted into iniquity. Incompetence is unethical when it involves the casual use of duct tape in a bypass operation because somebody sipped malt liquor and dozed through key lessons in medical school. Persisting as a foul-up heart surgeon is not merely inept; it is wicked. To fulfill certain obligations one must perform ably or step down.

There are other times when one must allow for innocent errors rather than pounce on them as an opportunity to make a few bucks. When you notice someone drop his wallet, you don't swipe the cash. When you get the wrong change, you inform the cashier. This is not just a matter of ethics but of civility. It would be exhausting to live in a world where one slipup meant death or replacing all your credit cards. Living an ethical life obliges us to tolerate imperfections in others (and to hope others will tolerate our own).

Ethics and Intent

No one deliberately sets out to become incompetent, but ethically, would it matter if someone did? Well, yes. In ethics intent counts. (This same principle appears throughout our legal system, where, for example, a distinction is made between negligence, manslaughter, and various degrees of murder, distinctions all having to do not with the act itself but with the intent of the actor.) There is a very different ethical meaning if I accidentally drop my bowling ball out the window than if I deliberately hurl it from the window to smite James Brown walking below, so angry am I at what he's been doing with that car of his. Although why I was bowling in my apartment to begin with is a reasonable question, and one my downstairs neighbors frequently ask. Samuel Johnson put it this way:

> The morality of an action depends on the motive from which we act. If I fling half a crown to a beggar with intention to break his head, and he picks it up and buys victuals with it, the physical effect is good; but, with respect to me, the action is very wrong. So, religious exercises, if not performed with an intention to please God, avail us nothing. As our Savior says of those who perform them from other motives, "Verily they have their reward."

This view is not universally held. Samuel Butler argued against it in *The Way of All Flesh*: "The more I see the more sure I am that it does not matter why people do the right thing so long as they do it, nor why they may have done wrong if they have done it. The result depends upon the thing done and the motive goes for nothing." (as quoted by Singer, p. 93)

And certainly, it may matter little to the recipient of charity what motivated the donor. Did she contribute a vast sum to build a new hospital out of piety, out of vanity, out of remorse for her tobacco company wealth, in pursuit of a tax break? To the utilitarian—or the patient—the important thing is the act itself. The motives are between the donor and her conscience and perhaps her therapist and accountant. Indeed, much of our legal system is designed to encourage or discourage particular acts. It doesn't matter to a state trooper if you obey the speed limit out of a sense of civic obligation or out of a fear of getting a ticket.

Even Johnson himself is oddly contradictory on this question, as we see in this conversation with Boswell about the social harm wrought by the writings of Rousseau:

> BOSWELL: I don't deny, Sir, but that his novel may, perhaps, do harm; but I cannot think his intention was bad.
>
> JOHNSON: Sir, that will not do. We cannot prove any man's intention to be bad. You may shoot a man through the head, and say you intended to miss him; but the Judge will order you to be hanged. An alleged want of intention, when evil is committed, will not be allowed in a court of justice. Rousseau, Sir, is a very bad man. I would sooner sign a sentence for his transportation, than that of any felon who has gone from the Old Bailey these many years. Yes, I should like to have him work in the plantations.

So where does that leave us? Doing the right thing for the wrong reason? Doing the wrong thing for the right reason? It leaves us with the ethical obligation not to be a boob. It is not enough to be well intentioned; one must strive to put those intentions into action in a capable way. One must consider the effect his actions will have on others. Looked at like this, to persist in ignorance is itself dishonorable.

Ethics and Dr. Johnson

Perhaps it is because I operate without reference to a formal system of ethics that I am drawn to a great moralist who did likewise, although it is true that what I sometimes do out of ignorance Samuel Johnson did out of inclination. Still, Johnson wrote from no particular system, although a strong and coherent sensibility emerges from his writing, particularly in his two series of essays, *The Rambler* and *The Idler*. He is informed by a knowledge of life, an understanding of the human heart, a love of sociability, a generosity of spirit, and an intimate awareness of life's hardships ("Human Life is everywhere in a state in which much is to be endured and little to be enjoyed"). It is a bleak view of life for so wise and good a man. ("The natural flights of the human mind are not from pleasure to pleasure but from hope to hope.") And if from our point of view, 250 years after his writing, he appears to be wrong at times, he is right as often as any person can be. While I cannot hope to be like him, this immortal genius, I can be grateful to him and strive to learn from his writing and his example.

Articulating no formal system, Johnson is very much a man of his time. He is informed by his Christianity, and shares the devotion of many of his contemporaries to an inflexible social order, a society dominated by a hereditary aristocracy, what Johnson called "subordination." However, his openheartedness and beneficence everywhere prevail. Despite his conservative leanings, he was quick to recognize the merit of others. And while he reveals a lamentable double standard about sexual behavior, finding adultery tolerable, albeit regrettable, in men but anathema in women, it is also true that he delighted in the company of women of accomplishment. Unlike his friend and biographer, James Boswell, Johnson took genuine pleasure in bluestocking society. For all Johnson's conservative—and sexist—proclamations, he treated people as individuals and was proud of his ability to converse easily and pleasurably with all whom he encountered.

It is Johnson's kindness and vitality that make him so appealing. He was bursting with life: While in his sixties, he joined some school boys in rolling down a hill; when quite elderly he stood up at a dinner for Captain Cooke to demonstrate the locomotion of a kangaroo by hopping around the room. He was, above all, the most sociable of men. "I consider a day lost," he said, "when I do not make a new acquaintance." As a consequence, his contemporaries didn't just respect him as the great moralist of his day, they loved Dr. Johnson.

To Johnson, matters of morality were not abstractions, they were immediate questions of how to live among others, and he enjoyed applying his prodigious learning and intelligence to the practical problems of daily life. There are narrower people who practice ethics without affection—little, crabbed people who need to be in the right, who adhere to social rules to feel themselves superior to others, who enforce moral precepts to avenge themselves on their antagonists or to air a grievance in disguise. But to Johnson, ethics was an instrument of benevolence and civility, an expression of our humanity.

Ethics and Authors

Be not too hasty . . . to trust, or to admire, the teachers of morality; they discourse like angels, but they live like men.

SAMUEL JOHNSON, *RASSELAS*

How to Read This Book

Each of the following chapters takes up the ethical questions of one particular aspect of life. I begin by considering some of the themes that will run through the chapter, and then turn to particular ethical questions. In addition, each chapter includes the following:

Ethics Pop Quizzes

Because the newspaper column replies only to actual queries from actual readers, there are many intriguing hypothetical questions I've not had a chance to consider. I pose some of these at the start of each chapter for you, the reader, to answer. You are invited to submit your replies to theethicistbook.com, or e-mail me at theethicist@randomhouse.com. The most interesting of these, along with my comments, will be included in the paperback edition of *The Good, The Bad & The Difference*.

Q & A

Each chapter includes some of my favorite questions and my answers, categorized for your convenience. Those few unsigned questions are hypotheticals, generated in-house in the early days of the column. All others, even those signed "Anonymous" are actual questions from actual readers of the column.

Guest Ethicist

Every ethics question can be answered many different ways. Another writer responding to these inquiries might employ a different methodology than I do, based upon values different from mine. To give some sense of the breadth of possibilities, each chapter features someone other than me responding to a question. I then take up the same question immediately after.

Arguing with The Ethicist

The columns that generate the most mail from readers are seldom those that discuss the great ethical issues of the day, like organ transplants or responding to Third World poverty. They are the small, homely questions. This should not be surprising: Such questions involve situations in which the readers have actually found themselves, questions they've asked themselves, and answers they've reached that are different from—and in the view of many readers, better than—mine, as they are quite willing to point out.

Readers often discern an aspect of the question I'd not considered or suggested another way to approach it. If I've seldom recanted a column as a result of this thoughtful correspondence, I've often revised my thinking. I'm able to respond to most of my mail, and these exchanges create a kind of dialogue around a particular ethical issue, a form of discourse that seems a particularly fruitful way to examine such questions.

I realize I may not be the first person to notice this.

I include just such dialogues under the rubric "Arguing with The Ethicist," presenting the original column and then a series of points raised by readers to which I respond. (When I do not cite a particular reader, I am paraphrasing arguments made by several people.)

Postscripts

Those who give advice for a living never hang around long enough to learn if they were of any use at all. However, I was curious to discover if the folks who wrote to the column took my advice or rejected it, and how their situations have since developed. Each of their questions is a kind of story, and I was eager to learn how these stories ended. And so I invited a few people to review my advice and to let me know how they resolved their problem. These follow-ups generally appear at the end of each chapter.

Commercial Life

Whoever commits a fraud is guilty not only of the particular injury to him who he deceives, but of the diminution of that confidence which constitutes not only the ease but the existence of society.

JOHNSON, *RAMBLER* #79 (DECEMBER 18, 1750)

That this is one of the book's longest chapters is unsurprising: It takes up the ethics of commercial transactions, our culture's most common sort of human interaction. One way or another, these questions involve money. In particular, they deal with shopping and with the essential conflict between buyer and seller. The former wants to pay the lowest price, the latter wants to receive the highest; the temptations of deceit are powerful. That is why the used-car dealer has long been depicted as a reviled and tormented soul. If the car had been invented one hundred years earlier, Verdi would no doubt have written an opera about a used-car dealer. (And he would have taken very different sorts of vacations, perhaps driving along the seacoast with a backseat full of kids singing "Are We There Yet?")

There is an entire body of ethics and a great deal of law designed to keep the wheels of commerce turning smoothly, and that's not entirely a bad thing. It's nice to be able to buy groceries knowing that your pound of coffee is an actual pound. And actual coffee. And it makes the shopkeeper's job more relaxing if he can be confident that you'll pay for it, rather than slip it down your trousers. (And it makes your guests happier, knowing they won't be drinking trouser coffee.)

Commercial codes are ancient and nearly universal; laws touching on business practices can be found among Roman law, and farther back among the Egyptians and Babylonians. The earliest such provisions were little more than *caveat emptor,* but we have made a kind of moral progress. In America, there has been something of a revival of such codes under the rubric of consumerism. Most Americans appreciate measures to ensure that today even the unwary are unlikely to buy tainted pork or a cardboard sedan.

But an uneasy tension persists between consumerism and commerce. We are, after all, a country that both discourages the sale of tobacco, a toxic product, and subsidizes its cultivation. Were you to introduce some other new product that killed off its users at so impressive a rate—some kind of exploding hat, perhaps—one suspects that Congress would take more vigorous steps to discourage its sale (at least to minors).

Health and safety are not the only factors in the creation of consumer law. Tradition and self-interest also play their parts. Philip Morris is reluctant to give up its enormous profits; tobacco farmers find a sentimental comfort (and a hardscrabble livelihood) in the family farm. Of course, similar arguments have been made by Colombian cocaine cartels and small coca growers. Someday, perhaps, a satisfyingly ironic solution to our tobacco problem will be found when the Colombian government sends us a billion dollars in foreign aid so we can attack the big tobacco traffickers and shift the small farmers to alternative crops, something less deadly and less addictive. Marijuana?

There are broad ethical implications in what is sometimes referred to as the "consumer movement." Its virtues are those of our democracy itself, high among them being truthfulness and the free flow of information that enables consumers (and citizens) to make informed choices, albeit when choosing breakfast cereal rather than a congressman (although, come to think of it, lately there may be less of a distinction here than the Founding Fathers could have anticipated).

And yet, conceding the righteousness of this crusading zeal, there is something in me that does not wish to be referred to as a "consumer." It smacks of the French Revolution somehow, only instead of being addressed as Citizen Cohen, I'm now Consumer Cohen, an honorific that rather overemphasizes a single sphere of existence. The problem is not so much that commerce dominates public life, it is that commerce *is* public life. It is often noted that too few of us vote, but we turn out in impressive numbers to any event that includes the phrase "10% Off!" We spend less time in the town square than we do at the mall, where there is, for example, no guarantee of free speech (although there is occasionally a nice free sample of cheese at that snack shop). All too often, shopping is what we have instead of civic activity.

The centrality of shopping is seen in the clash between those who cherish "life, liberty, and the pursuit of happiness" and the "life, liberty, and property" crowd. Indeed, the sanctification of property "rights" by the latter group has contributed much to human misery. It is difficult to make an ethical case for those whose worship of property has led them to challenge, for example, the very idea of environmental protection laws.

Such private property extremists dwell in a fantasyland of the rugged farmer living in isolation, on his autonomous homestead, out in the wilderness, where his actions affect no other person; except, perhaps, in the case of Jefferson and his slaves. But here on Earth, a more powerful case could be made that this solitary farmer is not so solitary, that his fertilizer washes off his field into the stream from which, many miles away, others must drink; that his produce is brought to market on roads others must pay for, in a truck that spews fumes others must breathe. He learned to do his crop calculations at a public school; he follows crop prices on-line, using the Internet created by government researchers.

It is environmentalism that provides a counterargument to the worship of private property, and it is a morally superior argument, not because it proposes a more austere lifestyle, but because it recognizes that we each live among others, affecting and being affected by one another. While honorable people may differ about any particular policy, this much seems unarguable. Those private property fanatics (to whom the current Supreme Court is increasingly and distressingly sympathetic) act unethically, not just because they espouse greed and relentless self-interest, but because their assertion of autonomy is intellectually dishonest. That is to say, that there can be no meaningful ethics that does not consider human beings as social creatures.

It must also be noted that profit is not the loftiest goal to which we can aspire, nor are commercial exchanges the most deeply satisfying human encounters. Much as one enjoys the mall, there is something to be said for the library or the school, the theater or the park, or indeed for the bedroom. Even in nineteenth-century London, that proud capital of a mercantile empire, the English dreamed of traveling to Italy; one reads so few novels where a woman from Tuscany yearns to live nearer the London Stock Exchange. A society where all human interaction is a form of commerce is hardly a society at all. In other words, if I ran my life the way I ran my business, it would barely be a life at all. Although I'd give more of my friend's coffee mugs with my picture on them. And I'd have a jaunty and memorable catchphrase to sum myself up. And my name would be written in an instantly recognizable typeface.

This is not to decry commerce, but to assign it a more reasonable place in human affairs. Johnson himself was not averse to commerce, which he knew improves the condition of humanity in manifold ways. After the death of his friend Henry Thrale, Johnson pitched in enthusiastically to help Thrale's widow sell her husband's brewery, showing an understanding of the buyer-seller relationship that presaged modern advertising's awareness that it must sell the sizzle, not the steak:

> . . . [W]hen the sale of Thrale's brewery was going forward, Johnson appeared bustling about with an ink-horn and pen in his button-hole, like an excise-man; and on being asked what he really considered to be the value of the property which was to be disposed of, answered, "We are not here to sell a parcel of boilers and vats, but the potentiality of growing rich, beyond the dreams of avarice."

But Johnson did not let his commercial zeal compromise his integrity, nor did this most sociable of men lose his awareness of himself as a person living among others.

THE GOOD, THE BAD

Ethics Pop Quiz

Below are four hypothetical questions for you the reader to answer.

Replies can be submitted to theethicistbook.com or e-mailed to theethicist@randomhouse.com.

Selected responses will appear in the paperback edition of the book.

Whenever I go to buy a nice pocket T-shirt, I worry that it's so affordable because it was probably made by some Pakistani kid who earns about 9¢ a day. If I buy the shirt, I'm exploiting him, but if I (and everyone else) don't buy the shirt, the plant closes and he's thrown out of work. Neither alternative seems very good. What should I do?

For years, I've patronized prostitutes, mostly through escort services. I practice safe sex, treat the prostitute with courtesy, and tip generously. These transactions, while illegal, are consensual, freely chosen by prostitute and client. Our interaction may not be based on love, but few jobs are. And it is certainly higher paying and less dangerous than say, working in a coal mine used to be. Is there some ethical objection I'm missing?

I've used the same excellent stockbroker for years, in part because of the first-rate job he does researching various companies. He's always up on who's about to launch a great new product or lose an important contract. Recently, he was indicted for insider trading for having just this sort of information. But isn't that what I pay him for?

Last week at the mall, the security guards evicted some folks outside a clothing store protesting Third World sweat shops. I say the mall had the right to eject these people; it's private property, and people come here to shop not for politics. What do you say?

Q & A

Entrance Exams

I was at the tailor when a young, casually dressed black man came in through the front door and said he was to meet a friend there. The shop owner (who is white, as am I) immediately told him that there was no one there, and closed the door, locking it behind him. But in fact there was a young woman in a fitting room—the friend in question—and, hearing his voice, she rushed out after him. Was the shopkeeper's lie blatantly racist? Should I have acted?

—ROBERTA POSNER, NEW YORK CITY

You could not be certain in that brief encounter if the tailor was being deliberately, malevolently racist—nor, I suspect, could he. He may well believe that he does not exclude men who are black, but merely men who look threatening. But if he considers every African American younger than eighty-five threatening, then regardless of his intent, the result is racial discrimination. And in any case, a quick glance through the door is a dubious way for anyone to spot a potential criminal.

The frail and elderly proprietor of the Delicate Lace Shoppe may bar her door to a menacing gang of club-wielding, beer-swilling teen thugs when her experience tells her that these louts are unlikely lace fanciers. That is, she may exclude them on the basis of their behavior, i.e., what they are actually doing. But barring people from stores based simply on how they look is a violation of the public-accommodations laws (and of fundamental decency) that, because it's so hard to prove, leaves victims with little recourse.

While the tailor's security is a genuine problem that must be taken seriously, the use of buzzers is not a good solution to that problem because, far too often, it becomes a device not to deter crime but to exclude African Americans. Another solution must be found. Neighborhood policing, for example, has been quite effective in dealing with just this sort of problem. So if the tailor is frequently robbed, he might ask his local precinct to put a cop outside the door, albeit not a New Jersey State Trooper if the tailor lives in the mid-1990s.

When you witness this kind of odious behavior, you could start by asking why you were admitted to the shop and the other customer was not. (If you are uneasy about a confrontation at that moment, write him a letter.) If you are unsatisfied with his response, tell him so. Then take the matter further. Write to the mayor, to your city council representative, to your city's human-rights agency, the Civil Liberties Union, and, indeed, to the newspapers. After all, this is a matter of social policy. You would be doing a fine thing to make this matter a part of our public discourse.

TICKET MASTER

My fiancé and I waited in line for four hours to buy tickets to a show. There were a limited number, so each person was allowed only two. We were approached by a man who offered us a $100 bonus to each buy an extra ticket. I was ready to accept, but my fiancé said it wouldn't be fair to those who'd waited in line. Was he right? What if no bonus money had been offered?

—R.A., CONNECTICUT

I'm with your fiancé. The money-waving guy was trying to cut in line, showing contempt for everyone behind you. And by offering money, he showed contempt for you, implying that even if you disapproved of his request, you'd set aside your values if the price was right. Furthermore, because tickets were in short supply, his jumping the line means that someone farther back who might otherwise have seen the show may not get to.

Even if this smoothie had offered no "bonus"—a delightful euphemism for "bribe," by the way—his behavior would still be objectionable because it undermines one of the small civilities of ordinary life. He affronts the sense of fairness, of equal opportunity, that distinguishes a line from a mob. But that's the kind of savage behavior people might have been driven to in a desperate attempt to see the final performances of *Cats*.

Until recently, I was too young to be admitted to R-rated movies. If my parents didn't mind my seeing a movie, was it wrong for me to lie about my age or buy a ticket to another movie and then sneak in? After all, I wasn't cheating the theater out of any money.

—DAN MARGOLIS, PENNSYLVANIA

If your parents are okay with your movie viewing, you have no ethical obligation to kowtow to the industry's ratings. That system might be defensible were it used merely to inform parents, but for a multiplex manager to rule on what someone else's children may or may not see is impertinent. A case could be made that when you engage in a voluntary act like going to the movies, you ought to obey the rules. However, rules ought to be reasonable, hardly the case with this capricious and arbitrary rating system (no to sex but yes to violence, vulgarity, and Chevy Chase).

When you lie to get into an unauthorized movie, you do the theater no harm: Indeed, you increase its profits without threatening its sanctimonious pose of social responsibility. However, if you buy a ticket to a G-rated movie and then sneak into an R, you deprive the creators of that movie of your nine dollars.

Lying is always unfortunate, but in this case it is a lesser transgression than sneaking, and it's not nearly as depraved as pouring a sinister glutinous substance onto popcorn and calling it "topping."

Of course, if that R-rated movie sells out, your stealth entrance may leave a late arrival seatless. So maybe the more honorable course is to lie about your age or to sneak into only unpopular R-rated movies: There's a rich cultural life.

To lie here is regrettable, but it is the less regrettable path. Your alternative is to truckle to an overreaching authority that imposes an unreasonable stricture simply to keep the wheels of commerce turning. Obedience to such rules isn't honesty; it is docility.

I am considering sneaking into the movies, but only into bad movies. I'll pay for independent films shown in small art houses, but not studio films in multiplexes. Given the quality of movies like *Mission to Mars* that leave me feeling as if someone stole my nine bucks, is it fair to say that until studios start making better films I may bend the rules?

—C. GILMORE, LOS ANGELES

I receive many letters from people eager to justify bad behavior, but yours is the first that attempts an aesthetic argument: It's okay to steal from those who make bad art. I admire your ingenuity but must, alas, reject your logic.

Ethics requires an examination of the act, not the person acted upon. If it is wrong to sneak into *The Producers,* perhaps the funniest movie ever made, then it is also wrong to tiptoe into anything that inflates a five-minute *Saturday Night Live* sketch into a ninety-minute feature. In short, no. You don't get to sneak into a bad movie. Not only is your proposal unethical, it's perverse: Anyone with a lick of sense wants to sneak *out* of a bad movie.

Let the Buyer Be Square

I recently bought a secondhand bicycle from a chap working out of an empty lot. He asked $75 for it—cheap, considering what I got. But now I wonder whether I ought to have been more diligent, and worry that there's a good chance my bicycle was stolen.

—F.S., NEW YORK CITY

Your concern does you credit—not as much credit as thinking of it before you bought the bike, though. Let's say partial credit. Sometimes there is an ethical obligation not to be a bonehead or, more kindly, not to become a partner in a famously questionable enterprise. In this case, you ought to have known that many used bikes sold in New York City are indeed stolen and you should therefore have made an effort to shop where they're not. Ask any bike shop employee to suggest a legitimate dealer. Incidentally, that three-card monte? A poor way to invest your aged mother's life savings. Magic beans, indeed!

TANK UP

When my boyfriend and I rent a car, the way he follows the requirement to "return the car with a full tank of gas" makes me uncomfortable. He has me sit in the driver's seat and call out when the gas gauge just touches the "full" line, hoping that this is gallons—and dollars—away from a full tank. He says he has no way of knowing that he received the car with a truly full tank. Is he right?

—ERIC WEST, WASHINGTON, D.C.

He is right on paranoia, wrong on ethics. The rental agreement he signed says fill the tank, not refuel until the semiaccurate gas gauge registers something vaguely fullish. His obligation is unambiguous.

It's true that he can't know if the car's previous renter topped up the tank, but that does not justify tailoring his own conduct to match that of the worst-behaved members of society. He also can't know if other drivers are carrying weapons, but he really ought not mount a machine gun on the roof of your rental car. (For one thing, he'd scratch the paint; that can be a pricey repair.) That there are petty scoundrels among us does not preclude the duty to behave honorably.

One technical consideration: On most cars, the gas gauge registers only when the engine is on. If your boyfriend insists on running the engine while he gasses up, he puts himself and anyone near him at risk of a dramatic explosion. This is a fine thing in a Schwarzenegger movie— it cuts down on the dialogue—but a poor way to economize.

A sign at the supermarket said "London Broil $2.67 lb.," but the actual packages were priced at $.07 a pound. I tried to buy two, but the cashier said the meat was mispriced. I think the store should honor the pricing on its packages and should have relabeled them as soon as they spotted the mistake.

—THERESA OGDEN, JERSEY CITY, NEW JERSEY

I don't agree. You knew perfectly well that London broil was not seven cents a pound. Taking advantage of an honest error is the improper act here. One must allow for the possibility that people make mistakes; it's what happens next that separates the ethical from the unethical.

Stores, of course, may not promote a product at one price and then refuse to sell it. This is not just a matter of ethics, but in many places it is a matter of law. But what you describe is not "bait and switch"; it's a comical foul-up. And while the store should certainly correct errors promptly, its behavior suggests a maladroit manager, not a moral transgression.

A heads-up for the future: General Motors does not currently produce a three-dollar Buick.

TWO LEFT FEET

I just purchased a pair of sneakers and did something I had contemplated in the past but never did. My feet are two different sizes, which has always been a source of frustration. This time, I switched sizes in the box and so, although buying only one pair, I have one of each size. I am not feeling particularly guilty but am wondering what you would say about this.

—J.N., CAMBRIDGE, MASSACHUSETTS

Were I not the amiable fellow I am, I'd say you stole a pair of shoes. But it's such a nice day out, so I'll say you, in effect, stole a pair of shoes. It is unfortunate that shoes are sized the way they are, so unrelated to everyone's asymmetrical feet (and I won't even go into my own pants problem), but the solution can't be for you to render another pair unsalable.

Of course, the store may be able to return them to the factory, and the factory may be able to find each of those solo shoes a mate, but that's not your decision to make. You really ought to have asked.

But happy running. Away from the security guard.

NOTE: Many readers wrote to say that the department store Nordstrom offers properly sized shoes, even if the customer wears two different sizes, by breaking up pairs. No additional charge.

SWEATERS BORROWED, USED, RETURNED

My sister was going to buy some colorful sweaters to use in a family picture and then return them for a refund. When I chided her on this, she said it was the same as when I went to Barnes & Noble and looked up European restaurant numbers in the *Michelin Guide* without buying the book. What do you think?

—M.L., VERMONT

Here's one way to sort it out: Ask a clerk's permission, or at least imagine asking a clerk (who could be incredibly charming and attractive; after all, it's your imagination). I suspect that the B&N clerk would let you look up a couple of numbers, but I'd be astonished if the clerk at the clothing store would let you borrow a wardrobe. There is not an absolute distinction between these two acts, but there is an absolute door to the store, and when merchandise passes through it, things change. At least your sister didn't plan to photograph a family dinner; it's so hard to return even a slightly used pot roast.

WINDOWS SHOPPING

I needed a video camera, so I went to a department store where the clerk educated me on the various models and let me try them out to see which I liked best. Then I went home and bought it for $100 less on the Internet. I feel bad about it, but not $100's worth. Is that terrible?

—W.W., LUBBOCK, TEXAS

It depends on your motives. If you were determined to buy your camera on-line, it would have been exploitive to enter the store intending to use it only as a source of information. But if you entered the store with an open mind, then you're in the clear.

Many shoppers would be happy to buy their video camera at a bricks-and-mortar operation (what we old-timers call a "store") if the price is right. In fact, many would pay more to buy it at the store, but not infinitely more. And no one is obliged to buy it at the store if it costs, say, a million dollars more. Entering the store does not obligate you to buy the camera there at any price. Just as you can shop around, checking prices at other stores, you are free to shop around on-line.

One thing you might have tried is haggling. If you'd returned to the store and said the same camera was a hundred dollars cheaper elsewhere, they might have been willing to lower the price.

However, your nonterrible behavior can lead to terrible results: If everyone does what you did, the store will go under, and you'll have nowhere to try out new cameras. You must make a rational calculation of what is in your best interest—short-term savings or long-term shopping opportunities.

Ultimately, this problem may be resolved by changes not in the buyer but in the seller. To survive, stores must provide incentives for people to shop there: helpful staff, quick repairs, great service, free pony rides for the kids. Otherwise, they can't vie with on-line outlets that have advantages of their own: low overhead, no sales tax, huge inventory. It's that edge that lets a savvy outfit like Amazon lose—what is it?—a billion dollars a minute?

WITH CERTAIN RESERVATIONS

Last night, my wife and I went to a popular local restaurant, where we were told there'd be a 1½- to 2-hour wait, so we found a spot at the bar. Twenty minutes later, they told us our table was ready. After seating us, the captain said, "Enjoy your dinner, Mr. Towns." We'd been given someone else's table. Not wanting to return to the bar for another hour, I chose not to correct his error. Was I wrong?

—ANTHONY LETO, LIBERTYVILLE, ILLINOIS

You were wrong, partly because you jumped the line (even if without knowing it), but mostly because poor Mr. Towns is probably still at the bar. The captain believes they've seated him; he must be getting awfully hungry. You should have told the captain that you'd like to keep your seats, but he should attend to poor starving Mr. Towns. All you would have risked is your table; losing it, while regrettable, would have been only fair.

Politics and Shopping

BOYCOTT COORS

When my pal ordered a Coors at lunch the other day, I read him the riot act: "You can't drink that; they're treacherous right-wing fanatics." He countered that an evil of McCarthyism was denying someone a livelihood because of his beliefs. Maybe he had a point. If it was wrong for Jack Warner to fire a movie actor for being a Red, isn't it equally wrong to shun Coors for its nonbrewery politics?

Each of us is free to follow the dictates of conscience in the beer aisle, but the question gets more complicated when you move beyond an individual act to a boycott with economic consequences. In your case, the big guy–little guy argument obtains. Your action may have the form of a boycott, but unallied with any organized movement, it's really just a way to display your anti-Coors sentiments. And unless I underestimate your beer-drinking capacity, you'll have no effect on the company you disparage: The ineffectualness of your protest becomes its justification. Jack Warner, on the other hand, was powerful enough to throw people out of work and wreck their lives—and to set a standard for the rest of his industry.

But what if your actions were part of an effective organized movement (such as that against Domino's, the perfect pizza not to eat with that beer you're not drinking)? Donna Lieberman, an attorney with the New York Civil Liberties Union, approaches the question differently. "You boycott Coors," she says, "because they use their profits for political activities you despise. Jack Warner blacklisted writers not for anything they did, but simply for having unpopular ideas." No one believed Zero Mostel was a threat to public safety. So you'd be wrong to organize a boycott of a company just because you didn't like the boss's thoughts. But when he uses your beer money to put those thoughts into action by supporting causes you oppose, you have every right to find another brand.

There is an alternative that obviates your Coors conundrum. Each day for much of his life, former Indian Prime Minister Morarji Desai drank his own urine, so he always knew the political implications of his beverage. He lived to be ninety-nine.

GERMAN CAR EMBARGO

Because of our national and religious background (English and Jewish) my family does not purchase German automobiles due to the sorry wartime history of BMW, Mercedes, and Porsche. Having said that, I really like the BMW Z3. Can I make an ethical case for buying a used one because no additional dollars will flow to BMW?

—STEPHEN E. WIMBOURNE, CHICAGO

If you decided simply to drop your embargo, you might make a persuasive case. Few, if any, people at those companies were adults during the war; most of the current employees weren't even alive then. However, if you choose to maintain your embargo, your used-car argument is unpersuasive. The point of such an action is not merely to deprive a company of profits. It can be a refusal to show forgiveness, even symbolically, for the enormities a company perpetrated. And it is a statement made not just to the company but to the world at large. As such, it can be a means of pressing a company and, in turn, a nation, to confront the past. And it could be argued that such efforts are partly behind the extensive reparations Germans have paid to Israel and to individual Jews.

Sorry, I'm afraid that BMW has driven you to rationalization.

APOTHECARY QUERY

It seems unethical for Wal-Mart, which does sell guns, to refuse to sell Preven, a morning-after contraceptive. Would I be in the right to protest Wal-Mart's policy? After all, my bookstore doesn't carry every book.

—ANN MOLLIVER RUBEN, MIAMI LAKES, FLORIDA

Many factors influence how a store selects its merchandise; some good, some not so good. Few would object when, due to lack of demand, a pastry shop declines to sell mint'n'bacon doughnuts. And there are times when ideological criteria are reasonable. Laissez Faire Books sells works with a right-wing slant; Revolution Books stocks its shelves from the left.

But our health care system only works if pharmacists distribute the medication doctors prescribe, not veto intimate medical decisions. A bookstore that doesn't stock your book will still order it, and there are few books one can't wait a week to read. But Preven must be taken quickly—ideally within twelve hours of unprotected sex, seventy-two hours at the absolute latest. (That's why Washington State now permits women to get Preven directly from their pharmacist, without visiting a doctor first, and why Britain is considering making it an over-the-counter drug.) The largest retail chain in the world, Wal-Mart is often the only or one of a very few pharmacies in town. A bookstore's values might inconvenience a customer; a drugstore's can put her in peril.

That is, if values comes into it. "This decision had nothing to do with our morality," says Jessica Moser, a Wal-Mart spokeswoman. "We look at many factors, including customer demand, what we already stock, and the expected sales of a product." And Wal-Mart does fill prescriptions for birth control pills, which can also be prescribed as emergency contraception.

But the company has a history of letting pressure groups dictate its inventory. Wal-Mart refuses to carry stickered music, though much of it goes Top Forty; they don't carry adult videos, yet surely we Americans have a hardy appetite for pornography.

While Wal-Mart did once sell handguns, says Ms. Moser, they now do so only in their stores in Alaska. And recently Wal-Mart has responded to its critics. In a policy change praised by Planned Parenthood, Wal-Mart ordered its pharmacists either to fill all prescriptions or to refer the customer to a pharmacy that will. This is a real improvement but still far from ideal. While Wal-Mart certainly has the right to decide if they want to operate a pharmacy, once they choose to do so, they have an ethical obligation to fill any legal prescription. It does them no credit to stand between a woman and her doctor's advice. And as this book goes to press the chain still refuses to carry Preven, so protest away. America is a free market, not just of doughnuts but of ideas.

Guest Ethicist

CAR TALK

I have been taking my car to the same great mechanic for years. Today I called to change an appointment; I'd forgotten a lunch date with a friend and, as I happened to mention, his boyfriend. Upon hearing this, my mechanic spewed forth a torrent of antigay rage. I was offended and horrified, and I told him so. Obviously, I'm not paying him for his personal beliefs. So am I justified in never taking my car to him again? Or should I overlook his nasty beliefs and keep patronizing his shop?

—E.S., ITHACA, NEW YORK

My son-in-law, who is a native Spanish speaker, recently had the good fortune to find a taxi during a New York City rainstorm. The cab driver, not thinking that he may be Jewish, proceeded to make various slurs against the Jews in the city. My son-in-law kept quiet. The driving was bad enough already and he did not wish to further endanger his life. As far as the tip was concerned . . .

Reflecting our particular dilemma I ask myself what I would do if my barber made anti-Semitic remarks. This, in fact, is unlikely since he is Israeli! I naturally would not return to his shop. Shouldn't I feel almost equally upset when other groups are maligned? Furthermore, if I still maintain a relationship with such a hateful person, surely I would be condoning his behavior.

In many ways it is easy for me to be so high-minded living in a large metropolis, for I have a wide choice of good mechanics. However good this particular one may be, I could go elsewhere.

Jewish law and tradition teaches that one should keep far from an evil person. Certainly, one can try to persuade such people of the errors of their ways. This, however, goes just so far. If after repeated attempts to reason with the other party he fails to respond, then the advice I would give would be to look for another mechanic. Surely, I should expect decency and ethical behavior from everyone with whom I do business, regardless of their job or profession.

MY OWN RESPONSE HAS A DIFFERENT EMPHASIS:

While his technical skills are paramount, they are not the only reason you have chosen this mechanic. If his shop were downwind from a rendering plant, you would feel free to avoid it. And so you might reasonably drive—or push—your car down the road to the shop with the Alpine air and enlightened crew.

But you must not retreat too quickly. Having known the mechanic for years, you have a chance to change his mind. So why not take up the debate—softly, calmly, reasonably? You'll feel better about yourself if you don't allow his intolerance to pass without comment, and it will do him good, too. Perhaps if you deploy all your rhetorical powers, he'll be doing free repairs on the floats at next year's Gay Pride Parade.

Of course, you may end up provoking yet more rancor. If after one of your discussions your car starts making eerie noises and bursts into flames, it's time to find a less hostile mechanic.

As you suggest, you don't need philosophical consensus to get your car fixed. A diverse and tolerant society does not require each shop to tack an ideological summary to its door, like a restaurant posting its menu. But once your mechanic thrusts his beliefs forward so venomously, you must respond. Stay or go, you cannot let his vitriol pass in silence.

Shoppers' Special

THIEVIN' GRANNY

At the supermarket, a charming woman in her seventies paid the checker, then popped a box of cereal, which had not been scanned, into her bag. A cheery "Good-bye" and off she went. I wanted to ask, "Did you forget to pay for that?" but I couldn't. What was my responsibility?

—MAUREEN ARMSTRONG, NEWTOWN, CONNECTICUT

No one wants to encourage crime, but neither does one want to violate the benign injunction to mind his own business. If we each saw everyone else as eager to turn us in for every petty infraction—drinking a beer in the park, jaywalking—we would inhabit a tense and intolerant world (or Switzerland). On the other hand, tolerance can be a pretty name for indifference to other people's distress. So how do we strike a balance?

Many people who would like to think they would intercede to aid Kitty Genovese would be loath to rat out that thievin' granny. For one thing, people are reluctant to yell "Stop, thief!" when they're not certain that what they're witnessing is a crime. (What if your cashier had simply rung up that woman's cereal by hand?) And they're especially reluctant when the hypothetical criminal is so charming. For another, Genovese was the victim of a violent crime, not a petty theft. But also, it is an attack on a particular individual, rather than on a vague corporate entity. Some hesitate to turn in a shoplifter because the consequences to the criminal seem overly harsh (go to jail, lose a job, be humiliated before family), while the harm to the store is diffuse and already budgeted for. What's forty dollars to Kmart? This argument is not morality, it is rationalization. But it can inhibit a potential Samaritan. Just as there are hierarchies of crimes and punishments, there is a more emotional triage of victims. Help protect Kmart? Probably not. A neighborhood deli, maybe. A neighbor's car, definitely. A friend's skull, instantly.

So where does that leave you? Ethically you are indeed obliged to alert the clerk when you spot someone stuffing a sweater or a pot roast into her shoulder bag. But you won't enjoy it. To witness a small crime against a big institution is to be afflicted with unwanted information, which is why I resent the incompetence of our nation's thieves. A really skilled shoplifter wouldn't let you see his sleight of hand; you wouldn't be made an involuntary accomplice. There's just no pride in craft.

CLASS ACTION

I've been invited to join a class action suit against the manufacturer of a computer I recently purchased. I've had no problems with the machine; in fact, I can't even understand the techno-legalese description of its apparent defect. But I'm advised that I may be entitled to over $400 in compensation. Is it ethical for me to join the suit?

—JACK GISIGER, WASHINGTON, D.C.

Your first task is to get a clearer idea of what may be wrong with your computer. It is possible to be cheated without knowing it: A work crew comes by and offers to "reseal your driveway"—you might not realize until years later that they'd merely painted it black. (And stolen your dog. And painted him blue.) Similarly, it may turn out, as you hack your way through the thicket of legal prose, that your computer may burst into

THE GOOD, THE BAD

flames in eighteen months or, on its own volition, crank out a Danielle Steel novel. Frightening flaws. And ones that might impel you to join the suit. However, if after becoming apprised of the problem, you remain content with your computer, then—as you seem to know perfectly well—you ought not participate in the litigation. A class action suit is not a lottery. It is a way to compel a company to compensate those it has injured, and to discourage it from doing future harm. No injury, no compensation.

BANK ERROR

More than twelve months ago, our bank overcredited our checking account. I pointed out their $400 error twice, in person and with full documentation. When each monthly statement arrives—service charges have now reduced the balance to $385—I wonder, "Should I just ask for the balance, and send it to a couple of charities?"

—R.B., DALLAS, TEXAS

Even if the tellers are surly, the lines are endless, and the Muzak is some horrible marching band medley, you still don't get to keep the $400. The bank's error—no matter how persistent—does not justify theft.

Your situation is undoubtedly frustrating. If you'd found a bag of cash that no one came forward to claim, you would eventually be allowed to keep it. But all you've discovered are numbers on a bank balance. Such are the vexations of the cashless economy. That, and the fact that you can't tip an attractive waitperson by making an origami bird out of a Visa card.

While these monthly reminders of the bank's ineptness may be irksome, they are not malevolently intended, and they do you no real harm. The simplest solution is to send the money back. A certified check sent to the bank via certified mail will provide you with a reliable record of the transaction. A more poetic, if riskier, approach is simply to let the money sit there. It will gradually decay and be absorbed back into the bank in nature's timeless cycle of service charges. It's humbling, really.

FRANC IN SENSE

When I got home from an outlet of a fast food chain I discovered that my change included an old French franc instead of a quarter. May I pass the franc on to the next victim? Could I bring it back to the restaurant that gave it to me in the first place?

—LARRY HEROLD, NEW YORK CITY

Your suffering a loss does not entitle you to make it up by cheating the next sap you encounter. You can try to exchange the franc at the fast food place (although I wouldn't count on success) or simply endure your loss with courage. As for fobbing it off at the same place, well, there's a kind of rough justice in that, but if you believe that passing bad money is wrong, it remains wrong even at McBurger's.

The saddest part of the story is that some poor French family finally arrives in America, and instead of enjoying our native cuisine, they're eating deep-fried who-knows-what. At least that would be the sad story if we had a native cuisine. The happiest part of the story is that this old franc will turn out to be incredibly valuable and you've eaten your last meal on a bun. *Bonne chance!*

The most metaphysical part of the story: It's alchemy. As long as you and everyone else don't realize you're handling a foreign coin, that franc has in effect been transformed into a quarter. After all, a coin is only a symbol, and for a while the franc worked fine. Indeed, in border regions, many people accept the currencies of two nations interchangeably. It's only when you realized what it was that it turned back into a franc, and then you had to endure your small loss rather than pass it on to another person. I suppose this is yet another case when ignorance yields greater happiness than does knowledge. (And yet I persist in sending my daughter to school. Some people—me—never learn.)

CAR SEAT OF THE PROBLEM

We are cleaning out our basement, selling a few yard sale items and giving others to charity, including two child-safety car seats built five years ago. At that time, they met all safety standards, but they fall short of today's stricter standards. Is it ethical to sell them? To give them away? What if a warning is provided?

—JACK CUSHMAN, BETHESDA, MARYLAND

Your intentions are honorable, but at least two of your yard sale choices are ill advised. There is something unseemly about selling subpar baby seats to the poor (or the overly frugal). Surely we don't want a society with one set of safety standards for those with money and a set of inferior standards for those without.

Giving away your car seat might remove the taint of financial gain, and providing a warning allows the recipient to make an informed decision. He's made the wrong decision, however, if he decides to use the car seats, according to Liz Neblett of the National Highway Traffic Safety Administration. In addition to today's stricter standards, "The Juvenile Product Manufacturers Association recommends that seats not be used after six years, and some manufacturers have adopted a five-year standard because of the possible degradation of material," she says.

Don't be swayed by the argument that an inferior car seat is preferable to none, either: "There are organizations in almost every state that make seats available free or at reduced prices to those who truly can't afford them," says Neblett.

Certainly, as standards are upgraded for various products, we needn't discard all of our old stuff. For example, you might ethically sell a used car that lacks air bags. But in this case the NHTSA's position is wise, car seats being relatively inexpensive and children relatively fragile.

WHAT A TANGLED WEB SITE WE WEAVE . . .

Many Web sites require you to register to gain access, the equivalent of being asked to produce ID and a personal history to walk into Macy's. Sometimes I give false or partial replies on their surveys. They get some data (but not private info) for their database, and I get to cyber-window-shop in peace and anonymity. Sound fair?

—A.M., TEL AVIV, ISRAEL

It's fine to omit personal information, not fine to lie. Fortunately, there is a technical solution. While many boxes on these questionnaires must be filled in before you gain access to the site, this can be done in a variety of ways. Rather than insert a fake address, for example, type in your protest: "This question is intrusive." You'll gain access to the site, and the proprietor will understand your objection and have a chance to change his ways.

Of course, you always have the option of not visiting a Web site that you think is making impertinent demands. Incidentally, your Macy's/Web site analogy is an imperfect one. On the Internet, no one sprays you with perfume samples; Web technology is, mercifully, in its infancy.

CARD SHARK

After using it only twice, I lost a $15 MetroCard, which means it had 9 bus or subway rides remaining. My brother is a student and is given a free unlimited-use MetroCard. Notwithstanding that it is illegal, would my personal ethics be compromised by using his card nine times, just for the rides I've already paid for?

—MORRIS GINDI, BROOKLYN, NEW YORK

If it were just a matter of your personal ethics, you'd be in the clear. By finagling only those nine rides for which you'd paid, you'd not put the scales of subway justice out of balance. But there's more to it than that.

Part of what makes civility possible is a sense that one is part of a community of honest people. Your proposed act of petty deception would undermine that sense, much as the spectacle of turnstile jumpers discourages other riders from paying their fare. (Unless, of course, you pass out handbills to bystanders explaining about your lost MetroCard.) Were there an open unattended gate and no witnesses, you might slip in nine times. But I doubt that a transit cop would be impressed with this reasoning.

There is another problem with your plan: It drags your brother's innocent student pass into a web of deceit; if you get caught, it's that pass that'll have its picture plastered across the front page, shaming it in front of all the decent honorable passes. While you're certainly entitled to the nine rides you paid for, you're not entitled to commit fraud to get them. Or to hire a steel band to distract passersby while you limbo under the turnstile.

One way to think about it is this: Is the MetroCard analogous to a train ticket or a dollar bill? To me the distinction has more to do with behavior. If your MetroCard is truly lost, i.e., not likely to be used by another, then the train ticket analogy seems superior; if it is likely to be used by another, then I'd go with the dollar bill model. My experience with lost objects leads me to prefer the former. (I know my card is around the house someplace!) A ticket is only an enforcement mechanism to ensure that we pay our fare. Thus, it hardly seems unethical for you to take the rides you paid for if there were a way for you to do so without committing other transgressions (which, alas, there may not be).

Losing things is not a moral failing; if there's a way to soften the blow, that's all to the good.

Keep It Real Estate

CO-OP COP

I am a member of my co-op board. A prospective buyer's tax return showed that she had deducted the entire cost of her Ivy League MBA, a clear violation of the tax laws. I am appalled by her deceit and wonder if it is a legitimate reason to reject her application. Should I report her to the IRS?

—ANONYMOUS, NEW YORK CITY

You should neither reject her application nor report her to the IRS, at least not based on what you've described. You have no idea if her deduction was deceitful or an honest error—or if, indeed, it was an error at all. "If education or training is undertaken to qualify you for a new profession, it is not deductible," says Curtis Arluck, a partner in the accounting firm Weikart Tax Associates. "But if it's further training within your field, it may be deductible." Either way, the case should be settled by the IRS, not a co-op board. And the IRS has every opportunity to do so if it wishes: The woman declared her tuition on her tax forms, after all.

While you have a legitimate interest in assessing a prospective buyer's financial strength, you should use each applicant's private information for that purpose only, not to snare tax cheats or otherwise clean up Dodge City. Unless you learn that an applicant is engaged in a serious and ongoing crime—a string of grisly murders, say, or touring with 'N Sync—then you must respect her privacy.

PSYCHICS DOWNSTAIRS

Our landlady decided to sell our apartment, and people have started coming over to see it. A storefront in our building is owned by a family of psychics, who blast music at all hours, yell at one another a lot, and are completely unreasonable if anyone complains. My husband insists that we have a duty to inform potential buyers of this nuisance. Not wanting to anger our landlady, I wonder if we should say something only if asked about problems. What do you think?

—E.T., BROOKLYN, NEW YORK

It sounds to me (over the yelling from downstairs) that we've entered Golden Rule territory. If you were the potential buyer, surely you'd want to know all you could about the building. While your landlady, as the person actually selling the apartment, has a greater ethical obligation than you in this case, you ought not be a party to deception. And so, while you don't want to make the place harder to sell, thereby making life more difficult for your landlady, you should not cover up a serious problem.

This means you should not wait passively for the buyer to pose a specific question about every possible exigency. If, for example, he wonders about vermin, he need not inquire about each mouse by name. Instead, you should voluntarily tell him how much you've enjoyed living in your apartment, despite some drawbacks, preceding your account of the psychics with this tactful phrase: "As I'm sure our landlady mentioned . . ."

And by the way, with psychics right downstairs, why are you seeking advice from me?

FREE SKI

Telemarketers offered us a free weekend at a fabulous ski resort if we attend a one-hour sales presentation. I'd love to go, but my husband thinks it would be unethical since we have absolutely no intention of purchasing a time share. What do you say?

—CAROLYN THORNBURROW, KINGSTON, ONTARIO

I say go. You're not misleading the telemarketers: They asked you to take a certain action, not to have a particular attitude. And you may not be as adamant as you think. Your feelings may shift once you savor the sight of the pine trees and the scent of the skiers. (Or have I got that jumbled?) That's why the telemarketers want to get you there.

To ease your conscience, when you call for a reservation share your feelings and let them decide if they want you. I suspect they'll be undeterred by your declared immunity to their fabulous time-share opportunity.

A note of caution: Many telemarketers believe if they can just get you there, in range of their glib line of patter and twinkly blue eyes, they can have their way with you. Or maybe they say that about the young Paul Newman. But either way, don't be so certain you're immune to their marketing charms. Your free ski weekend could turn out to be a very expensive vacation indeed.

Arguing with The Ethicist

On a recent airline flight, I had eased my seat down when the hulking guy behind me shouted, "Hey, it's tight back here" and ordered me to return to upright. When I wouldn't, he actually kicked my seat back in place. Worse, when I called the flight attendant, all she did was harrumph, "Miss, I do think you should put your seat up." The guy in front of me had his seat back, so I would have been forced into a cramped little rhomboid had I complied. What should I have done?

—K.R., NEW YORK CITY

You should have held your tiny ground. When you buy an airline ticket, you purchase more than a chance to re-create the confinement of a galley slave on a Greek trireme at the Battle of Salamis. You rent a slender swath of space, both vertical and inclined those few, almost imperceptible, degrees.

Of course, if you can, accommodate the passenger behind you. That's a courteous thing to do, but it is not an obligation. And it is certainly not a courtesy he may demand pedally.

Next time it happens, ask the flight attendant if she can move you to another seat, or the obnoxious guy behind you to cargo.

DAVID OWENS ARGUES:

As a six-foot five-inch frequent traveler of over twenty years, I beg to differ. Nowhere on my tickets has it ever said the passenger in front of me can put his/her seat back, thereby removing 10 percent or so of my space. When I squeeze into a typical coach seat, my knees are literally jammed into the seat in front of me. It's usually so tight, I remove the in-flight magazine for an extra quarter inch. I've had many an encounter with passengers in front attempting to recline their seat, only to be met by my kneecap. Reclining of one's seat requires the concurrence of the person behind you!!

I REPLY:

I sympathize with your suffering, but the party who inflicted it on you is the airline, and it is to them you should complain, rather than attempt to gain more space at the expense of the passenger in front of you. The size of airline seats is not an immutable law of nature; it is a deliberate choice by the airlines, willing to trade your comfort for their profit. Rather than fighting for crumbs with the passenger in front of you, I encourage you to write a fierce letter to the airline.

RICHARD MERSON DEMURS:

The consensus among travelers is that reclining a seat is RUDE—with the exception of early-morning or late-night flights when the seat is reclined to enable the passenger to rest more comfortably.

I REPLY:

I'm curious about your assertion that yours is the consensus view. It is obviously not the view of K.R. Is there someplace I might read the study that backs this up?

A.S. WARINNER PROPOSES A TECHNOLOGICAL SOLUTION:

The suggestion has been made, which is a long way from gathering steam, that airline seats be modified or come equipped with an enabling button on the back that can be used by the passenger sitting behind to limit the reclining travel of the forward seat when both are occupied.

I REPLY:

An interesting idea. But how about the suggestion that the airlines might actually provide a humane amount of room? Why should passengers be so docile in their dealings with the real source of their misery, and so fierce in battling one another?

A FINAL THOUGHT:

Nearly all the men who wrote in—many of whom noted their height— argued that K.R. ought to have remained in a locked and upright position. The few women who wrote defended K.R. against her neighbor's bullying. K.R. is herself a woman. Gender plays its part here, not just in the size of the passenger, but in her vulnerability to bullying and his sense of entitlement.

At an annual charity quilt auction for a Mennonite camping associ-ation, prices were running lower than usual, so I bid up the price on a quilt I didn't want but could see that another guy really wanted. Eventually, he got his quilt and the camp got some extra money. But was I wrong to cause him to spend more than he oth-erwise would have?

—ANONYMOUS, COPENHAGEN, NEW YORK

You did nothing wrong. Indeed, you abetted the mission of the event, which was to attract charitable contributions, not just bargain hunters.

Unlike auction scams where a dealer's shills bid up a price, you'd have had to pay for the quilt had your bid prevailed. That is, you would have had to take responsibility for your actions, one aspect of ethical be-havior. In addition, the other guy was free to drop out at any time. While your motives were different from his—philanthropic rather than acquisitive—there was no deceit, no compulsion, and no impropriety.

A READER BEGS TO DIFFER:
A bid means you want the object. If you do not want the object and bid on it, you are telling a lie. In this case, The Ethicist is saying "the end justifies the means."

I REPLY:
A bid is a promise to pay, and he'd have kept that promise. Not dishon-est in the least.

LEONARD BERKOWITZ ARGUES:
A shill is a shill. Despite the fact that Anonymous risked actually buying the quilt that he bid up in price, the action was not philanthropic but

deceitful. He gave no money from this transaction to the cause. Bidders at charity auctions, probably not experienced in the ways of big-time auctions, expect a level playing field.

I REPLY:

In an auction-house fraud, the shill is not really bidding at all. He is an agent of the auction house and, if his bid prevails, no money changes hands; the item simply goes back into inventory. Our guy is not a shill; he's an authentic bidder. If his bid prevails, as it well may, he's bought himself a quilt. Both bidders are doing the same thing—bidding on a quilt—albeit with different motives. You might not like his motives, but I'm not so sure they're relevant. It is his actions we must judge, and they strike me as reasonable and honest.

MP3

I am a college student who listens to music I download from the Internet. This is probably illegal and in a sense it is stealing. However, I do not want to buy CDs just to listen to one or two songs. Can I continue to do it, just as many ethical people jaywalk? Or is this akin to walking into a store and stealing something?

—ANONYMOUS, NEW JERSEY

To download music from the Net illegally is theft, depriving songwriters, performers, and record companies of payment for their work. It is not so iniquitous as tossing a canvas sack over Elton John's head and swatting him with a stick until he sings "Candle in the Wind" (or stops singing it, depending on your taste), but it is dishonest, and you should not do it.

Your temptation is understandable. In a perverse kind of social progress, the Internet makes it easy to steal songs right in your own home while you're still in your pajamas. You might almost make a case that it is unethical of Napster, say, to tantalize honest music lovers beyond human endurance. This is a ticklish line of reasoning, however;

perilously close to blaming the victim. That is, even if I sashay around town in a sport coat made of hundred-dollar bills, your robbing me is unethical. Unethical, but understandable.

Yours is an intriguing sort of mischief, less likely to be deterred by calls for individual rectitude than by technological innovation. What stops many people from photocopying a book and giving it to a pal is not integrity but logistics; it's easier and inexpensive to buy your friend a paperback copy. Similarly, technologies will soon be in place to encrypt music so it can't easily be stolen and that make it convenient to pay for just the songs you want.

"There will be all kinds of new ways to legally download music—by single cut or for a limited number of plays or for a limited amount of time," Marc Morgenstern has told me. He runs new media activities for ASCAP, an organization that protects songwriters' rights and collects their royalties. "We're going on the assumption that people want to be good, and we're looking for ways to help make it easy for them to do the right thing."

In fact, ASCAP seems less interested in helping people be good than in making it impossible for them to be bad. But if their system means that songwriters can make a living and college students can walk in the sun once again, that's not such a terrible thing.

SIVA VAIDHYANATHAN, DEPARTMENT OF CULTURE AND COMMUNICATION AT NEW YORK UNIVERSITY, MAKES THE COUNTERARGUMENT:
You should not rely on the testimony of interested parties such as AS-CAP when determining the terms of your ethical calculus. Contrary to conventional wisdom (and the efforts of media companies), copyright is not property. It's the result of a complex series of deals that publishers have made with the American people over the past 210 years. We allow them to set monopoly prices and create false scarcity for a product for limited purposes and limited times. This creates an economic incentive to publish that might not exist under perfect competition. This is very different from property. Copyright is a state-granted limited monopoly.

When I was fourteen years old, a friend played for me his copy of The Clash's album *London Calling*. I loved it. I put a tape in his deck and recorded it. I listened to it for about a year. When I turned fifteen, I earned a bit more money. So I bought the album and recorded over my tape. Is this theft? Is it unethical?

I REPLY:

If you phrase your argument as impoverished young hipster versus bloated parasitical record company weasel, well, it's hard for me to type with my eyes so clouded with tears. But if you acknowledge that the music you're downloading is by the very emerging and cutting-edge artist you champion, it looks a little different. It may indeed be in their interest to have you do so, but that's their decision, not yours.

SIVA SAYS:

When Sheryl Crow released her second album, many of the cuts received substantial airplay on FM radio and VH1. I liked all the songs I heard and enjoyed hearing them for free. I even turned up the volume when they came on. But I never bought the CD. I enjoyed the music enough for free, and felt no urge to pay eighteen dollars for them. This is private, noncommercial use. I paid nothing. Is this theft? Is it unethical?

What is the practical difference between listening to downloaded music in the privacy of my apartment and listening to broadcast music in the privacy of my car?

I REPLY:

Here's the difference: The band gives its permission for the airplay (indeed, their record company has no doubt sent a CD to the station, which in 1957 would have been accompanied by a delightful bribe. Nothing says "play my song" like a thick slab of untraceable cash), but they've not given you permission to download. I'm a big big fan of the artist having control over his work. If he wants to give it away, fine. Quibble all you want about the word, but when you take someone's work without his permission, stealing seems a serviceable term.

I see all this from a slightly different perspective. The history of popular culture is a continuous struggle on the artist's part not to get robbed. As I'm sure you know, R&B artists in particular were generally shafted by their record companies. And it took a series of painful strikes before scriptwriters won royalties for their work. It seems to me that what MP3 does is democratize the ability to rip off an artist. And what's particularly galling is that you not only want to do it, you want to be praised as a social progressive when you do.

SIVA GETS THE LAST WORD:

I do not mean to glorify or even encourage the further exploitation of artists by anyone—consumer or corporation. What I meant to do with my examples was to complicate your analysis. You believe that ASCAP still defends the mythical artist. It was started for that purpose, but it in fact defends the established artist and taxes the emerging artist.

MP3 democratizes many things. But it is a mistake to see the rise of tech and its use by young people as exclusively exploitational. As I said, it depends on the use, extent, and context. It is a mistake to assume that the potential for mass piracy equals the existence of mass piracy. Again, there is no evidence that MP3 actually hurts artists in any tangible way. No one can deny the potential to hurt artists. But piracy is already actionable and unethical, as it should be.

LADIES' NIGHT

Yesterday we were walking in Park Slope and noticed an unusual sign in the window of a kids' clothing and toy store: "Lesbian Moms, 10% Off." Is this sort of discount ethical (not to mention legal)? I can't imagine a store boasting a sign stating "White People, 10% Off," for example. This line of thinking started my friends and me wondering about those "Ladies' Night" discounts offered by some bars. Are they ethical?

—GINA D., MANHATTAN

By filing complaints against Ladies' Nights with the D.C. Office of Human Rights, John Banzhaf, a law professor at George Washington University, and his students forced several bars to abandon this practice. But while this argument is right on the law, it's wrong in the heart. Of all the places to demand strict economic equality, it would be cold and unfeeling to start, say, at the movie theater box office. Pay up, Granny! And you, too, little baby! You infants and oldsters have had a free—or at least moderately discounted—ride for too long.

Equal pricing is fair only in a world of equal paychecks. If women earn less than men, why not offer them nickel beer? If lesbian moms are hard pressed in other ways, what's the harm in giving them a break here? While these pricing policies are certainly not meant as economic justice, they do provide a kind of unintended compensation.

Professor Banzhaf and his team were on stronger ethical ground when they filed suits against the all-male Metropolitan and Cosmos clubs, and when they forced dry cleaners to charge women the same price as men are charged for cleaning shirts. The former was an egregious policy of segregation, the latter a failure of the law to recognize the decline of the elaborately pleated blouse. But courtship and mating—and surely that is at the heart of Ladies' Nights—are different.

The ethics of such policies must be judged by the actual effect they have on the society and not only by their adherence to abstract legal principles. Ladies' Nights subsidize a supply of amorous tipsy women to attract thirsty and infatuated men. If the result is sociability, flirtation, and an increase in the supply of human happiness, drink up. If the result is drunkenness, despair, and grim misalliances, it is not just the pricing policy that discredits this institution.

SHERI WEINSTEIN SAYS:

Ladies' Nights have NOTHING to do with reparations for unequal pay. If anything, they work to ensure age-old strategies for male privilege and advantage. Ladies' Night is based on the premises that women need to be lured to a bar, and don't "naturally" enjoy drinking as much as men do; a bar without women is useless; the drunker the women, the more fun for the men.

And have you noticed that any and every bar advertising Ladies' Nights is invariably a cheesy, meat-market, Jell-O-shot, wet-T-shirt-contest bar? I challenge you to show me a jazz club, a comfortable cigar bar, or a place for people over thirty (the age at which society begins to deem most women no longer sexy, or "bar worthy") that advertises Ladies' Night.

I REPLY:

Yours is a good point, and it is just the argument Banzhaf made (successfully) in his D.C. lawsuit. But while the intent of Ladies' Nights is certainly not reparations, the effect may be. And while gender (or age) discrimination is unsupportable, I don't have it in me to begin my social reforms by taking away my grandmother's movie discount or my sister's nickel beer.

The atmosphere in the bars you describe seems more a matter of taste, age, and social class than social justice, although I'm afraid I'm baffled by the phrase "comfortable cigar bar." I keep picturing Donald Trump and hideous respiratory diseases. But romance is such a personal thing.

SHERI WEINSTEIN COUNTERS:

Your grandmother does not get a movie discount because she is female, but because she is elderly. Your sister does not get beer for a nickel in bars that aren't based on a theory that drinking women need to be bribed, seduced, and patronized. But here's an idea: Why not have women carry a general "gender card" around with them? It should, according to your argument, be good at restaurants, dry cleaners, and especially be good at getting women's clothing and haircuts down to the prices of men's.

I REPLY:

My point is that we ought not begin by leveling down, i.e., by removing these petty forms of discrimination that if anything benefit the disadvantaged group, albeit in small ways; rather we should turn our attention to genuine social reform.

I love your idea of the gender card as long as it can be expanded, through an elegant and refined set of computations, to include more members of the society: The more disadvantaged you've been, the less you pay for a haircut. It seems a lot better than the current system of tax breaks for millionaires and free parking for celebrities, all glossed over with a veneer of pseudoequality that enables both Bill Gates and my hypothetical granny to pay the same ten dollars (oh yes! It's New York) for a movie.

Postscripts

Microsoft recently offered a $400 rebate to people who bought a computer and subscribed to its on-line service. To comply with a state law, the company added a clause about California consumers being able to cancel the service anytime. Many people took the rebate and immediately canceled the service, pocketing $400. Since Microsoft must have anticipated that some people would do this, is it unethical?

—T.J., CALIFORNIA

If you signed up for Microsoft's on-line service intending to use it but then canceled because you were dissatisfied, enjoy your $400. But if you signed up only to cadge a rebate, never intending to use the service, then you have behaved badly. That Microsoft anticipated this sort of thing doesn't alter the equation. Banks anticipate getting robbed, and so they install big, heavy vaults; that doesn't make robbery acceptable. Foreseeing crime, I stuff mousetraps into my pockets, but that doesn't make pickpocketing okay, and now I stink of cheese.

I reach this conclusion reluctantly, because if the tables were turned and you offered a $400 rebate to Bill Gates, there's every reason to believe he would take it, and your car, and your house, and your immortal soul. At least that's the impression one forms from the government's investigation of Microsoft's business practices.

Full disclosure: For several years I regularly wrote for *Slate,* an on-line magazine that is owned by Microsoft. But then again, what isn't?

T.J. FOLLOWS UP:
I did take your advice and promptly returned the DVD player I received for free, courtesy of Microsoft, as I never intended to subscribe to MSN. Your amusing advice only made me a stronger believer of what I knew in my gut to be right anyway.

On a side note, Microsoft was notified by the State of California a few days after their rebate news spread that they had misinterpreted California law. Originally they had allowed customers to buy, then cancel, an MSN subscription but keep the rebate, thinking this was required by law. In fact, they *can* require that a customer purchase something noncancelable (the MSN subscription in this case) in order to receive a rebate. By the time they pulled the rebate promotion, most of the damage had been done: Thousands of customers had received millions of dollars' of merchandise with the rebates, and immediately canceled their MSN subscription. Microsoft said they believed most people would not take advantage of them. Clearly, they didn't anticipate how enticing such a loophole can be to people. You were right to say that it is unfair, even for Microsoft, to be taken advantage of in this manner.

SNEAKY SENIOR DISCOUNTS

My friend and I buy senior tickets through Moviefone, which does not define "senior." The theaters we attend offer lower prices to those over 62; we are both 55. However, we are members of AARP, which you can join at 50, so by that measure, we are seniors. The ticket takers never notice the type of ticket, and given how outrageous movie prices have become, is what we are doing unethical?

—J.N., QUEENS, NEW YORK

I'm afraid that what you're doing is indeed unethical. You're going to the movies on tickets to which you're not entitled. Your saying AARP defines senior as fifty years old is beside the point. I define senior as "anyone older than me," but that has little clout at the box office. The movie theater is entitled to set its own prices. And while tickets are indeed expensive, so are beachfront houses on Cape Cod, and you don't get to work a little fiddle to get yourself one of those either, which is too bad, because I love the beach. Furthermore, while a ticket taker may be inattentive, that does not mean you get to slip her an unauthorized ticket or swipe her wallet. Much that is possible remains, alas, unethical.

I did not take your advice with regard to the senior tickets. My friend and I still do it, although I perhaps feel a bit more guilty about it (she doesn't at all) once I received your opinion on the subject. On the other hand, I wouldn't be seeing a lot of those movies in the theaters if I were to pay full price, so at least the theaters get some business from me. As far as the theaters are concerned, I have not polled them to ascertain their thoughts on the subject.

Work Life

Every man, from the highest to the lowest station, ought to warm his heart and animate his endeavours with the hopes of being useful to the world, by advancing the art which it is his lot to exercise; and for that end he must necessarily consider the whole extent of its application, and the whole weight of its importance.

JOHNSON: *RAMBLER* #9 (APRIL 17, 1750)

Workplace ethics is generally taken to mean, or at least to overlap with, something called "professional ethics"—legal ethics or medical ethics, for example: a code of conduct, usually devised by fellow practitioners, admonishing colleagues against the most vulgar abuse of the clientele. Such codes generally come with penalties, the most severe of which, banishment from the guild, is seldom applied (like capital punishment for rich white folks). Professional codes are a fine thing, as far as they go, and often rest on the firm moral foundation of honesty and service to others. However, such codes also tend to ratify the status quo. If, for example, the poor are deprived of legal services, the code of legal ethics is not likely to confront that, at least not in an effective way, at most urging some pro bono work, but hardly enforcing that recommendation. Such codes are not blueprints for reform.

Such codes are the rules for professional guilds; they are compacts of equals, like doctors regulating doctors. But most people's jobs are far more hierarchical: There are bosses and workers, managers and interns. That is, there are great inequalities of power. To be useful, professional ethics must address these things. It might also dictate that working conditions be humane, or question how the profits are meted out among the staff. And to be really useful, such codes must offer a way to question the job itself: Should we really be selling, say, deep-fried doughballs for kids—now with twice the sugar? And should they explode when dropped?

But, of course, one must eat, and the opportunities to live one's values are few for all but the saintliest among us.

Most codes of professional ethics simply assume that the profession is worth pursuing. Many movies, conversely, challenge the validity of a profession itself. In many an Act III, a boxer hangs up his gloves, a sheriff hangs up his gun, a cop hands in his badge, each having learned that the profession itself is not an honorable pursuit. This sort of thing rarely happens at the American Bar Association. It did happen to Michael Douglas in the movie *Traffic,* when he finally rejects the job of America's drug czar. He has, however, not walked away from acting. And thank goodness.

I receive only a very few questions about the nature of the work itself: I am employed at a nuclear weapon's facility, at a plant that discharges toxic waste into the groundwater, at Fox television. Indeed, to date I've received no mail of any kind that begins: "I am John Ashcroft and about to lead a prayer breakfast at the Justice Department . . ." But hope springs.

What I do receive are letters from workers surprisingly willing to abandon many of their fundamental civil rights the minute they get to the office: the right to privacy, to be treated with respect, to have a life away from the office, even the right to the protections afforded by law. My mail shows a distressing willingness toward the view "Your job— love it or leave it." It is a position few would take outside the factory (for themselves, though they might suggest it to other people). It is as if decades of labor law had never happened. (Hey, if the boss doesn't want to pump clean air into your coal mine, find another job; it's his coal mine.)

At first I interpreted this attitude as a distressing willingness to prostrate one's self before authority. If he wants to fire you and hire his nephew, tough; it's his steel mill. But that wasn't the case. It's abasing oneself to property, to capital. It does seem that for many who write to the column, property rights supersede human rights. My correspondents seem to believe that ownership of, say, a Kinko's, gives one powers in excess of what a British captain had onboard his ship in Nelson's navy, and they could flog a disobedient sailor or hang a homosexual. (But they couldn't make color copies instantly!)

Given this docility among my correspondents, even at a period of low unemployment, little of my mail seeks an ethical argument for workplace reform. And yet, it is curious in a nation that makes such a display of its devotion to democracy that these principles are not carried into the workplace. Are there guarantees of free speech on the job? Does everyone have a share in decision making at the office? Is there real equality of opportunity? If these ideas are worth cherishing in a vague Fourth of July–ish sort of way, surely they are worthy of inclusion for the fry cooks and counter help at McDonald's.

There is another, more limited, sort of professional ethics that serves less to define honorable behavior than to codify common practice. Such a code is less ethics than anthropology; that is, one might well find a code of conduct for, say, seventeenth-century slave dealers: Always give correct change, don't lie about the number of teeth, never have a ringer bidding for you, that sort of thing.

And, of course, it can be a defense in, for example, a medical malpractice case to assert that one has adhered to the standard behavior of one's colleagues. Further, it is not entirely fair to judge those living in another time or place by the values of the here and now. However, in the here and now, one could examine the professional ethics of, say, the Russian mafia, and find it wanting. Or the American Congress, for that matter. Which is, I suppose, another way of saying that the legal and the ethical are not necessarily synonymous. Campaign contribution (even to both candidates in a race), legal; bribe illegal. Shooting a member of a rival crime family legal, sorry, acceptable professional practice; shooting a member of one's own crime family, unacceptable (unless you shoot sufficient members to vanquish all opposition and become head of the family). I'm not sure what the parallel would be in the U.S. Congress. But I'll bet the Majority Leader is.

Ethics Pop Quiz

Below are four hypothetical questions for you, the reader, to answer.

Replies can be submitted to theethicistbook.com or e-mailed to theethicist@randomhouse.com.

Selected responses will appear in the paperback edition of the book.

I am a copywriter at a big ad agency. At some cost to my career, I decline to work on ads for cigarettes or SUVs, products I loathe. But lately I wonder if my entire profession isn't suspect. Rather than provide a full and honest view of a product, we deliberately mislead, trumpeting its merits but omitting any mention of its defects. Isn't this just lying? Must I look for another line of work?

As the CEO of a large corporation—you'd recognize the name and the irritating jingle that promotes our most famous product—I'm paid about 20 times the salary of an average employee. My predecessor made only about 8 times the worker average and certainly did no worse a job than I do. I don't really need, oh, let's call it 10 million a year; I'd happily do my job for around 2 million, but if the board of directors wants to pay me 10, am I wrong to accept it?

Despite my repeated efforts to help him improve, one of my employees isn't cutting it; I plan to let him go when his contract expires next month. I've no legal obligation to give him any advance notice, and if I were to tip him off, I'm sure he'd do an even worse job as well as hurt the morale of his colleagues. However, I happen to know that he's about to close on an expensive new house. So what do I do? Would it change your answer if it weren't just one person, but all the workers at an unprofitable factory whom I was going to lay off?

I'm the editor of a Chicago newspaper. To keep my best reporter (let's call her "Hildy") from quitting and running off to Albany to marry an insurance man, I've had the sap arrested on trumped-up charges and tricked Hildy into covering one more story for me; I've got her hiding an escaped murderer right now. In my defense, it's the only way I know to get the story, free an innocent man, bring a corrupt city hall to justice, and save Hildy from a miserable marriage. Plus, I love her. And remember—Albany. So am I all square here?   —WALTER BURNS, CHICAGO

Q&A

We begin with one of the three audition questions for "The Ethicist"; it was the first to run in the column.

Privacy

READING A COLLEAGUE'S E-MAIL

As I was dropping a memo on a colleague's desk, I glanced—inadvertently, I promise—at her computer screen, and saw my name. She had written an e-mail to our boss deftly attributing the failure of a recent project to me. That was a rash overstatement, but how can I defend myself without acknowledging my inadvertent e-mail read?

Reading the first few words may have been inadvertent, but reading further was clearly volitional. Were you wrong to do it? Well, yes, of course you were, as you know. But the sight of one's own name is so alluring.

To withhold even a glance would reveal not an excess of virtue but a lack of vitality. However, reading too far is wrong. So what do you do now?

It depends where your office is located. If it is in a TV sitcom, this will all turn out to be a merry mix-up; you think she's planning to stab you in the back, but she's really planning a surprise party. If your office is in Elsinore, you've understood exactly what Hamlet's up to, but in a moment you'll be stabbed through the arras. Either way, there's little for you to do.

If your office is not located in a work of fiction, if you deal with actual people, trust is required. We make a kind of bargain: I agree not to pry; you agree not to make me a sap. No embezzling, no stealing military secrets, no adulterous liaisons. The shock of marital infidelity is as much the anguish of trust betrayed as it is outrage at sexual transgression. Coworker, soldier, spouse—each stakes a claim to privacy; each tacitly agrees not to abuse that privacy. Your deceitful colleague has violated her part of the bargain, but you will not improve your circumstances by violating hers. So what do you do?

In a few days, send a memo to the boss: "I've been thinking about the project, why it didn't work and what we can learn." In writing, in private, in pencil, with a chance to revise, you'll behave better than you would in a showdown. Acknowledge your own shortcomings in the project. Consider how it might have been handled differently. Do not criticize your coworker; she's already gone wrong by blaming you, as your boss has probably noticed. Do not confront your deceitful colleague; you shouldn't have been reading her mail. While tactics like hers may be a routine feature of office life, like casual Fridays and inevitable Mondays, you can transcend her treachery, at least on paper.

Above all, resist the temptation to seek rougher justice. You could spill a cup of coffee into her keyboard, destroying the instrument of her perfidy. But office coffee is always so weak; you must be strong.

PRIVATE PRACTICE: READING EMPLOYEE E-MAIL

I discovered that my supervisor routinely reads employee e-mail. Legal issues aside, is this ethical? I can understand doing so if a crime is suspected, but not as a matter of routine. It feels like a violation of my privacy. What do you think?

—ANONYMOUS, NEW YORK CITY

While it is indeed legal, I agree with you: Your supervisor should not routinely read employee e-mail. The right to privacy does not vanish at your office door. That the employer owns the computer system is not germane. The company presumably owns the rest rooms, but the boss doesn't get to spy there.

Absent suspicions of specific wrongdoing, one justification for this practice is to ensure that employees use work time for work. This argument is not enough. Every worker every day has passing thoughts unrelated to the job. We all need to make a doctor appointment or contact a child's school. While your supervisor has a valid interest in learning if an employee is a habitual slacker, there are less intrusive ways to do so. Surely the quality of a layabout's work—or lack of it—will be apparent (as will the gentle snoring sounds emanating from his cubicle).

Also, many e-mails that are work related—an early draft of a report, comments about a coworker—are not something you necessarily want scrutinized. A desire for privacy is not an admission of wrongdoing, and to assume otherwise is to rupture the bonds of trust between employee and employer. If every legitimate activity were subject to constant monitoring, we'd all be flossing our teeth on prime-time TV. Naked. On CBS.

UNFAITHFUL ORGANIST

I recently started a temp gig at a church, and they've intimated that they would like to hire me. I'm concerned that they'll ask me what my faith is (I'm an agnostic on good days). I think they may have gotten the wrong idea because they saw me reading the Bible in the chapel. Is it wrong to work for a church and not believe in God?

—J.H., TORONTO

If your work is technical in nature—bookkeeping, say, or plumbing, or even organ maintenance—your own theological opinions are beside the point. This is not hypocrisy; it's tolerance. I doubt that the minister would object to his car being repaired by a Hindu, Muslim, Jew, or atheist. Unless you have strong personal objections to that church's teachings, there is no reason you shouldn't work there.

If, however, you're actually conducting services or otherwise participating in the church's spiritual life, all concerned would probably feel much better if your personal beliefs were in accord with the congregation's. And if you refrained from playing that "Charge!" thing stadium organists are so nuts about.

PROPRIETARY INFO?

I work for a small dot-com that is developing a service that will be available in three to five months. I have been courted by a much larger dot-com, and during our meetings I learned that they will launch a similar service in two months, decimating the one offered by my current employer. I have not yet signed with the larger company. Do I tell my current employer about their plans?

—C.M., AUSTRALIA

You should alert your current employer to this powerful threat lurking over the horizon. You might save your boss a lot of money and help your coworkers keep their jobs. Unless the interviewers asked you to hold the conversation in confidence, you are free to discuss it; they certainly know where you work.

If you plan to jump to the big dot-com, you may be tempted to keep this information to yourself rather than help what will soon be a rival. However, as long as you work for the small dot-com, you should show some consideration for its fate. In any case, if the big dot-com is as big as you say, you'll do it no harm by warning your current boss.

And consider the tiny Hitchcockian possibility that the big dot-com is nowhere near perfecting that new service and is using you to carry disinformation behind enemy lines and scare your boss from the field. One misstep and you could be an innocent man swept into a whirlpool of intrigue.

My stockbroker executes trades for the private client accounts of a nationally known and highly successful mutual fund manager. My broker will often tell me what stocks the fund manager is buying for those private accounts. Should he be offering me this advice? Is it okay for me to listen?

—ANONYMOUS

Your broker is betraying a client's confidence, a breach of professional ethics. He should not do it, and you should be wary when he does.

Joseph Cohen—no relation—a spokesman for Merrill Lynch, says his company "takes client confidentiality very seriously. You should not share information about one client's activities with another." The firm's "Compliance Outline," an in-house code of conduct, specifically instructs the staff: "You should not piggyback: that is, enter transactions after a client's trade to take advantage of a perceived expertise or knowledge on the part of a client." This view is espoused, at least officially, throughout the industry, Cohen says.

It is a reasonable policy, intended to ensure that a broker recommends a trade only because it is in the best interest of his client, not to grease the skids for some other deal he's eager to make. And while the Securities and Exchange Commission does not explicitly forbid this practice, it warns that such information sharing can lead you into treacherous waters where you risk breaking a variety of laws; for instance, those related to insider trading.

Despite these warnings, this stricture is certainly not universally obeyed. And so, when considering any stock, you should buy it on its merits, not because your broker tells you that financial giant Warren Buffet or soon-to-be-divorced Tom Cruise bought a thousand shares. If your broker is willing to breach client confidentiality, can you trust him to be honest about something as important as a stock's value or Tom Cruise's marital status? Indeed, your broker might be such a scoundrel that he is lying about betraying a confidence, claiming that soon-to-be-divorced Tom Cruise bought a stock when in fact he did not. He might not even be divorced all that soon. A tip from a broker is just another tip, so *caveat emptor.* One longtime market observer, Colin Negrych, notes, "On Wall Street everyone lies to each other, but the good thing is that no one is listening."

References and Résumés: Job Seekers

I am 7 weeks' pregnant and looking for a new job. When should I tell prospective employers? Is it unfair to look for a job at this time?

—L.C.

Of course it's okay to look for a job; everyone must make a living. And when you meet a potential employer, what you should talk about are your qualifications.

In an unfair world, where women are penalized for being pregnant, you have good reason to keep your condition to yourself. In a humane world, where pregnancy is not a liability but an ordinary fact of life, your condition would be irrelevant. Either way—self-protection or personal privacy—you need not discuss it in an interview. Indeed, at seven weeks, many women have not even discussed it with family.

The Federal Pregnancy Discrimination Act forbids companies of a sufficient size from discriminating against a pregnant woman in hiring or promotion as long as she can do the job. "If you're being hired to move pianos and can't do heavy lifting because you're eight months' pregnant, you can be turned down," says Donna Lieberman of the New York Civil Liberties Union. "The law allows flexibility on both sides, but your employer is supposed to make a good-faith effort to accommodate you."

Sadly, even liberal-minded institutions don't always comply. Women academics, for example, can face heavy pressure to schedule childbirth during the summer; junior faculty, reliant on the goodwill of their superiors, are especially vulnerable.

Indeed, in any job, you need the trust of your boss, and so as a practical matter you should mention your pregnancy as soon as you comfortably can, perhaps once you have an offer on the table, perhaps later, when you're more sure of your job and your pregnancy. Your boss can't legally retract the offer, but the reality is that he may feel betrayed, as if he'd been tricked into hiring you—especially if you have skills that are not easily provided by a temporary replacement—and that would be an unfortunate way to start any professional relationship.

But inconvenient as it may be for the boss, pregnancy is a fundamental experience that society must accommodate, rather than ask individuals to cobble together their own solution. On the other hand, if you'd like to make your every human need subservient to the demands of commerce, you might try this strategy: Pledge to deliver your baby in the employee lounge during your break, making a little cradle out of an empty box of file folders. That'll show you're a team player.

MODERNITY LEAVE

My wife and I excitedly expect a child this year. Her employer provides paid maternity leave. But she is unsure whether she will want to return to work after the child arrives. Would it be proper for her to take the paid leave and then quit the job without returning? Should she, in that event, repay any of the money she received?

—ANONYMOUS, ATLANTA, GEORGIA

Since your wife is unsure about her future, she should take the leave without the least hesitation. In such a life-changing situation, few of us can be absolutely certain how we'll feel six months later. Circumstances change—emotional ones as well as financial ones. Right now she may think she'll itch for her old desk, only to discover later that she yearns to have another child. Or vice versa: Maybe she'll end up wanting two or three more desks.

Should she ultimately decide not to return to work, your wife has no moral obligation to return any of the money (unless, of course, her company has a policy that requires her to do so). Her situation is analogous to a worker out with an injury who, upon recovering his health, decides not to return to his job. Certainly no one expects him to return his disability payments.

If your wife were certain she'd never return, then she doesn't want leave, she wants to quit, and she should tell her boss as much. First, she owes him an honest account of her situation so he can plan accordingly. And second, she should consider the other workers who will be affected by her actions. Some employers are reluctant to offer paid maternity leave (the Family and Medical Leave Act mandates only unpaid leave), fearing that their employees will never come back. Were your wife to hide her intentions, it would reinforce this negative view of pregnant workers. One hopes that upon learning of her situation, your wife's boss will still grant her a paid leave in the same spirit as she'd be given her accrued vacation time.

One caution: You may want to check with a lawyer to make sure that, under the provision of your wife's particular leave, she is not obliged to repay any benefits should she decide not to return.

TEMPORARY INSANITY

I am a recruiter for a temp agency. Many companies that use us practice nationality-, sex-, age-, or race-based discrimination. I can cooperate, making me personally guilty and legally liable. I can dispatch applicants solely on ability, knowing they are not welcome. Or I can cease to deal with such clients, forfeiting revenue. Is there a positive alternative to simply leaving the industry?

—ANONYMOUS, NORTH CAROLINA

What you describe is not only unethical, it is criminal. "This has been illegal since July 1965," says Daniel Pollitt, the Kenan Professor of Law Emeritus at the University of North Carolina. "Title VII of the Civil Rights Act of 1964 forbids most of this. Age and disability discrimination were added later."

While it is difficult for a single individual to resist such pervasive iniquity, passive acceptance is not an honorable option. Fortunately, there is the positive solution you seek. Call the Equal Employment Opportunity Commission, the federal agency charged with enforcing Title VII. And, Pollitt adds, the E.E.O.C. is conveniently located: "They've got offices in Charlotte and in Raleigh."

DOCUMENTARY DISCLOSURE

Please help me with this unsettling "don't ask don't tell" misery. After working as a production assistant on a documentary on gay and lesbian issues, I had a job interview with a conservative magazine. I described my duties on the film but avoided mentioning its subject. My hollow rationalization was that since I'm not gay, I wasn't betraying my identity, and that it was senseless to jeopardize my chances for this job by bringing up something controversial. But now I'm afraid that I treated homosexuality as shameful and secretive. Still, since the film's subject wasn't germane to my qualifications for the job, was it necessary to bring it up?

—ANONYMOUS, MICHIGAN

When describing your professional experience, the particular subject of a documentary is irrelevant and so need not be mentioned. I might work on a movie about house cats, but that needn't mean that I want some creature clawing up my sofa and shedding hair all over the apartment; that's *my* job. To work on a documentary implies neither approval nor disapproval of its subject. In any case, you gave your prospective employer an honest account of your skills; he's not entitled to a summary of your values.

The danger here, of course, is not betraying the trust of your interviewer, but betraying your own principles. So why not be more candid? Your prospective employer may not be the prig you suspect; he may rise to the occasion and find your documentary a fascinating project. On the other hand, if he is as stiff-necked as you fear, you might not want to work for him. Your job interview is an opportunity for each party to learn about the other.

One more thing: Your not being gay doesn't really come into it. It is not just Jews who should resist anti-Semitism, or only African Americans who should oppose racism. These are obligations for us all.

I'd say that you wish you'd been more forthright about your last project, and while you needn't be ashamed of your job interview, next time speak more freely.

GOING BACK ON JOB OFFER

I recently received a job offer, which I orally accepted. When I approached my current employer with my resignation, he made a counteroffer. I now wish to remain with my current employer. Is it correct to revoke my acceptance of the original offer?

—ANONYMOUS

The most virtuous thing to do is stand by your word unless your prospective employer is willing to release you. He probably will. No one wants a disgruntled worker on staff. But while garnering offers is fine, accepting them isn't, at least not if what you prefer is to keep your current job and get a nice raise. Next time don't be so quick to accept an offer you may not want.

If you do decide to stay where you are, there are a couple of ways to make it up to your would-be employer. First, promptly inform him of your plans, to minimize his inconvenience. And second, be candid. Tell him why you've changed your mind. Who knows, he may match your counteroffer—to which I hope you'll not blurt out another reckless acceptance.

Be grateful that your indiscretion involved an actual contemporary job offer and not a marriage proposal in a nineteenth-century novel: You'd be horsewhipped and driven from the county.

HANDYMAN'S REFERENCE

When the handyman in my building lost his job recently, I felt bad—not that he was especially handy, but he was friendly and re-

liable, and it seemed that he was forced out over a personality clash. So when I got a call from a landlord who was considering hiring "Freddy" as a super, I gave him a bigger thumbs-up than he perhaps deserved. Was I right?

—D.R., NEW YORK CITY

While that landlord needs a decent super, he doesn't need a super super, a candidate for the supers' hall of fame. Freddy, however, does need to make a living, and that's a reason to err on the side of praise. And while your letter of reference must be honest, it may be phrased in the traditional style of the genre. Just as the convention of love poetry is one of overstatement, so the language of the reference letter often drifts away from scrupulous assessment toward praise. Indeed, a moderate recommendation is generally taken to be no recommendation at all. You do nothing dishonorable by adhering to the conventions of the form (although you probably should not send love poetry to your super, who ought not combine his professional and personal lives).

Were he offered a job piloting an airplane while performing heart surgery for the United Nations, you'd have to be more fastidious, but in this case the consequences of your hyperbole are easily borne. If Freddy is inept, the worst that happens is someone's shower doesn't work, a minor problem easily remedied by the fellow who replaces Freddy when he gets fired.

And who knows? Perhaps he'll be handier than you expect. Maybe he'll grow into his new job much as did Harry Truman, who liked to putter around the White House making small repairs. When he left the presidency, there wasn't a dripping faucet on Pennsylvania Avenue, or so I learned in my junior high history class, which may have been taught by an indifferent teacher whose letter of reference was stuffed with inflated praise.

PRAISEWORTHY?

The head of my academic department is stepping down and we are all being asked to sign a card saying "job well done." But I think

THE GOOD, THE BAD

the job has been done very poorly. How do I choose between the honesty by not signing and the camaraderie in participating?

—ANONYMOUS, ARIZONA

Dr. Johnson, that most punctilious of men, ruled on this more than two hundred years ago: "In lapidary inscriptions a man is not upon oath." So err on the side of generosity: Sign the card, and delight in the fellow's departure.

Perqs or Pilferage?

FREE CHAIR TO PROP GUY

To supply props for a movie, I rented chairs from a fancy furniture company. When the movie came out, the company sent me one of their most expensive models "as a courtesy." The job is over, so it's not exactly a bribe. Can I keep it?

—ANONYMOUS

You're not going to like this answer, so you'd better sit down. On something you paid for yourself. Corruption requires nothing so vulgar as a quid pro quo. A politician may defend his junkets and gifts by insisting that they brought no specific favor in return, but they create, if only unconsciously, expectations for the future. Even if you never again patronize that company, your future prop choices will be influenced by the possibility of finding some equally comfy "courtesy" in your mailbox (if it is a very big mailbox or a very tiny chair).

In a pristine world, a drama critic would know no actors, a fire inspector would meet no landlords, and military pilots who kill skiers would be tried in front of a jury of skiers, not military folk. We cannot demand such fierce isolation, but we can easily avoid retroactive corruption. Buy your own chair, and enjoy good posture and a clear conscience.

The company I work for rents a skybox to entertain customers at football games, and so is allotted a certain amount of Super Bowl tickets. Our general manager wrote a personal check for these tickets and then sold them at a profit. Since he paid for them himself, he feels he did nothing wrong. Did he?

—ANONYMOUS, ST. LOUIS, MISSOURI

Your GM used his privileged position to buy a company asset for less than he knows it to be worth in order to sell it for personal gain. That cheats the company and, even worse, it cheats me. Those tickets are a deductible business expense, that is, subsidized by taxpayers, that is, me. And your GM never even sent me one of those giant "No. 1" foam rubber hands. That's not just unethical, it's ungenerous.

INDECOROUS DECORATOR

When I worked for myself as an interior designer, I registered with a carpet store that offered me a 10 percent commission on any business I referred them. Now I work for someone who was unaware of this store until I told him about it. Recently I sent that carpet store a customer who placed a big order. Can I keep the commission or must I split it with my boss?

—S.R., LONG ISLAND, NEW YORK

Neither of you should take the commission. The kind term for this practice is "conflict of interest." Rather than direct your client to the store where she'd get the best product at the best price, you sent her to the place where you'd make a profit. That she is happy with the carpet is neither here nor there. She'd be even happier if the 10 percent price reduction went to her, not you. The unkind term for this practice is "kickback."

That said, the "Code of Ethics and Professional Conduct" of the American Society of Interior Designers permits such commissions as long as the client knows about them and forbids only "undisclosed compensation" from those with whom you do business. (Then again, this is a code of ethics that allows you to put a red velvet sofa in a lime green room.)

In some professions and many parts of the world the payment of such commissions and fees (what many Americans would call "bribes") is standard procedure, but just because a practice is commonplace does not exempt it from ethical scrutiny.

AT THE SPARTAN MOTEL

Two of us at work travel to the same city to check on our project. One stays at an expensive upscale hotel and receives frequent-flyer credits. The other chooses to stay at a much cheaper hotel, closer to the job and equally nice, but without that bonus. Is the first person taking advantage of the corporation?

—B.K., TWIN CITIES, MINNESOTA

If your bonus-loving colleague adheres to the company's rules on travel and is honest with the boss, he's doing nothing underhanded. While it is a fine thing to minimize expenses to your employer, you are not obliged to squeeze dimes by pitching tents beside the interstates. In fact, choosing more austere quarters could be false economy. Your boss may prefer you pampered and pleased; that can make for a more productive worker. If frequent-flyer credits contribute to your coworker's contentment, there's no harm in that.

To forestall the resentment a frugal traveler may feel for a sybaritic colleague, you might suggest that your boss offer each employee a standard travel allowance and a choice: Squander it on high living or choose modest accommodations and pocket the savings. Or the boss might have one travel agent make the arrangements for all employees, booking everyone into similar accommodations. Or he could issue everyone a folding tent and a road map and enjoy the team spirit engendered by common suffering.

I teach driver's ed to senior citizens called in for reexamination because of an accident or traffic ticket. An eighty-four-year-old student who is really struggling announced, "If you get me through this, I'm going to give you a thousand dollars." My gut feeling is that this gesture is out of desperation and certainly out of proportion to the services provided. If he hands me a $1,000 tip, should I accept?

—DANIEL HOLLAND, WISCONSIN

I suspect that his offer, made in the heat of his trials, will not be repeated after the test is over. But if it is, unless your student is fabulously wealthy and absolutely lucid, I'd decline that tip. It is indeed inappropriately large for the service rendered.

Here's a counteroffer: How about helping him fail? I know plenty of people who'd gladly chip in to keep a jittery, frequently ticketed driver of any age off the road.

UNINTENDED PAYCHECK

While working for a major studio, some coworkers and I were mistakenly issued extra paychecks. I suggested we alert the payroll department, but my friends disagreed. Since the show was almost over, payroll would not have time to uncover the mistake. Plus, we'd worked extra hours for a particularly parsimonious studio. I put my check away uncashed but never called payroll because that would be snitching on my friends. Was my response appropriate?

—ANONYMOUS, LOS ANGELES

Some people think that the American film industry has become stale and unimaginative, but I'm encouraged by the boundless ingenuity of your colleagues when it comes to justifying whatever happens to be in their interest. Of course you can't keep the money. And while you needn't explicitly inform on your friends, you must tell the payroll office about the mistake with your check.

Guest Ethicist

A friend, the former chairman of a large college department and still a vigorous force in the institution who could urge a candidate's promotion or not (mine, for instance), gave me his manuscript for a book to comment on. It was shockingly terrible: a sophomoric theme, poor sentence structure, incredibly shoddy grammar and spelling, you name it. As a subordinate to an executive, what was I to do?

—N.K., LONG ISLAND, NEW YORK

KATHA POLLITT IS A POET AND A COLUMNIST FOR THE NATION. HER MOST RECENT BOOK IS SUBJECT TO DEBATE: SENSE AND DISSENTS ON WOMEN, POLITICS, AND CULTURE. THIS IS HER ADVICE:
Once, a friend gave me his manuscript to comment on. Being young and foolish, I went through it carefully, annotating its numerous errors, solecisms, and clichés. You'd think my friend would have been grateful—I had, after all, saved him from having all these faults pointed out by book reviewers—but he was hurt and angry. Did he pick up on the smug superiority and needling exasperation that increasingly animated my blue pencil as I read? Could be. In any case, he didn't speak to me for six months.

This experience and others like it have taught me that writers may ask for "comments" but ninety-nine times out of a hundred what they really want is a pat on the head. As Joseph Conrad said, "I don't want criticism, I want praise!" Some writers have a few trusted souls of whom they demand and expect sincerity, but it doesn't sound as if this older professor has that kind of relationship with you. Perhaps he just wants a bit of encouragement—this you can ethically give, without getting into the details: fascinating subject; no one else has given it quite that twist; length is perfect; have you looked into this that and the other nook and cranny of that general academic area? I promise you, he's not going to ask a lot of follow-up questions, because he probably doesn't really want to confront this mess of a book you describe.

It is possible, though, that he knows it's a mess and wants to rope you into editing it, and this would be a disaster for you. As with me and my friend, your resentment and disapproval would cancel out any gratitude he might be expected to feel. So just before you hand back his pages, be sure to tell him of the terrible crisis that has just befallen your family, which is consuming every bit of your time and strength and explains the big black circles under your eyes.

I REPLY:

Ms. Pollitt suggests a more guarded response than I did, but she has, no doubt, been called upon far more often than I to edit a friend's book, and so speaks from far more experience. I advised less flattery, more utility, and by all means, brevity.

It is at best tactless of the chairman to put a subordinate in so awkward a position. But once there, you need not assess his book's rank in the literary hierarchy; your task is only to say something that will help him revise. Refrain from mentioning every solecism; he'll find many people to do that. Instead, try to offer one or two concrete suggestions to improve his book. Be specific, be brief, be kind. Avoid words like "sophomoric," "semi-literate," and "pig's vomit."

House Rules

FASTER FOOD

An intern at a Wall Street firm, I'm paid by the hour and they round our time sheets up. A 40-minute lunch counts as a full hour, losing me 20 minutes of earnings. Would it be fair if I were to round a shorter lunch down?

—ARI WALISEVER, NEW YORK CITY

Symmetry is the soul of ethics. If your boss rounds 46 minutes up to an hour, say, he should round 44 minutes down to a half hour. Thus, as a matter of fairness, you may indeed round down. In the long run, of course, your time sheets must be an honest indication of hours worked. Rounding off the figures is a bookkeeping convenience, not a way for your boss to cut his costs or for you to pad your paycheck.

In fact, it is your boss who may be doing something not just unethical but illegal. The Fair Labor Standards Act, so several lawyers inform me, provides that all nonexempt workers be paid at least minimum wages for all hours worked. It does not permit "rounding up" meal periods in cases like yours. You may want to mention this to your boss or speak to a lawyer. You could be entitled to do away with this practice and to collect back pay.

Another option: Consider that meal-in-a-pill that space guys enjoy in science fiction stories. Okay, not enjoy, but eat. And fast.

OFFICE PRAYER

Every so often somebody at a meeting decides to invoke God's favor for some commercial or competitive enterprise. All present are expected to bow their heads, look reverent, and say, "Amen." I am not a religious believer, however, and I feel the beginnings of intimidation. What should I do?

—DAVIDSON GIGLIOTTI, SARASOTA, FLORIDA

If your colleague opens the jet ski sales conference (assuming you are in the jet ski business) with a silent prayer on his own, he harms no one and is entitled to your tolerance and respect. (And who knows? Perhaps God likes jet skis and will miraculously boost sales.) Further, if he tactfully sounds out like-minded coworkers and invites them to pray in his office, invoking God's wrath on rival jet ski dealers, he's done nothing wrong.

It is when he imposes his religious practices on others that he is acting unethically. But confrontation is unlikely to settle the matter. Once he is in mid-prayer, there is little you can do. Instead, stop by his office later, gently describe your discomfort, and ask him not to lead any more prayers at meetings. If this fails, take it up with your boss. It is his responsibility to establish a policy that protects the rights of all employees, and to see that no individual takes heat for declining office prayer.

If neither approach works, remind your colleague that in our pluralistic society, invoking God for narrow self-interest in a distinctly secular setting is a practice customarily reserved for winners of a Grammy Award.

EXPORT JOBS

I work for a small printing house that provides redactory services (copy editing, technical editing, etc.). I have been told to begin using offshore services in India, as the cost is less than half what we pay domestic freelancers. I have been forbidden to tell my freelancers about the Indian company, though one of my associates has volunteered to e-mail them and take the fall. My associates and I have also discussed quitting en masse. What is the morally correct thing to do?
—ANONYMOUS

Sometimes the key to a question is not how it's phrased but when. As the ship is sinking, the only answer to a question about nautical safety may be "Don't elbow anyone into the water on your way to the lifeboat." The later you ask the question, the more limited your options.

Your concern is well founded. When a company leaves town, it has an ethical responsibility to the community and to its workers—freelance or otherwise—to give them fair notice, to help them find new jobs, and to maintain their health insurance and other benefits during the transition period. In many countries, this is not merely ethically correct, it is the law. But it is unlikely that your boss has any intention of honoring that responsibility, just as it is unlikely that she is pulling up stakes out of a desire to aid economic development in southwest Asia. And one should be particularly suspicious when such a move is planned in secret.

But this late in the game, your choices are few. Simply quitting is one form of protest, but, as you say, unlikely to help your freelancers. Remaining on the job won't help much either; it seems clear that you lack the power to improve your workers' circumstances or alter your company's plans. But stay or go, the one thing you must do is tell your workers the truth. You may also want to talk to the press. The publicity might make other companies think twice about skipping town in the middle of the night.

The answer to a question can also depend on how many people are asking. On your own, there is little you can do to change your company's behavior. But trade unions and other organizations have had considerable successes in this area. Sometimes the goals determined by individual moral choice can only be achieved by acting in concert with others; sometimes the dictates of ethics are best expressed as politics.

CROSSING THE LINE

After eight weeks on strike, after most of my union colleagues returned to work under threat of being replaced, I, too, crossed my own union's picket line. I'm still struggling with my actions. I was required to join the union (it was a closed shop). I came to view the leadership as incompetent and just plain wrong. When we tried to dissent, we were hooted down. In the meantime, I was in real danger of losing a job I held dear. The "moral" position seemed to be to stick with the union; but is it not moral to decide for oneself when one disagrees with one's representatives?

—HRK, DETROIT, MICHIGAN

A well-run union is a democratic union, one that gives its members a chance to be heard, to dissent, and to vote on policy, particularly on something as serious as a strike. Sticking with the union, then, is a matter not only of morality but of self-interest.

And while, as you say, one must sometimes dissent from a democratic decision, you may do so only as a matter of high principle, not simply because you find yourself on the losing side of a vote. Nor can crossing your picket line be justified because your union is a closed shop; so is America; so is every nation. And so as long as you reap the rewards of past and present collective effort, you cannot cavalierly ignore the decisions of representative government, even when its leaders are, as you say, imperfect.

However, it is hard not to question your facts here. What one person calls "hooted down," another calls "vigorous debate." And I wonder about your certainty that most of your fellow union members had returned to work. In a recent Detroit newspaper strike, for example, both of these assertions were made by some who wished to cross the picket line and return to work, and both assertions were denied by many who stayed out.

That said, if you are correct, and if most of the members have returned to work, the strike has failed, and the rank and file should have a chance to vote on ending it. That you didn't have such an opportunity only makes your circumstances more painful. As an institution becomes less and less democratic, the obligation to abide by its decisions diminishes. If most members of your union want to end the strike but are denied a chance to express that view, you are free to choose for yourselves.

This is an agonizing decision, and it is bound to provoke resentment from those who stay out, and, of course, your own disappointment at crossing the picket line. If your circumstances were indeed just as you described, then you have done nothing unethical by returning to your job, but it won't be a pleasant place to be.

BIDNESS ETHICS

Is a supplier who submits a bid after the deadline entitled to have it considered? Recently, my company sent a letter of intent to the successful bidder. Learning this, another bidder submitted a new bid, drastically reducing the price, which would, of course, benefit my company. Is it ethical to accept this new bid?

—ANONYMOUS, NEW JERSEY

THE GOOD, THE BAD

If you established a deadline, you ought to stand by it. That's the right and honest thing to do. It's also smart, practically speaking. Just as you expect your suppliers to submit genuine bids, they expect you to abide by the conditions you impose, and while you might gain in the short run by accepting the new low bid, in the long run you'll erode the trust that makes doing business possible. By standing fast, you let your suppliers know that they must make their best offer the first time out; they won't get another chance.

An imperfect but not utterly debased solution is to extend the deadline for everyone. Be candid with all the participants, announcing that you received a late bid from a company you are eager to include, and invite all to make another bid. But you might want your company's lawyer to look at the letter of intent first; it may preclude a new round of bidding.

ATTILA'S GARDENER

I've been offered a job at a questionable law firm. I'd only be working on civic-minded pro bono cases, not the dicier corporate accounts that pay the firm's bills. Should I take the job?

—L.A., NEW YORK CITY

We professional ethicists call this the Attila the Hun's Gardener Problem. Is the fellow who prunes the Scourge of God's forsythia, while steering clear of any actual looting and pillaging, doing anything wrong?

Such associations are perilous. The trouble starts with tiny requests. When the plundering guy is on vacation, or half the ravaging department is down with the flu, you may be asked to pitch in. It will be awkward to decline. And beyond what you do for the firm is what the firm does to you. If your potential colleagues are doing things that you find contemptible, do you really want to spend every day with them?

In a world of vast corporations with diverse holdings, though, it is difficult to determine the limits of personal responsibility. NBC is owned by GE, a company much in the news for refusing to clean up the PCBs it dumped in the Hudson River. But a script assistant in Burbank can't reasonably be held accountable for safety standards at a reactor across the country (though she'll have to answer to her own god for *Suddenly Susan*). Consider a few guidelines. For starters, remember that the more the laudable and the discreditable interact, the more perilous your position. Beyond that, look at the work you'd be doing from your employer's point of view. What's in it for her? It may be tolerable to work in a benign and autonomous branch of a dubious company, but not if your essential function is to burnish its image. (For example, you wouldn't want to run an animal sanctuary if the company that owns it is just trying to distract people from its otherwise awful environmental record.) And finally, the larger the public relations staff, the more suspicious the enterprise.

So where does that land you? For the saintly person who can take vows of poverty there is always work. But for the ordinary honorable person, employment options are fewer; compromise is sometimes an unfortunate necessity, and rationalization a persistent risk. Bottom line: If you need the job, take it, but be on your guard. And be prepared to quit if, in the future, more is demanded of you than you're comfortable doing today.

TOBACCO LAWYER

I am the attorney for a former employee of a tobacco company who has evidence that it purchased tobacco contaminated with radioactive residue for use in cigarettes. His wife has prevailed upon him not to allow this information to be made public, because it might affect his future job prospects, although he bears no responsibility. The Virginia State bar advises me that I may not violate attorney-client privilege here. What should I do?

—NEIL KUCHINSKY, COLONIAL HEIGHTS, VIRGINIA

In Virginia, as in most states, the code of legal ethics forbids a lawyer to disclose a client's "confidences and secrets" without his consent, unless he plans to engage in a future criminal act or to lie to the court. Neither exception seems to apply here.

Few people would consult a lawyer who might spill their secrets to the cops. Nor could they give their lawyers all the information needed to mount a defense unless they could rely on the lawyer's silence. While you are constrained by this provision, your client is not.

"The American Bar Association recognizes the authority of the lawyer not only to counsel the client on strictly legal matters, but to advise on moral matters," says Stephen Gillers, vice dean and professor of legal ethics at New York University School of Law. "The lawyer is free to, and should, bring to the client's attention the moral implications of his circumstances."

A TAXING DILEMMA

A woman cleans houses for several people. One withholds taxes; the others do not. But that lone tax form covers so little pay that she fears the IRS will figure out she's also working off the books. She doesn't want to abandon the employer in question, and with a child to feed, she also needs her undocumented income. She doesn't want to get into trouble with the law. What can she do?

—ANONYMOUS, NEW YORK CITY

When New York City offers corporations multimillion-dollar tax breaks to do nothing and the federal tax code is the least progressive it has been in decades (making it ever more possible for a housekeeper and Bill Gates to pay the same rate), it would be churlish to chide someone so hardworking and modestly paid. However, while working off the books might be justified ethically, working on the books is actually a better policy financially, thanks to the Earned Income Credit and the Child Tax Credit. And that means that the employer who files taxes is the one looking out for the housecleaner's best interests.

Say the woman in question cleans five houses a week at $60 a pop. That comes to about $3,000 from each employer, or a total of $15,000, a year. "Just considering federal taxes, with one child and an income of $15,000, the housecleaner would owe nothing—that's a $500 tax, less the $500 child credit," says Jim Weikart of Weikart Tax Associates.

"Her EIC will be $1,600—and that's not just taken off her taxes. She gets to keep any money left over—in this case, the full amount of $1,600. Now, if her employer withheld her share of Social Security, she would owe $1,147.50 there, which the EIC would cover. In fact, it nets the housecleaner about a $450 refund."

The employer's filing does put the housecleaner on the IRS radar, but it also means more money in her pocket, and it does her good in other ways. It earns her Social Security coverage when she gets older, protects her and her child if she becomes disabled, and makes her eligible for unemployment compensation. It also rescues her from the perilous position of breaking the law. So, instead of worrying about whether she should abandon that employer, she would be better off trying to encourage the others to follow that lead.

What's more, Weikart points out that it may be easier than the woman thinks to persuade them to change their ways. "Many household employers want to do the right thing," he says, "but have had bad experiences with government. But recently these procedures have been streamlined, and it's much easier to comply."

And if the woman is lucky enough to clean for clients who aspire to seats on the Supreme Court, persuading them to file should be easier still.

AGENT HARASSER

My agent hit on me in an aggressive, annoying way. I should have fired him, but a project was pending, and to my regret, I decided not to. The project was awarded to me and I had only to sign the contract when he hit on me again. This time, I fired him. The next day I was off the project. Should I tell his wife what a scum he is? Is revenge so bad?

—ANONYMOUS, NEW YORK CITY

You should not call your former agent's wife. You'd be directing your anger at an innocent person, and besides, such a call would probably be ineffectual. If she is unaware of her husband's character, a single phone

THE GOOD, THE BAD

call from a stranger is not apt to enlighten her. In any case, you should not pursue cheap (albeit enormously tempting) revenge of any sort; you should seek justice.

While your ex-agent's behavior does not meet the definition of sexual harassment for Title VII—he was not your employer—he may have violated your professional relationship in ways that a lawsuit can remedy. "It would be worth it for a person in her situation to have a consultation with a lawyer," says Anne Vladeck of Vladeck, Waldman, Elias & Engelhard, a firm that specializes in employment law.

Furthermore, he may well have violated the civil rights laws of your city or state; contact the appropriate agencies. And you can certainly talk to your former agent's boss, who, if he knows you will not merely let the matter drop, may be anxious to resolve it promptly.

The one thing you should not do is passively accept this treatment. While you may understandably want to put this unpleasantness behind you and simply find a new agent, it would be exemplary if you could give a thought to the next client who'll walk through this guy's door. Take action now, and you may spare someone else the same mistreatment you received.

HAPLESS HARPISTS

I enjoy teaching music, but very rarely do I have a student with absolutely no ability. My sister, a fellow musician, says it is unconscionable to keep taking money from these hopeless musical misfits. If I gently suggest that the harp is not the best instrument for everyone and the student still insists on continuing, am I morally obliged to terminate lessons?

—ANONYMOUS, NEW YORK

If your student asks your opinion of her talent, you owe her the truth. And certainly if she is contemplating a professional career, you must provide a candid assessment of her chances. But if she is pursuing music for the pleasure of it, then you're free to teach her as long as she enjoys (and you can tolerate) the lessons. Being a bad amateur musician is no worse than being a bad amateur golfer, or sitting around watching TV, or driving a bucket of balls into a TV (assuming it is one's own TV).

While your student may be guilty of aesthetic crimes, you are innocent of any ethical offense by continuing her lessons. You would, however, be committing a crime against good manners if you were to wear earplugs. Most professional music teachers consider it tactless.

DOGGED PURSUIT

After a year of perfect behavior, our dog, Jasper, was expelled from his dog-walking group when he and another dog had an altercation. (We paid the vet bills and the emergency room bills for the dog walker.) Are we obligated to tell new dog walkers about this isolated event? Jasper is usually friendly, and his therapist did not consider this to be one of his issues.

—TED SUTTON, BOSTON

Once the words "emergency room" appear in a question, the words "full doggy disclosure" must appear in the answer (along with a less disingenuous synonym for "altercation"). The new dog walkers are entitled to know what they're getting into, and the better they understand Jasper, the better they'll be able to do their job. You should provide an honest account of your dog, placing his anomalous misbehavior in context by also detailing his many fine qualities: He's affectionate; he's good with kids; he volunteers at a soup kitchen; he's a terrific dancer—whatever they happen to be. But such a list must include his biting, something you'd want to know if you were taking up work as a dog walker. You might also want to research your potential legal liability should you, knowing Jasper has once bitten someone, conceal this information.

But all this obfuscates the real matter at hand: Your dog has a therapist?! I can't even persuade my imaginary Uncle Milt to go to counseling—and talk about issues!

I'm an assistant to a screenwriter in Los Angeles. Here your boss is your mentor who will guide you to Your Next Big Opportunity. I believe in this system and I depend on it, as it has served me well, but now I'm being held back. Our scripts are valued at over $100,000 a draft, and these days every script is half mine. Meanwhile, I can't afford a new muffler for my car. It would be simple to get a job if I told the executives that the pages they were "loving" were mine. But this would mean breaching a business relationship with my boss. May I do it?

—ANONYMOUS, LOS ANGELES

Let me make sure I understand the system you've come to believe in and depend on. You help your boss get credit for work he didn't do, and in return, he helps you get ahead through influence and connections. Well, you've certainly found the right industry and the right town for you.

I admire your faith in those studio executives and their ability to recognize merit, and that they'd of course believe you when you say the really good work in those scripts is yours. But here's another view.

"Almost everyone who contributes anything to a script develops the delusion that it's 'half mine,'" says the screenwriter Lorenzo Semple Jr., whose credits include *Three Days of the Condor* and *The Parallax View,* "so I strongly doubt that going to studio execs with this plaint would make it 'simple to get a job.' On the contrary, he'd be labeled a disloyal nutcase and be booted out the gate."

But to answer your question more directly, no, you may not violate your agreement with your boss. Fortunately, you have more honorable options. You can tell your boss what you've told me. If he places the same value on your work that you do, he might be willing to promote you from apprentice dupe to journeyman dupe and share credit and money on your next project. Or he'll find some other hungry young writer to exploit.

You can quit. Then go home, write a spec script on your own, sign your name to it, and sell it on its merits. (You are free to use your contacts to make sure your script lands on the right desk.) Of course, relying on your own ability is a risky strategy, particularly in your business, where nearly everything that's written fails to sell.

You can work for someone better. That is, for a more honest thief, someone more likely to keep his end of a corrupt bargain. I suggest Satan. But it is surprisingly hard even to get an appointment without the right connections. Maybe your boss can hook you up.

Arguing with The Ethicist

ART OF THE MATTER

I am an artist, and I support my family by painting reproductions of the work of more famous artists, a common practice in the tradition of painting. However, some say this is akin to stealing the famous artists' work. Is it right for a wealthy client to commission a copy of a work available in the original? Is it wrong for an artist to accept the job?

—RAY ABEYTA, BROOKLYN, NEW YORK

All artists are influenced by their precursors, and as you note, some art deliberately makes other paintings its subject. What's more, adopting a style—as many painters embraced Cubism, for example—is not just honorable, it is inevitable. This appropriation and transformation of ideas is what culture is. Your work may differ in degree, but it is not different in kind from what every artist does. So long as you do not commit fraud by passing off your work as that of another artist, you do nothing unethical by catering to your client's desire.

As for your patrons, with great wealth may come great responsibilities, but buying an original by, say, Brice Marden, is not one of them. If a client is happy to own something merely Mardenish, that's no crime.

In a sense, great work is immune to imitation. It's one thing to say you're going to paint a picture in the manner of Pollock, quite another to do it well. Your knockoff will inevitably lack essential Pollock qualities. The words "bad imitation" are a tautology: All imitations are inferior to (or at least different from) the original. To modern eyes, what is most striking about those convincing counterfeit Vermeers of the nineteenth century is how little they now resemble Vermeer, and how much they look like nineteenth-century paintings.

People buy things for many different reasons. When someone pays $1 million for an original Brice Marden painting or $6,000 for an original Vera Wang dress, one of the things that confers value is its status as an original. Neither your $500 mock-up in the manner of Marden nor the $300 knockoff shmatte ought to diminish the original (though brand watchdogs will bark, of course). The customer for one is not the customer for the other. Indeed, the copy can enhance the value of the original by declaring it a work worthy of imitation.

These issues are much debated in the art world as both ethical and aesthetic questions, and there are painters who would resent what you are doing. However, artists as various as seventh-century Chinese calligraphers, Marcel Duchamp, and Sherrie Levine have challenged the idea of the proprietary original. If you get busted for your artistic endeavors, and those folks are on the jury, you'll walk.

DAVID WALL COUNTERS:

I'm not an expert about art or the law, but it seems to me copying a piece of art is distinct from imitating the style of an artist. Is there no copyright protection law surrounding works of art? I can't imagine there's not. If I read your article, paragraph by paragraph (which I did!), and then typed each paragraph in my computer from my memory, and then sold it to another newspaper for very little money claiming that I wrote it as well as admitting it was a copy of your work, would I be on a solid legal and ethical foundation?

I REPLY:

I'm not a lawyer either, but as I understand it, copyright protects only specific expression and not an idea. Many artists would argue that the copy is a very different sort of specific expression from the original. It is similar only in crude outlines. The idea here, much discussed in the art world, is that all those details of brushstroke and color are quite different in the copy, and as such it is a distinctly new work. The argument runs that no work springs from nothing; all work has its sources and influences. That is no more true in this copy than in any other painting. This argument—and I find it persuasive—challenges the meaning of "originality."

It is, paradoxically, essential that the artist sign his own name to his copy and not that of the person who painted the original. To sign someone else's name would not be giving credit, it would be counterfeiting.

Were you to reprint my column under your name, you would be taking my specific language, my means of expression, and that is protected in law and, in my opinion, in ethics.

ROGER FAMILY WRITES:
Reproducing art for pay is unethical if not illegal, especially if the original in question is by a living, possibly struggling, artist.

I REPLY:
One of the many interesting things that I discovered in talking to artists and critics while working on this question is that wealthy clients do not commission copies of starving artists. There's no need to. They can buy such paintings. The only copies commissioned are the work of incredibly successful artists.

SIMON FRANKEL SAYS:
As an intellectual property and art law lawyer, I was surprised by your response. Your answer did not mention a real legal (and ethical?) risk of "copying" the work of a famous artist: copyright law. If an imitator merely copies the "style" of a recognizable artist, and clearly sells the work as such, then the work is unlikely to run afoul of the copyright laws. But if a person creates an imitation of a famous work that is still under copyright law (say, a work by Jasper Johns) that would be a violation of the artist's copyright. It's hard to say whether the artist would assert a claim of copyright infringement or agree with you that "the copy can en-

hance the value of the original by declaring it a work worthy of imitation." But it is certainly an issue for would-be imitators to consider.

I REPLY:

I defer to your legal knowledge, but note that Mr. Abeyta would argue that his "copy" is profoundly different than the original and so ought not run afoul of copyright laws. As I noted in my column, he signs his own name to his paintings; there is no attempt at fraud. Further, one of the things that gives an original its value is that it is an original. So Mr. Abeyta's Picasso-ish work has no value to an actual collector and does not diminish the value of an original Picasso. Thus I see no problem here as an ethical matter.

LAURENCE CUTTER COUNTERS:

There is nothing either flattering or sincere about ripping off the works of Jackson Pollock, especially by making exact copies of his works. In a world flooded with Pollock clones, the work of the artist is demeaned and its value lessened, not to mention the introduction of increased efforts in the art world that are now needed to discern this fraud. And the owner of the original is now left in the position of having to defend its true character.

I REPLY:

To me, the ethical question pivots on ideas about originality, influence, and what it is to make art. This has been a subject of lively discussion in the art world over the last decade or two, and many (most?) critics—and most artists—would argue that the notion of Pollock's work as sprung fully formed from the wellspring of his genius, unsullied by influence, is false—a residue of romanticism with its idea of the heroic (generally male) creator. That is, Pollock has his antecedents, as does Abeyta. The question critics are likelier to engage is not "original or unoriginal?" but "good or bad?" This is in no way disrespectful of Pollock's accomplishment. Quite the contrary. It argues that Pollock is, in the most profound way, inimitable. And so Abeyta does him, and the culture, no wrong.

My efforts to find a job seem hindered by the fact that I have a Ph.D., which is unusual for someone in my field. So I want to remove it from my résumé. Some friends think this is a sin of omission, and therefore okay, as opposed to a sin of commission, where I would say I possessed a degree I did not. What do you think?

—ANONYMOUS, ST. LOUIS, MISSOURI

No doubt many people wish your friends' theory were true. I suspect that Kevin Costner would like to omit that water movie and that mailman movie from his résumé, but he should not: They are a part of his professional history, about which a potential employer may reasonably inquire. And while a Ph.D. may not seem as discreditable as *Waterworld,* that's not for you to say. Your obligation is to give a prospective employer an honest account of your professional and educational history. Perhaps he's found that the overqualified grow restless in that particular job, or maybe he's anti-intellectual, or maybe he's jealous because he never finished his dissertation. You must be honest here regardless of his leanings. Perhaps you'll have a chance to reassure him at the interview, if you don't slip in too many Latin phrases.

You do have another option. You are certainly free to give your prospective employer something less formal than a résumé. You might say, "Here are some things I'd like you to know that make me a great candidate for the job." Then you can choose what to include.

However, your desire to omit your Ph.D. is a desire to deceive, and that you may not do. A résumé is assumed to be a complete education and professional history. If you provide a résumé, it must be an honest one. As people get older and their professional experience increases, they necessarily omit early positions from a résumé, lest it end up ten pages long. But in doing this sort of editing, you must prune the minor experiences and retain the major ones, and that includes your Ph.D.

There are, of course, limits on what an employer may ask about you. Your peculiar hobbies, your erotic life, that weird noise you make when you eat? None of his business. But when an employer requests legitimate information, you must answer honestly.

As a vocational counselor I have not only recommended to others but have myself obtained jobs by omitting a degree or so. Instead of looking at the subject from the "ethical" point of view, think of it in a pragmatic way. Why should I, or any prospective employee, hinder our own opportunity to get a job that we might want (or need!) in order to be "totally truthful"? While you cannot say you have a degree that you do not have because a simple background check will uncover this, no one could possibly know that you had another degree that you forgot to mention. This is only a sin of omission, and a pretty small one at that. I would like my name withheld because right now I have such a job!

I REPLY:

Well, yes, if I take your advice and "[i]nstead of looking at the subject from the 'ethical' point of view, think of it in a pragmatic way" there's all kinds of things I can do, like slip into your house and take your TV set. That I won't be caught (I'm capable of fabulous stealth, much like your résumé) has nothing to do with an action's rightness or wrongness. I grant you that leaving something off your résumé is a small wrong (I never claimed otherwise) but we were not arguing about its size, only its propriety. One inconvenient thing, I would have to change the name of the column to "The Pragmatist." And put sturdy bars on my windows.

EDWARD FRIEDMAN ARGUES:

You would complain mightily if an employer profiled someone by saying "Women aren't as accomplished at math as men," or "Blacks seem to have fewer job skills than whites." But you have no problem accepting the profiling of Ph.D.'s: "Perhaps he's [the prospective employer's] found that the overqualified grow restless in that particular job, . . ."

I REPLY:

While I was speculating about a prospective employer's reasons for wanting that information, I was not endorsing them. Indeed, such an employer would be foolish to make the assumptions I described and would often deprive himself of excellent employees. And as I suspect you know, were an employer to make hiring decisions based on the prejudices you enumerate, he'd be not just unethical but in violation of federal law.

ELIZABETH FRANK ASSERTS:

I used to put my published novel as a credit on my résumé, hoping that it would indicate to prospective employers a basic knowledge of grammar and assurance that I was accustomed to, as they say, "heavy document input." I took it off because I received too many charges that I was overqualified, that I would become "bored" (with a word-processing job in a law firm? Naah—who could be bored with that?). Sometimes it is necessary to keep your light under a bushel in order to keep bread on the table.

I REPLY:

The expectation is that your CV provides a complete educational and professional history, and thus to omit so significant a segment of one's education as a Ph.D. seems deceptive. I do think you could make a case for keeping quiet about your novel, however, as it involved no employer-employee relationship and could, alas, be considered a private pursuit, not germane to a job interview.

A Postscript from the Original Job Candidate

I decided not to include my Ph.D. on my résumé as a rule, but did in certain situations. But it got to be too much trouble remembering who I had given which info. So, since my rabbi agreed with you and I was getting nowhere anyway, I began including it in all résumés and letters. Since that time (early last summer) I have had NO interviews. Previously I had been getting about a 30 percent response.

I have now essentially given up trying to find a job in my field. I think being 50 years old, with 20 years experience, frightens employers in St. Louis. Not working in my field for several years is also a hindrance.

So, I have decided to see if I can learn enough to make a living selling jewelry or art. I currently work part-time in a gallery selling both. Unfortunately, my research thus far tells me that it's next to impossible to make a living in these areas without working in a commission environment. And I hate the environment commission sales breed. So, my career search continues to be a work in progress.

Another Postscript

One of the references I used in a job application is my former boss, whom I am now dating. We were not romantically involved while we worked together, and she says our current involvement has no bearing on the recommendation she would give me. Am I obliged to reveal our relationship to my potential employer?

—ANONYMOUS, BOSTON

Even with a sincere determination to be punctilious, your former boss faces a conflict of interest in writing a reference for someone she's seen naked. If no one else at the old firm is in a position to write you a recommendation, then she may write it, but she should acknowledge your personal connection and leave it to your potential employer to gauge its effect on her comments. Her disclosure can be brief ("As someone I have known both personally and professionally . . .") and need not extol your kissable lips or that funny way you crinkle your eyes in a moment of passion.

ANONYMOUS FOLLOWS UP:
One factor influencing my decision was the fact that my former boss was (and still is!) a woman, as am I—a facet of my life of which my employer was not aware.

What I ended up doing was going out to lunch with my new boss in the small Internet company I was joining, and revealing to him that (1) I was living with a woman, and (2) she used to be my boss and I used her as a reference. I offered to give him another reference to check if he wanted. He said that it was not a problem for him at all, that he really didn't care that much about my references, and that he knew he wanted to hire me even before he checked any of them. (He was also support-ive about the personal revelation I had made to him.) I asked that he not reveal this to his partner, as I am not friends with him, and didn't want him to know at that point that I lived with a woman. As far as I know, he hasn't.

I feel that telling him about my reference conflict, albeit after the fact, cleared this issue up. For me, the important factor was not whether or not he thought it was important, but that I had been honest about my relationship with the person I had used as a reference. In retrospect, I should have done what you suggested [and] casually told my new boss that one of my references was a friend as well, and told him I had a girl-friend more on my own schedule.

Civic Life

The apparent insufficiency of every individual to his own happiness or safety compels us to seek from one another assistance and support. The necessity of joint efforts for the execution of any great or extensive design, the variety of powers disseminated in the species, and the proportion between the defects and excellences of different persons demand an interchange of help and communication of intelligence, and, by frequent reciprocations of beneficence, unite mankind in society and friendship.

JOHNSON: *RAMBLER* #104 (MARCH 16, 1751)

By civic life, I refer to those times when we are out in public among strangers but not shopping. If we're not at work, not at home, and not at the house of a friend, as likely as not we're buying things. We do this in places that are partly public and partly private. Every store or restaurant is governed by the laws of our society, but each may also establish various rules we must obey or risk finding ourselves dragged away from the salad bar and tossed into the street. This section, however, is concerned with those encounters that are not shaped by getting and spending, but by what we have of public life. It is here where we see demonstrated those values held in common by all Americans—and the conflicts that arise from the clash of values that are not.

Dr. Johnson understood that individual ethical choices affect more than the people directly involved; they contribute to the tenor of the entire society. But while Johnson could articulate the values esteemed—if not actually practiced—by nearly all educated people in eighteenth-century London, our age lacks such consensus.

What shapes our public interactions is uncertainty. We cannot be sure that our own ideas about ethics, about how one ought to behave, are embraced by everyone, or anyone, else. This is a country of enormous variety, with respect to income, education, religion. It is a country of immigrants: 11 percent of us were born in another country; 40 percent of us are the descendants of Ellis Island arrivals, who brought with them great diversity of values. A conflict is harder to resolve when those at loggerheads make fundamentally different assumptions about right and wrong. Making wise ethical choices is a tricky business in a country where we don't even agree if it's okay to talk at the movies.

I see this uncertainty in the many letters to the column asking when one should intervene in the affairs of others. How do you respond to the cry of "Stop thief!"? What do you do when you're on the bus and you see a mother slap her child? Civility and tolerance mean that there are times when we must mind our own business. But compassion and a concern for others means there are times when we must go to the aid of those in need. But which is which? What is caring and what is meddling?

If we are too reluctant to intercede, we create a bleak and indifferent society in which each of us struggles alone with no expectation of kindness from anyone else. New Yorkers were horrified by the prospects of just such a society when Kitty Genovese was attacked and murdered as her cries for help went unanswered. If, however, we intercede too readily, we create an intolerant society where everyone spies on and interferes with everyone else. And while it would be a fine thing if no one were to throw so much as a gum wrapper on the sidewalk, not everyone wants to live in Singapore.

When considering the ethics of civic life, it is not just the behavior of individuals that can be scrutinized but also the objects and institutions we have created. We can, for example, consider an SUV, think about its design, and consider the effect it will have on others. We can ask if this is an ethical object.

Similar questions can be asked about public space itself. In their wonderful book, *The Park and the People,* Roy Rosenzweig and Elizabeth Blackmar recount the history of New York's Central Park in a way that touches on fundamental ethical questions. How are we to behave in such a space? Who is the park for? Who pays for it? Who makes decisions about its use? In describing, say, a 1981 ruling by Park Commissioner Gordon Davis denying the artist Christo permission to build a massive installation in the park, the authors show how public space is an expression of the ethics and values of the society. Here is ethics expressed as horticulture.

Indeed, for Calvert Vaux, who, along with Frederick Olmsted, designed Central Park, it was not merely a space for recreation but an essential element of democracy. Vaux believed that a free and egalitarian society required great public institutions—parks, libraries, schools—if it was to flourish. Olmsted and Vaux were very much aware that no individual Manhattanite, however wealthy, could have a backyard like Central Park, or for that matter, a private library like the New York Public Library, or private tutors like the faculty of City College. These were municipal treasures that could only be created through group action and that were to be enjoyed through mutual interaction. The park was a creation of civic life and to use it was a reward of civic life. Indeed, to use it was a way to learn what it meant to be a person living among others. In the following chapter, I'll take up some questions about how to behave ethically within these public spaces.

Ethics Pop Quiz

Below are four hypothetical questions for you the reader to answer.

Replies can be submitted to theethicistbook.com or e-mailed to theethicist@randomhouse.com.

Selected responses will appear in the paperback edition of the book.

I am the leader of a large Western nation (you'd recognize the name) that trumpets its devotion to democracy. In the election that brought me to power, I received far fewer votes than my opponent, but our peculiar rules made me the victor. (It's a wild story.) For me to continue in office is legal, but is it ethical?

My country is waging an unpopular and, I believe, unjust and tragic war against the people of a tiny nation. I've just been drafted, and I plan to lie and say I am a homosexual, quite enough to keep me out of the army. I realize that if I don't serve, someone else will be sent in my place. And I know that my motives are not just opposition to the war: I'm scared for myself, too. Is my plan an ethical one?

—ANONYMOUS (AGE 19), 1968

Like most Americans (more than two-thirds according to a study I ran across) I favor capital punishment. I know it might not actually deter any murderers and that most Western nations have forsworn it, but my religious beliefs lead me to support it, if only so society can send the message that murder is wrong. What do you think?

My company typically makes a campaign contribution to the congressional candidate we think most shares our interests. No problem there. Lately I've learned that a competitor routinely contributes to both candidates in the race so they'll have access to whomever wins. Granted this is legal, and there is no quid pro quo here, but it sounds a little fishy. Is this a bribe or is it just good sense for my company to do the same thing?

Q&A

Concede or Intercede

I was on the subway when I saw a frustrated mother slap her child for crying. She didn't hit him hard enough to endanger his life, but the scene suggested something equally scary: an eternity of whacks, verbal abuse, and humiliation. I was afraid to say something, lest I make the mother even angrier at the child. Should I have?

—A.K., NEW YORK CITY

In a diverse city like New York, there is no consensus on child rearing. There's not even consensus on using a cell phone in a restaurant. Many parents consider spanking of any kind to be cruel; others see harsh discipline as a duty. (Scriptural justifications for spanking abound on the World Wide Web.) And people who are sure they're right aren't moved by a stranger's remonstrance. But it sounds as if this isn't discipline, it's just someone lashing out at her child. Slapping, after all, doesn't deter tears, it causes them.

Ignore the impulse to voice your outrage for its own sake, and subject your actions to one simple test: "Will this help the child?"

Addressing the subject directly risks causing offense, especially where differences of race, class, or religion apply. And if the mother is capable of this violence in public, she could be capable of much worse at home when she's offended, and unobserved. So proceed with caution.

Elisa Koenderman, who oversees all domestic violence cases at the Bronx District Attorney's office, points out that the woman doesn't seem to be breaking any laws. Still, Koenderman suggests intervening, but gently. "The parent may be acting out of frustration and rage," she says. "By saying something like 'Hey, take it easy,' you give the parent a moment to stop and think. And it is good to demonstrate that you as a member of society disapprove."

This point will not be lost on the child. After a few years of getting knocked around, many kids come to believe they deserve their fate. Hearing another adult take issue with the treatment he's receiving might help counteract that effect.

Even if your rebuke doesn't have immediate results, someone else might hear you, and may speak up next time, too. And after that, who knows? Not so long ago, corporal punishment in schools was commonplace. Today, several countries have made it illegal for even a parent to spank a child.

If you're worried about saying the wrong thing, try distracting the mother instead of forcing a confrontation. Ask her for directions, or about how to switch trains. As long as your intervention wins the kid a moment of peace, it's a risk worth taking.

LIBRARY COPS

At our local library, a guy who seems unbalanced has been viewing Web sites on how to build bombs. I mentioned this to the librarians, but they did nothing. In the aftermath of Columbine, I wonder if I should go to the police.

—R.F., HARTFORD, CONNECTICUT

People read murder mysteries without then killing their neighbors. People read Pat Riley's ludicrous motivational twaddle without then destroying the beauty and poetry of basketball. In America, you may read whatever books you wish. And the Internet operates on the same theory, albeit if you surf the Net in the tub you risk a painful electrical shock.

There are many excellent ways to thwart violent crime. Creating a Library Police is not one of them. The Columbine shooters you refer to were reported to the police at least six times, not for reading about bombs, but for actually making bombs, as well as engaging in other criminal activities. Your librarians were right not to act; there can be no free exchange of ideas when government officials collect reading lists.

THE GOOD, THE BAD

I recently confronted a stranger for wearing a fur coat, denouncing her for the violence and cruelty that went into making her unnecessary garment. The friend I was with said what I did was wrong, but I think I was simply speaking out against an evil. What do you think?

—KEVIN O'CONNOR, NEW YORK

You denounced her? The fostering of social progress sometimes obliges one to jettison civility, but you seem to do so with an alacrity reminiscent of the McCarthy hearings. While the animal rights folks may have the ethical high ground here, I'm not so sure that haranguing strangers on the street is the ideal form of protest, although it no doubt kindles within you the warm glow of moral superiority. Vigorously advocating your point of view is entirely appropriate, but a burly guy (assuming you've achieved burliness) browbeating a lone woman (the sex that predominates in the fur-wearing classes) is not advocacy, it's bullying.

There is a hierarchy of wrongdoing that calls for a hierarchy of responses: the greater the wrong, the more vigorously one may oppose it. It would have been ludicrous in 1850, for example, to urge Frederick Douglass to soften the tone of his abolitionist editorials in *The North Star.* In addition, one must match means to targets. Thus, you ought not harass my imaginary Aunt Mimma for wearing the fox stole she has owned since 1956. Instead, hand her a leaflet. And then rally your confreres to picket the biannual fashion shows in Bryant Park, which could be to antifur protesters in 2001 what the Pentagon was to antiwar demonstrators in 1967.

When you are in doubt about a particular tactic, here's a helpful guideline: Ask yourself, "Am I working for social change, or am I venting?"

BAD BOYS ON THE BUS

I board a bus where three young men are engaged in loud and vulgar conversation. As their talk turns more violent, some passengers move away. The young men begin taunting other passengers with racial slurs. After a few more stops, they approach an elderly woman and demand her purse. She refuses. A few more insults and they leave the bus. The driver remains silent throughout. At what point is one compelled to intervene? Complicating matters, I am white, the young men are African American, and the slurs are directed at people of Asian descent.

—J.C., SAN FRANCISCO

Anyone who's been on a city bus when school lets out knows that an adult's idea of loud and vulgar may be a kid's idea of high spirits. And so you were wise to avoid a confrontation when the young men were simply being inconsiderate. The harm to others was minor, and you rightly avoided escalating the tension. Censorious stares or moving away are apt responses.

When the kids taunt another passenger, circumstances change. They've gone from at least ostensibly self-contained rudeness to harming others, and those others are entitled to your support. You might begin by alerting the driver; he may be unaware of what's happening at the rear of the bus. But once he knows, you can demand that he respond. He is not a police officer, of course, but he can officially call for orderly conduct. This can be less contentious than your speaking directly to the kids.

It is when the kids attempt to rob an old lady that every other passenger on the bus is obliged to come to her aid, even in as simple a way as speaking up and demanding that they leave her alone, or asking the driver to radio for help. Several sociological experiments suggest that getting the first person to intercede is the difficult thing. Many people are reluctant to do so, partly out of an understandable fear, but also by a dread of embarrassment. However, once a single person steps forward, others are often willing to join him.

I don't want to minimize the risk involved. A group of young men harassing people on a bus is frightening and confusing. (And as you note, our sense of danger is easily skewed by ideas about race.) Certainly, had the young men been armed, there would be little the passengers could do. But if any of us were attacked in the circumstances you describe, we'd want our fellow passengers to come to our aid; I hope I would have the courage to do likewise.

On the bus the other day, I glanced at the woman next to me. She was working on a special-education student's evaluation form, showing the child's name, the school's name, and all of the child's problems and diagnoses. She should not have been doing confidential work in a public place. Should I call the school and tell them without mentioning the therapist's name, or chalk it up to a momentary lapse in professional judgment?

—C. COHEN, FOREST HILLS, NEW YORK

Alas, I think the lapse is yours for the (admittedly minor) offense of snooping. A "glance," as you call it, would not have revealed as much information as you took in. With all due respect, for civil society to be possible, there are times when we each must mind our own business.

Give this poor, hardworking special-ed teacher a break; let her catch up on her work on the bus. While she should, as you note, be more careful about confidentiality, it does seem unlikely that any misuse of the information could come from the casual glance of a fellow passenger. Something as simple as covering the name of the student whose records she is working on would solve the problem, and you could certainly have gently suggested that to her, although reporting her would have been a bit extreme.

If, however, you'd like to do some glancing on that commuter spy bus that runs through Los Alamos, you might qualify for a part-time job with the FBI.

Public Space: Disposed and Indisposed

Say I see something in my neighbor's trash that catches my eye. Say it turns out to be an antique worth a lot of money. Do I have to tell my neighbor? Or did it cease to be his property when it hit the curb?

—ANONYMOUS, NEW JERSEY

As an ethical matter, you may invoke the ancient and honorable rule "finders keepers." The result, happiness. You gain a magnificent, if malodorous, antique; your neighbor cleans out his closet; and the city has one fewer bibelot to haul to the dump. Everyone wins.

As a legal matter, it is not so different, says David Goldberg, a lawyer with an astonishing amount of knowledge on this subject. "Garbage is considered the paradigmatic case of abandoned property, meaning that the finder should win (so long as the trash can is not on private property), but some courts, invoking the common law's 'aim' of 'reuniting true owners with their property,' apparently treat the 'abandoned' category as a disfavored one, meaning that the owner might have some argument if the object was mistakenly thrown in the trash." In this, too, ethics and law converge. If the neighbor inadvertently tosses out a cherished antique, you ought not take advantage of his bungling. Try leaving a note if you're scavenging from individual houses in the suburbs.

Goldberg cautions that the garbage owner's privacy also enjoys protection. When the U.S. Supreme Court took up the issue in *California v. Greenwood,* Justice Brennan had this queasy-making assertion: "A single bag of trash testifies eloquently to the eating, reading, and recreational habits of the person who produced it."

Allow me to sum up: You may not go through Bob Hope's garbage and read his mail, but if someone deliberately throws Bob Hope—certainly a cherished antique—into the trash, you may keep him, although you can't sell him without violating the 13th Amendment.

FOUND MONEY

I found a roll of money in a restaurant rest room, presumably lost by another patron. I could (1) keep it, (2) ask the restaurant to return it if the owner comes looking, or (3) leave it in place, figuring that the restaurant could not be trusted and that the rest room is where the rightful owner would look. I chose option three. Which would you choose?

—MICHAEL LEWYN, ATLANTA, GEORGIA

I choose "none of the above." Option one is out: You can't keep the money because it's not yours. If you trust the restaurant, option two is fine, but only if the money's owner comes to claim it. If he doesn't, the restaurant, no more entitled to this found money than you, ends up with it. Option three just punts: No harm is done, but no solution is found. And if you don't trust the restaurant, why trust its patrons? Why assume that the next guy in will be more honest than the staff? (In a wacky sitcom, the next guy in would be a time-traveling George Washington. While scrupulously honest, he'd be confused by the indoor plumbing and frightened by the picture of himself on the money, so he'd flee back to his own time.)

So my solution is to tell the staff what you found (without specifying the amount, of course), leave your number, and hold on to the money. If its owner returns, they can refer him to you. If after a reasonable wait he does not return, the money's yours. (Of course, if you've discovered a huge sack of cash, you may want to call the police and have them deal with it, as is your legal obligation in some jurisdictions.)

NAKED NEIGHBOR

My neighbor, a 20-something and quite good-looking, never draws his blinds. The view from my apartment is extraordinary. Every night at 8:15 he returns from jogging to shower and prepare for bed, which I enjoy watching. Am I wrong to do so?

—ANONYMOUS

If the dreamboat across the way forgot one night to draw his blinds, you should respect his privacy: It would not be right to exploit a moment's carelessness. However, if he leaves them open every night in a big city where he obviously has neighbors, you can assume he knows what he's doing. To persist in such behavior is analogous to his going to a nude beach (and with no risk of sunburn). So enjoy! It would be almost insulting to avert your glance. Like the Wrigley Building or the Museum of Science and Industry, naked neighbors are part of the scenic splendor that is Chicago (if that is your kind of town).

Alas, while there may be no ethical impediment to your hobby, it is not without legal risk for both the observed and the observer. In many cities, municipal regulations proscribe various "offenses against public sensibilities," and although one is unlikely to be convicted of such a charge, the arrest alone can be quite unpleasant.

THE DEADBEAT'S DAUGHTER

I have an acquaintance who is, frankly, a deadbeat. For years, although able, he has worked only sporadically. Recently, his daughter was admitted to college, and received a free ride, based on financial need. Our children will be entering college soon, and they will receive little aid. This seems grossly unfair. What would be a more ethical alternative, a system that would not punish the daughter for her father's indolence, yet not penalize hardworking parents? Or should we just go on a mad spending spree between now and the first tuition payment?

—K.P., MASSACHUSETTS

I admire your eschewing a Dickensian system where the deserving poor attend college, but the undeserving poor—and their unfortunate children—are excluded. As you note, while parents should be financially responsible for their children, one must avoid punishing the child for the sins of the father, and punishing the larger society by creating a huge class of uneducated young people.

Perhaps the alternative you seek is true public education, including higher education. A nation as wealthy as ours could guarantee everyone the necessities of life—food, clothing, shelter, health care, and education (including higher education). Those who want more than the basics would pay for it themselves. This was once how we tried to provide all Americans with libraries and parks, fine public schools and free broadcast television, in the halcyon days before gated communities and pay-per-view.

Of course, even a system of free college education won't entirely address your question. Your neighbor will have contributed little in taxes; you'll have contributed a lot. But don't be too quick to condemn the grasshopper next door. One man's layabout is another man's philosopher. All you've really said about him is that he hasn't earned as much money as he possibly could. Any cosmetic surgeon or stockbroker could level the same charge against every fourth-grade teacher or firefighter or Vincent van Gogh. But even if your neighbor isn't painting masterpieces in his garage, don't judge him too harshly. Living in a civil society means being tolerant of those who live differently from ourselves.

On the other hand, maybe you are being overly frugal and would feel better if you indulged yourself just a bit. If you do go on that mad spending spree, please note that my shirt size is 15/34.

FASTIDIOUS LETTER CARRIER

A letter carrier for 16 years, I worry that I do wrong by delivering solicitations from "religious" organizations to people of limited means. I just don't feel right helping those snake oil salesmen get one cent richer. Which is the lesser of the two evils: throwing away a piece of Deliverable Bulk Business Mail (junk), or being a middleman for those sophists?

—ANONYMOUS, BRONX, NEW YORK

As a mail recipient, the last thing I need is a government official—that would be you—censoring my mail. That would be repellent. Your job is to deliver the stuff, not decide whether it is acceptable for other people to read. If carrying certain publications is an insuperable affront to your values, the honorable course is resignation.

For all of us, the appropriate response to unpalatable ideas is counterargument, not suppression; the soapbox, not the trash can. (Similarly, I don't want an AT&T operator screening my phone calls, even from my most idiosyncratic relatives. Hanging up on cranks is my job.)

There is a distinction between ideas and actions. You must not stifle the former, but in some cases you may thwart the latter. For instance, you should decline to deliver a ticking time bomb. But postal regulations already prohibit sending hazardous materials, so as it turns out, by adhering to department policy you'd be doing the right thing.

This analysis does leave some ambiguous cases, admittedly. Consider the J. Crew catalogue: ideas or actions? I say even when dealing with the most frightening sweaters, the mail must go through.

CAR-POOL CUNNING

To use the car-pool lanes during rush hour, we must have at least one passenger in the car. To avoid the clogged roadways when driving my child to an event, I sometimes pay another child five or ten dollars to ride with us so I can use the car-pool lane on the return trip, saving me 30 to 75 minutes. Is this ethical?

—D.M., GAITHERSBURG, MARYLAND

Nope. You clearly understand the law's purpose, which is to reduce the number of cars on the road by having folks travel together who'd otherwise drive separate cars. Your letter-of-the-law maneuver is ingenious, it is convenient, and it gives a kid a chance to take a fascinating car ride rather than squander her time doing homework or playing outside, but it conflicts with the intent of the law, and so you must forswear it.

Sometimes a law's intent is ambiguous—the tax code, for example—and one's best course is to stick to the letter of the law, but this is not such a case, and you should honor the law's spirit.

Meaning, too, no inflatable dummy in the passenger seat. In fact, it is a dependable general rule: "Beware of all enterprises that require an inflatable dummy," as Thoreau did not say.

Guest Ethicist

I'm about to buy a cool SUV, but my friends act like I'm some kind of criminal. Am I?

MICHAEL KINSLEY IS THE EDITOR OF *SLATE.COM*. THIS IS HIS RESPONSE:
Underlying this SUV issue are three more abstract questions. First: Are we as individuals under some sort of ethical obligation to consume less energy than we would otherwise be inclined to, given our particular resources and tastes? Second: If the answer to the previous question is "yes," does that make it unethical to drive an SUV? Third: Energy aside, in a crash between an SUV and one of the few remaining normal-size cars, the chance of the smaller car's occupants getting killed and the SUV's occupants getting a story they can dine out on for years is higher than if both combatants were driving normal cars. Is this unfair?

The answer to the first question is yes. Even the most pigheaded (and pig-hearted) enthusiasts for capitalism—short of Ayn Rand cultists—acknowledge an ethical obligation not to consume to our full potential but to reserve some of our resources for selfless good works and charity. Ordinarily, though, there is no ethical obligation to rise above our own preferences among the myriad choices about what to consume. Capitalism really is an efficient machine for assigning relative prices to different goods and services in a way that automatically aligns our incentives with society's interests. In this sense, it may be piggish to spend $60,000 on a consumer indulgence of any sort, but the choice between an SUV and, say, 60,000 Hershey bars is ethically neutral.

What makes energy different is the simple Econ 101 concept of "externalities." When I consume gasoline, I reimburse the oil companies for the cost of drilling, the cost of refining, the cost of bragging about how wonderful they are on noncommercial television noncommercials. But my consumption also imposes the costs on you of pollution, global warming, the risk of finding yourself at war to protect some loathsome foreign government that happens to be sitting on oil. For all that, I pay you nothing. The proper solution is for society to realign individual incentives with social costs by raising the tax on energy (and lowering some other tax, such as the Social Security payroll levy, by an equal amount). That would be unlikely even without an oilman in the White House. In its absence, there is an ethical obligation to consume less energy than you desire and can afford at current prices.

But does this mean no SUV? The answer to the second question is not necessarily. Hell, it's no, not at all, not by a long shot. Let's even make the question tougher by assuming we have no real need for an SUV, even for our pleasures, let alone for our basic needs. (Yes, there was that time three years ago when our Honda Accord couldn't make it across the pass in a snowstorm, and only last month the SUV was damned useful in helping to shovel Aunt Martha into that nursing home. But who are we trying to kid?) Even so, driving an SUV says almost nothing about whether you are doing your bit to conserve energy.

For example, if you choose to live near your work and drive an SUV, you'll use less energy than if you commute from far away in a regular car. If you're a member of a large family, it could take two regular cars to replace the SUV, which would be no energy bargain. If you recycle fanatically, set your home thermometer at 55 degrees, drive slowly, and go around turning off light switches, you may feel entitled to an SUV indulgence—and you'd be right.

But what about the third question: SUVs as prophylactics for their occupants and carriers for everyone else? Ethical? The answer is, it depends. Do SUVs increase the net number of crash fatalities? If so, there's a case. But assuming that lives saved and lives lost roughly cancel each other out, it's hard to see an ethical obligation to voluntarily increase your own chance of being roadkill by denying yourself the vehicle you want. Everyone is free to buy an SUV, and when everyone has done so (about three weeks from now in the Seattle area) the relative advantage will be gone. Crashes between two SUVs are less likely to be fatal than crashes between two regular cars, so the net effect on car safety will be positive (except for that small problem of SUVs flipping over during dangerous maneuvers like a left turn).

Of course, not everyone can afford an SUV. This means the spread of SUVs, on average, increases the safety of richer people and reduces the safety of poorer people. Can it be ethically okay to improve your own safety at the expense of people in general, but not okay if the people in question are likely to be poorer than average? Well, the sad truth is that poverty is dangerous to your health in any number of ways, of which the added risk of injury or death because you're less likely to be driving an SUV must surely rank quite low. Although I haven't begun to do the numbers—and wouldn't know how—I would bet (is that ethical?) that an SUV indulgence would be properly priced at around $50. So give $100 (just to be safe) to a homeless center, and enjoy your SUV.

I REPLY:

It depends where you drive. If it's on the unforgiving lunar surface, no harm done. If you do a lot of off-road driving here on Earth, you might need an SUV. But if you do most of your driving on paved American roads, then your friends are right.

SUVs are inherently dangerous, not for their own passengers but for everyone else. The National Highway Traffic Safety Administration reports that the height and weight of SUVs make them responsible for 2,000 additional deaths a year; they are twenty times more likely than a conventional vehicle to kill other motorists in side-impact collisions. If you have no compelling need for the SUV's off-road features (i.e., if your sport utility vehicle has no utility) there's no way to justify endangering others so you can play cowboy. Why should your fellow motorists support your lifestyle with their life span?

If you do your driving in a city where the roads are paved, the population dense, and the public transportation excellent, it's abhorrent to drive any kind of car at all. Last year in New York City, 193 pedestrians and bicyclists were killed by cars and approximately 15,800 were injured. And that's not the half of it. "When you talk about damage caused by cars," says John Kaehny, executive director of Transportation Alternatives, "you also have to talk about emissions; noise (as a threat to both quality of life and health); damage to buildings; delays to motorists, ambulances, and deliveries; damage from fuel extraction and shipping; and the cost of national security to secure oil lines." And that toll ($19 billion a year by one credible estimate) is shouldered by all citizens, though fewer than half actually have a car.

Even beautiful preserves like city parks allow motorists to speed through, disrupting family picnics in the name of a quicker route to the store. Surely a benign urban vision requires a distinction between a park and a parking lot.

So if you're planning to drive that SUV in a big city with decent public transit, pack a suitcase into your roomy cargo area, because you're driving straight to hell.

NOTE: Mr. Kinsley and I each wrote our responses without reading the other's, so what is presented here is not a debate. It does seem relevant to mention how each of us gets to work. Mr. Kinsley drives a Nissan Xterra, two years old, 19 or 20 m.p.g. I walk from the bedroom to the living room, in the same pair of slippers I've had for years. When work does compel me to leave the house, I get around mostly by subway, but then again, I live in a city with fine public transportation while Mr. Kinsley lives in a region with excellent rock climbing.

Charitable and Uncharitable Impulses

FAITH, HOPE, AND CLARITY

I am on the board of a health facility raising funds for a much-needed extension. A local businessman with known ties to organized crime has offered a substantial donation. Should we take the money?

—S. WAGNER, STAMFORD, CONNECTICUT

If by "ties to organized crime," you mean that your would-be donor is proffering a cut of his loot, you must decline. Receiving stolen goods is illegal for a charity, just as it is for an individual. If, however, the money is legitimate but you're troubled by an association with an unseemly figure, you face a tougher decision. It is unsettling to believe that your charity serves to buff the image of a scoundrel, and many fundraisers seek to avoid this. Andy Tiedemann of the Harvard Alumni Affairs and Development Office explains his institution's approach: "If we felt the money was illegally gained or ill-gotten in some way, we would not accept it." They have no written policy defining "ill-gotten," though, and Tiedemann could not immediately recall a single instance of a donation being rejected on those grounds.

Awkward as that position may be, it is the only one our society offers. In his play *Major Barbara,* George Bernard Shaw poses the question of whether or not the Salvation Army should take money from an arms maker. In his introduction to the play, Shaw answers, "It must take the money because it cannot exist without money, and there is no other money to be had . . . The notion that you can earmark certain coins as tainted is an unpractical individualist superstition."

The world being what it is, you can do no better than follow Shaw's advice and Harvard's example. As long as the money was obtained legally, accept it. Thus, while the Homestead Strike would provoke you to revile the name of Andrew Carnegie, at the end of his life when he offers your town a library, you would be foolish, and a bit of a prig, to rebuff his largesse. (One might argue that relying on charity is no way for a democracy to solve its social problems, as I do below, but while awaiting the reforms I yearn for, you might well be guided by Shaw.)

One exception to this policy: Decline money from a group whose actions directly clash with the stated goals of your organization. The Sierra Fund, for example, ought not accept a donation from General Electric and thereby share the profits of a major polluter of the Hudson River. In the past, I have argued against a health care organization's accepting tobacco money. My case was as much aesthetic as ethical: It is simply too ironic for those producing a product causing 400,000 deaths a year to contribute to a hospital, unless such a contribution is accompanied by an acknowledgment of responsibility. That is, a hospital could welcome money to build the "Marlboro Lites Emphysema That We Caused and for Which We Are Really Sorry" Wing.

UNCHARITABLE VIEW

The company I work for is active in several well-known charities, and yet many of my coworkers refuse to participate in any of our fundraising activities. Aren't they just being selfish?

If your coworkers' resistance is merely an excuse for fecklessness, sloth, and watching a lot of sports on TV, then there is certainly nothing admirable about it. But if they're acting on principle, they may have a case, for despite what good it may do, even the best-intentioned charity is no friend of democracy.

In a democracy, we (or our representatives) gather publicly to identify common problems, devise solutions, and establish accountability. Charity shifts these activities to unelected celebrities and private councils. What kind of society leaves the solution of its social problems to the whims of people like me and Rosie O'Donnell?

The more that private money supports parks and libraries, the more easily a city abandons its responsibility to them. (In many cities, public funding for these treasures is at historic lows.) And though the N.Y.C. Parks Department, for example, is responsible for patches of green all around the city, private donors may limit their contribution to their own (wealthy) neighborhood. As a consequence, parks in middle-class neighborhoods are glorious while those in poorer districts are in disrepair, and magnet schools attended by middle-class kids receive a lot more gifts than those serving poorer kids. This is no way to build an egalitarian society.

Furthermore, having helped to improve schools and parks in their own neighborhood, wealthy people may well become less ardently committed to the cause of improving services citywide. This is no way to encourage a broad sense of shared civic life.

It is often the case that corporate donations, for example, are intended to promote not genuine social change but good public relations. In the world of corporate giving, no good deed goes unpublished.

Finally, charity cloaks corporate greed. A corporation that dispatches teams of lobbyists to drive down the tax rate still expects to be applauded for the money it spends, say, planting trees (or perhaps cutting them down—it's so hard to keep these ideologies straight). When a thief, having stolen your wallet, hands you back carfare, it's tough to mutter much of a thank you. Similarly, nice as it is that Bill Gates gives money to libraries, a decent country would tax Microsoft at a rate that lets cities buy their own books.

Of course, when there is human need, one must act. So if you're moved by a charity's appeal, then do what you feel is right. It is better to do some small bit of good than not to. It's just hard to be enthusiastic about this particular form of benevolence.

My friend and I play tennis at a neighboring town where only residents who pay a yearly fee of $50 may use the courts. They are unsupervised and one or both of them is always vacant. We are not preventing any resident from playing. Are we committing an unethical act?

—SHANE MULLANE, WESTCHESTER COUNTY, NEW YORK

I'm afraid you are acting badly. This is a version of what economists call the "free rider" problem: For instance, is stealing cable really theft? You add no cost to the cable company and prevent no one else from using cable. Yet if everyone stole cable, the company would go under: no more cable TV, no more *Sex and the City* (which many economists would consider pitiable, although I don't recall why). Hence your obligation to pay your share of any such service.

However, while you behave badly, that neighboring town behaves worse by giving you no way to pay your share even if you wish to. The town does have a legitimate interest in funding its facilities and regulating their use, but this can be done without pulling up the drawbridge.

Residents-only policies, redolent of gated communities, are disturbingly undemocratic and too often have the effect, if not the provable intent, of excluding minorities and the poor. Happily, in most American towns, public facilities like museums and ballfields, libraries and playgrounds, are open to all. You don't have to show your papers to enter Lincoln Park in Chicago, even if you hail from Westchester, New York.

I am a Lutheran pastor living in a parsonage. Our school district is debating a building project to be funded by increased property taxes, a proposition I support (although I do not have any children enrolled in the system). As the parsonage is exempt from property tax, is it right for me to vote in the election, considering that, should the project be approved, my portion of its taxation is passed on to neighbors?

—DOUGLAS S. LARSON-SELL, LONSDALE, MINNESOTA

Your exemption from property taxes is not germane. Many people own no property and hence pay no property taxes: They still get to vote. America long ago abandoned owning land as a prerequisite for voting (and I understand that in many states women have been granted the franchise).

As a citizen, you are to vote on all ballot issues, even those that don't seem to affect you directly. Otherwise, only motorists would vote on highway bills; only backpackers (or bears) on funds for national parks. But these issues concern the entire society. For instance, the bill you describe funds school construction, and even those without children have a stake in an educated populace. Democracy works best when people have a broad sense of community, shared experience, and mutual responsibility; that is, of civic life.

Although I must say, why church property like your house is exempt from taxes is a mystery to me.

Criminal Justice

UNCOMPROMISING COP

A senior police executive, in another city on a personal matter, was attempting to rent a car. The clerk said he couldn't because his driver's license had expired 3 months earlier. Needless to say, his wife rented the car and did the driving for the three-day trip. What should the policeman do, knowing now that he had driven illegally for several months? I'll tell you what I did. I had another cop write me a $100 ticket for an expired license. No one would have known, except me.

—J. GRAHAM

If you are determined to be so scrupulous, why ask for only a single ticket? Why not a hundred, one for each day you broke the law over those three months? Why not two or three hundred, one for each instance of unlicensed driving?

I incline toward a gentler view of your circumstances. Your intentions were honorable. As soon as you realized your license had lapsed, you stopped driving until you renewed it. A civilian in similar circumstances could do the same and maintain his self-respect. After all, a ticket is the unfortunate consequence of getting caught; it is not a fee you pay for the privilege of driving with an expired license. I see no reason for you to pay this artificial fine.

I hope that you'll allow for human fallibility and give some other unintentional offender the benefit of the doubt, just as I'm going to let you off with a warning: Sometimes excessive fastidiousness is not ethics; it's vanity.

COP LINE

A police officer, I sometimes handle phone inquiries from family members about persons just arrested. When a wife asks about charges, and her husband has been arrested for soliciting a prostitute, I can withhold the information in hope that he has learned his lesson, sparing her pain and humiliation, and perhaps preserving a marriage. But is a husband who violates the law and his vows entitled to my protection? And worse, withholding the truth could put the wife at risk of contracting a sexually transmitted disease. Should I tell or not?

—ANONYMOUS, NEW YORK CITY

You should tell. Your consideration for your callers is admirable, but your job is to provide public information, not preemptive marriage counseling. You ought not pick and choose among crimes, covering up some and revealing others. I may believe that Pizarro learned his lesson and genuinely regrets murdering Atahualpa and conquering the Incas, but if Mrs. Pizarro's ghost calls, I'm obliged to tell her what he's doing time for.

Different relationships entail different obligations. In deciding whether to tell a friend about a straying spouse, your actions will be variably influenced by your intimate knowledge of the friend, the friend's desires, the circumstances of that particular marriage. But when responding to the public in your official capacity, you should treat all callers and crimes consistently. And so you must give that wife the information she is legally entitled to. This will not only enable her to protect her health, but to make her own decisions about her marriage.

Incidentally, when you shield a prostitute-patronizing husband, what do you suppose he tells his wife when he gets home? "Don't worry, honey, it was only grand theft auto"?

SECRET GARDEN

I own a weekend house in rural Pennsylvania. Recently I noticed that my neighbor is growing marijuana on his land, and some plants are actually on my property. I don't want to confront him, and I don't want to turn him in, but I don't want to get in trouble myself. What should I do?

—ANONYMOUS, PENNSYLVANIA

You should gently ask your neighbor to uproot his plants from your property; you need not put yourself in legal peril so he can conveniently raise a cash crop or chemically raise his spirits. However, I'd continue your good neighbor policy and say nothing about the plants on his land. As I, a nonlawyer, understand it, you have no legal obligation to report this crime and no moral obligation to enlist in the drug war.

One caution: In the antidrug mania that grips some jurisdictions, conspiracy laws have sometimes been applied with disconcerting haste. To chat with your neighbor about his horticultural pursuits, or even to know about his crop may put you at risk for such a charge, which, even if utterly groundless, would no doubt be an unpleasant situation. You might want to check with a lawyer before doing anything.

In 1979 I was sentenced to life in prison, with the possibility of parole in 2003. One of the principal factors in winning parole is an admission of guilt. But I am not guilty of the convicted offense, and I am loath falsely to state otherwise. Claiming to have "found Jesus" also greatly enhances one's prospects, but that would be contrary to my true beliefs. I am content to remain honest and spend the rest of my life in prison. But my incarceration has hurt my family greatly and I hate to inflict more pain. Should I lie?

—J.Q., FLORIDA

One speaks truthfully not because he believes the people he's speaking to are honest, but because he believes it right to be truthful. It is an internal choice, independent of circumstances. To act otherwise is to embrace Mafia morality, or at any rate, Mafia movie morality: Deal honorably with our friends and treacherously with everyone else. This is not ethics; it is tactics.

However, if you are caught in a system that is not just slightly dishonest but egregiously unjust, your obligation changes. You need not testify truthfully at the Salem Witch Trials or before the Spanish Inquisition, for example, since these tribunals were not actually pursuing truth. To lie in this situation is to commit, at worst, a small wrong to counter a great wrong.

Sadly, this may be your situation. Your prospects are dim no matter what you tell the board, says Martin McClain, an attorney with the Legal Aid Society's Capital Defenders Unit (and an expert on Florida law). The parole board probably isn't interested in how you answer their questions. "This sentence for first-degree murder was adopted in the seventies as another option to the death penalty. The first people receiving it are just now coming up for their hearings. I don't know of anyone who has actually received parole. I don't know any lawyers there who expect their clients to get paroled, certainly not in their first hearing. The politics in Florida have many people concerned whether parole will ever be exercised."

If your conviction was truly unfair, if you are genuinely innocent, and if what you say to the parole board will not harm others and might secure your release, then you have the right to lie without hesitation or inhibition. In this case, however, the very circumstances that make lying justified also make it pointless. If the parole process is a sham, if no one gets out on parole, then there is no reason to lie. It is a grim paradox. In such circumstances, when all action is equally futile, stick to your principles and what comfort they may provide.

Arguing with The Ethicist

UMBRELLA EXCHANGE

One rainy evening I wandered into a shop, where I left my name-brand umbrella in a basket near the door. When I was ready to leave, my umbrella was gone. There were several others in the basket, and I decided to take another name-brand umbrella. Should I have taken it, or taken a lesser quality model, or just gotten wet?

—I.F.S., NEW YORK CITY

If your umbrella was actually stolen, then your taking another one means that some poor sap will end up umbrellaless, get soaked, catch a cold, and die! You'll feel—what's the word?—terrible. Your having been robbed does not justify your robbing someone else.

It is more likely, of course, that your umbrella was exchanged inadvertently, and so your taking an equivalent one provides a kind of rough justice. Everyone leaves with an umbrella more or less equal to what he arrived with, and everyone stays dry. This system works only if people are honest and don't try to trade up. To be safe, you might want to err on the side of taking a lower-quality umbrella, thus letting everyone rest easy when leaving an umbrella at the door.

One caution: This is a casual system best applied to inexpensive items. I don't recommend it for cars left in a parking lot.

A READER FULMINATES:

I was appalled to read your response to I.F. S. in New York. Since when does right and wrong come with a dollar amount assigned to it? Petty crime is okay, just not grand theft? If the umbrella was taken inadvertently rather than on purpose, this is rough justice?—F.A.U., Los Angeles (Even in L.A., we know better!)

I PERSIST IN MY FOLLY:

But there was no crime—that is the point I was trying to make. The question pivots on a cultural assumption. Do you think the umbrella was stolen, or do you think—as I do—that it was an inadvertent exchange of two essentially identical objects? If one standard-issue three-dollar umbrella is accidentally swapped for another, a routine occurrence around here, no one is harmed, and everyone leaves with pretty much the same umbrella he had when he came into the store. The result is that everyone stays dry. With your solution, someone ends up wet, and at the end of the day there's an unclaimed umbrella in the lost and found. How is that better? But perhaps there's so little rain in L.A., and so much underground parking, that the routine transactions of walking around a city have faded from memory.

HAT IN HAND

I often ride my motorcycle without a helmet. Our state helmet law basically applies to motorcycle riders under 18. I figure I'm not putting anyone but myself at risk. My friends say that this is tantamount to suicide. But isn't it just one of many risks all of us take every day?
—KELLY KREBS, MINNEAPOLIS

If riding without a helmet affected only you, then helmet laws would be intrusive and paternalistic, and you'd be doing nothing unethical by riding bareheaded. An autonomous rider living free of the larger society is an attractive and romantic idea, but like most romantic ideas, it has little correspondence with actual life. Should you get in an accident, you are likely to be more seriously injured than you would be had you been wearing a helmet, and thus you'll consume enormous medical resources. And should you die, your dependents might need a variety of public assistance. In other words, all sorts of social costs will increase, from insurance to emergency services; other people will be paying the price of your riding with the wind. And that is unethical. So I'm afraid that, law or no law, you've got to wear the helmet.

However, if you remain determined to feel the wind in your hair, you can ride without your pants, which will not greatly augment your chance of dying, except of embarrassment.

M.A. OF SAN FRANCISCO DEMURS:

Should no one skydive, mountain climb, or mine coal because we might inflict injury upon ourselves? Perhaps my diet and exercise habits should be determined by those who might pay for my medical care. If we all followed your advice on this matter, we would develop a society that was quite dull, if not totalitarian. Mr. Krebs may be foolish, but he is highly ethical.

I REPLY:

The helmetless rider is asking others to pick up the tab for his fun. If he were entirely insured, as some states require, he'd be endangering only himself, up to a point, and while he might be foolish it would not be unethical. I would like to add this less financial, less Adam Smith–ian caution: This rider's untimely death will have profound emotional effects on his family.

What's vexing about this rider is his unwillingness to take ordinary precautions, his frivolous and childish approach to life. We of course allow for dangerous pastimes. No one would say playing football, riding a bicycle, or climbing Mt. Everest is unethical, but we expect people engaging in such practices to exercise due caution to minimize the dangers.

There is also something to be said for the macabre counterargument. When helmet laws went into effect, there was a real decline in the availability of organs for transplants; healthy young men killing themselves in motorcycle accidents had been a major source. It is the helmet wearer who deprives so many ailing folks of life: How thoughtless. Plus, without helmet, quick death; with helmet, lingering, expensive life. So perhaps the most ethical position is to ride without a helmet. Drunk. Down Mt. Everest.

EXERCISING CAUTION

A woman who works out at my gym is skeletal to the point of appearing deathly ill, and yet she exercises for hours. I can't know for sure that she has a problem, but she appears to be wasting away, possibly killing herself. Does the gym have a responsibility to intervene? It could be sued if it denies her membership. Should I just watch her get thinner and thinner or should I confront her?

—B.B., WASHINGTON, D.C.

I see no persuasive argument against your approaching her gently. You risk nothing but minor embarrassment, and you might be of some help. If you have misdiagnosed her condition, apologize for intruding on her privacy. She may be impervious to the concern of a stranger, but that ought not be an excuse for inaction. The very fact that this emaciated woman is out there on a treadmill could suggest that she is desperate to be noticed. While the gym staff should certainly make sure that no one imperils her health on the StairMaster, this seems a curious time to bring that up. If this poor woman were on fire, surely you would put her out before pondering the gym's vulnerability to a lawsuit. Forget the gym's responsibility: Think first of your own.

R.B. OF WESTPORT, CONNECTICUT, REBELS:
Consider the following: You are in line at a Dunkin Donuts (for black coffee only, of course) behind a hugely obese woman with a fat child in tow. The woman orders a bag of jelly doughnuts and they both dig in. Do you approach her gently, voicing concern about the potential risk of diabetes, heart problems, stroke, etc. for both her and her child? My point is only that one must leave other people alone to make their own, often neurotic and wrongheaded lifestyle choices, both for themselves and their children.

I REPLY:

It would indeed be intolerable to live in a society where every portly fellow who went into a restaurant and ordered a steak was hectored by someone at the next table. However, B.B. described a woman who seemed not merely unhealthy but in immediate risk of her life.

Further, the intrusion I advocate is such a modest one, the worst it can be is annoying, no real harm done. I didn't suggest that B.B. wrestle that woman to the ground and force a protein shake down her throat, only that he not utterly ignore what might be the suffering of another human being. If ours were a society where the paternalism you describe were prevalent, I'd be won over by your argument. However, neglect and indifference seem so much the norm that to take a gentle liberty, even with another adult, seems called for in this case. I believe the harm it might do is small, and smaller still if one is sufficiently tactful.

A.M., CAMBRIDGE, MASSACHUSETTS, RESPONDS:

As a psychologist, I find your advice about the woman in the gym unlikely to be helpful. Someone in the throes of anorexia is basically in a delusional state, and it is unlikely that being approached by a stranger will have any effect. I would advise going to someone at the gym who has some authority. I don't understand why you sounded so scornful about B.B.'s question about the gym's responsibility. They should be responsible about making sure their equipment is not being used to someone's detriment (just as they warn people about symptoms of heart problems), and I think it is fair to assume they will have more leverage with their clientele than a stranger would.

I REPLY:

But of course I did write that the gym staff must ensure that no one imperils her health on their equipment. Presumably, they've cleared this woman to exercise and, from B.B.'s point of view, may have been lax in doing so. I also wondered if B.B.'s emphasis on what the gym should do was a way to avoid acting himself. However, on further consideration, your solution is a better one than mine, at least as a first step. While B.B. should indeed act if he sees someone at genuine risk, the action he should take is the one you suggest: Speak to the manager of the club. A staff member approaching the woman is more likely to be effective and less likely to embarrass her. However, if the gym does not respond, I maintain that B.B. should indeed speak to the woman. He ought not use the staff's inaction as a way to justify his own.

TOM MAGUIRE WRAPS UP:

A desire to defer to the proper authority in intervening in the lives of strangers does not imply either timidity or laziness. The proper authority in a bar to deal with drink orders from the inebriated belongs to the bartender. Seeking a parallel authority in the gym management for limiting use of its equipment for safety reasons strikes me as both sensitive and sensible. The dismissive tone of your concluding sentence suggests (inadvertently, I'm sure) a lack of recognition of B.B.'s obvious intelligence, integrity, and ethical sensitivity.

I REPLY:

You are entirely correct. Thank you.

DEMERIT BADGE

My son has been a Cub Scout for three years and I've been a den leader for one, a wonderful experience for us both. But I was appalled by the Supreme Court's decision upholding the Scouts' right to exclude gay people. I cannot feel proud to see my son wearing a uniform that represents bigotry, and so we are withdrawing from scouting. Many of my friends also oppose this discrimination but plan to continue in scouting anyway. Aren't they wrong to do so?

—LYNN WINTER, PORT WASHINGTON, NEW YORK

Resigning as you did is the ethical thing to do. Just as one is honor bound to quit an organization that excludes African Americans, so you should withdraw from scouting as long as it rejects homosexuals. That scouting has a legal right of free association does not clear you of this obligation. The right to shun Jews is no less anti-Semitic for all its legality.

Those who remain in the Scouts are on shaky ground even if they sincerely seek reform from within. That may have been a reasonable strategy while the issue was unsettled, but once the Supreme Court handed down its decision, the debate ended. To stay now is to accept—if not endorse—its policy. You need not agree with an organization's every principle, of course, but the matter in this case is too fundamental—and too cruel—to tolerate. Besides, all too often those who remain are not actually fighting from within; they're going on camping trips from within. Were you to find yourself transported to 1952, there would be no honor in lamenting Jim Crow and then sitting down at a segregated lunch counter and ordering a tuna sandwich.

Resigning need not mean giving up the struggle. Ex-Scouts can write letters, rally support, and seek to reform scouting in order to rejoin one day. In the meantime, there are other, more tolerant, youth groups. The Girl Scouts and the Boys and Girls Clubs of America have no similar homophobic policies; neither do many foreign scouting organizations. Scouts Canada, for instance, is particularly humane, not only rejecting sexual orientation as a criterion for membership but also authorizing specialized troops, including ones for Mormons, Cantonese speakers, and gay Scouts. Any chance of your becoming the first Long Island outpost for Canadian scouting?

A READER ARGUES:
Isn't this a matter of free association? The Scouts have the legal right to expel anyone whose behavior fails to meet their standards. Rejecting the sexual practices of homosexuals—as do most religions—is in no way analogous to racial or religious prejudices.

I REPLY:
The Supreme Court ruled that the right of free association allows a group to exclude people whose views conflict with that group's essential message. Thus, the Boy Scouts had to argue that being antigay was its essential message, a dubious position, it seems to me. But even if that were true, and expelling James Dale, the Scout master in question, were legal, it would still be odious. On the same grounds, the KKK has the right to exclude African Americans: legal, perhaps, but hardly ethical.

However, I see it not as a matter of free association but as a discrimination case, as did, incidentally, the New Jersey Supreme Court and four of the justices of the U.S. Court. The BSA is not a small group of friends gathering in someone's home; it is a huge national organization that frequently makes use of public facilities—school auditoriums, firehouse basements—for gatherings. Your argument seems awfully close to that which justified segregated schools in the postwar South.

What's key for me is that Jim Dale was by all accounts, including BSA's, exemplary both as an Eagle Scout and as a troop leader. For years, BSA regarded him as the very embodiment of its values. It is only the fact of his being gay, not anything that he actually did, that led to his ouster. Calling this prejudice "religious" does not make it right.

Scouting has absolutely no idea what Jim Dale—or any of its other Scout leaders—gets up to in bed. Nor should they. This is a private matter and none of BSA's business. Because they expelled Jim Dale not for anything he did but for the mere fact of his existence, I see the case as akin to discrimination based on race or religion, and something we all must resist.

D.C. OF BAYSIDE, NEW YORK, CHALLENGES CANADIAN SEGREGATION:
Scouts Canada has groups for Mormon, Cantonese-speaking, and gay scouts. Why shouldn't the gay scouts be in the same troop with the Mormons (or the Cantonese-speaking Mormons)? Sounds almost like separate but equal.

I REPLY:
There are two important differences between the U.S. and Canadian approaches. The more significant is this: gay Scouts and Scout leaders (or Mormon Scouts or Cantonese-speaking Scouts) are welcome throughout Canadian scouting; gay Scout leaders are expelled from BSA. And second, when a small group feels oppressed by the larger society— African American college kids attending a large, mostly white Midwestern university, for example—it is reasonable that they may seek the comforts of familiarity for a short time, as a transition to full participation in the general culture. This seems a small enough thing to ask, and is quite different from the dorms at that Midwest U rejecting black kids.

A Postscript from Lynn Winter

Half the families in our den never called or responded to my resignation in any way. I don't know and have not been able to find out if they continued in scouting or not since our children attended different elementary schools and the only times I saw them was at Scouts. Half followed my example and also quit. Two of them that did so said they planned to allow their older son to continue in Boy Scouts and one planned to enroll her younger son. Their reasons for quitting then seemed to be social and/or loyalty to me. One of these women has an openly gay brother-in-law living in the city with his partner. I recently spoke to her and raised the issue again and she continued to state she hopes her son, who was withdrawn when I resigned, will join the Boy Scouts with a leader in town that she likes and respects. This staggers me. She also will send both sons to Boy Scout camp this summer. She is also Jewish and I shared with her that the Reform Jews have sent letters to their colleagues asking that support for Scouts be withdrawn because of discrimination. She was aware of this. From local Scout leadership on up to the top I heard nothing.

I asked my son if he missed Scouts and he said he missed the meetings at everyone's homes but not the troop meetings. I miss Scouts and the connection with my son and his friends that we shared. We did a lot of fun things together and his involvement with other group activities does not necessarily involve me. I continue to be gratified when I see that another group has taken a stand and that the entire issue has not been swept under the carpet.

A Postscript

Called for jury duty, I was asked if I would be able to impose a death sentence. I am an ardent foe of capital punishment, but if I answered no, I would have been left off the jury and replaced by a juror who believes in the death penalty. If I had lied and said yes, perhaps I could have saved the defendant's life. What should I have done?

—A.B., PHILADELPHIA

Lying here is not only unethical, it corrupts the judicial process, and it cuts both ways. No one wants a cop on the stand to lie about a defendant he "knows" is guilty. However, excluding all jurors opposed to capital punishment can indeed produce a biased jury. "You do end up with juries entirely filled with pro–death penalty people," says longtime capital-cases defender Stephen B. Bright, director of the Southern Center for Human Rights. Furthermore, Bright says, "this tends to racially skew juries, because there is a higher rate of opposition to the death penalty in minority communities than in the general population."

You may have more latitude if the question were put to you this way: Are you too closed-minded on this issue to serve? You are free to hold the prosecution to the highest legal standards, to consider matters of race and class as they are presented in the courtroom. And you may well decide, weighing all mitigating factors, that the prosecution has not met the criteria necessary to impose the death penalty. You are not asked to forsake your history, your values, or your opinion of capital punishment. You are asked if you can be fair.

"It is similar to a juror who has been exposed to pretrial publicity," says Bright. "That in itself needn't disqualify him. He must answer this: Can you put that aside and decide the case on the evidence? Similarly, a juror must ask himself—and he'll be asked—if he can set aside his personal views and decide the case on its merits."

Bright's advice may guide an uncertain juror, but not one as clear in his position as you seem to be. If, like me, you could never impose the death penalty, you must say so, and you will be excluded, with the grim consequences you describe. (Indeed, if you express even hesitancy about capital punishment, you may be struck.) I'm afraid the real solution to your dilemma ultimately lies in political and not personal action.

A.B. FOLLOWS UP:

Like many who submit questions to "The Ethicist," or, at least, as I imagine them, I submitted this question in the hopes of being granted ethical wiggle room from a higher authority. We all know the basic rules of society: Tell the truth. Don't be selfish. Treat others as you'd have them treat you. The question is when, if ever, we reach the limits of those basic tenets.

When I was called for jury duty, I told the truth. No, I cannot vote to impose the death penalty. And I was asked to leave the room within minutes. While expected, it was not what I wanted.

So I submitted my question in frustration, hoping for your sanction to fib next time, place myself on the jury, and sabotage this system. As many times as I've reread this answer, however, I still can't find that wiggle room in your response. Lying does open up a can of worms here. What else would you be able to lie about in order to get yourself empaneled on a jury? Fact is, the law depends on truth telling from all involved, so there's really little choice here.

The sad truth is that political action is futile in this arena. Most Americans believe in capital punishment, no matter how many innocents are freed from death row for wrongful convictions. If sabotaging the system is unethical, all that's left for us opponents is to opt out of it, removing ourselves from responsibility for what is done ostensibly in our names. That's not comfortable either, but what else is there?

Social Life

After the exercises which the health of the body requires, and which have themselves a natural tendency to actuate and invigorate the mind, the most eligible amusement of a rational being seems to be that interchange of thoughts which is practiced in free and easy conversation; where suspicion is banished by experience, and emulation by benevolence; where every man speaks with no other restraint than unwillingness to offend, and hears with no other disposition than desire to be pleased.

JOHNSON: *RAMBLER* #89 (JANUARY 22, 1751)

By "social life," I refer to those encounters created not by commercial necessity, but by the pull of affection—our encounters with friends and neighbors motivated only by pleasure.

Aside from certain obvious strictures (i.e., even if your neighbor's dog barks all night, you ought not burn down his house—the neighbor's or the dog's), much that governs these relationships is classified not as ethics but as etiquette. However, the barrier between the two may be more permeable than it appears. Etiquette is small-scale ethics, those rules that regulate the interactions of small groups of people. But even in the modest exchanges of civility, much is at stake, believed Dr. Johnson, who averred that politeness was of great moment in society. "It is," said he, "fictitious benevolence. It supplies the place of it amongst those who see each other only in publick, or but little. Depend on it, the want of it never fails to produce something disagreeable to one or other."

This is etiquette as social lubricant. You say "Thank you"; I say "You're welcome." We both feel fine, and nobody gets shot. (Or, in Johnson's time, cudgeled.)

Some requirements of good manners are now so stylized, so divorced from their origins, as to seem entirely arbitrary, but often their original purpose can be traced. Shaking hands was once a way to show that your hand did not hold a weapon. A man's tipping his hat derives from a knight's raising the visor of his helmet to identify himself as a friend, although no one is certain what became of men's hats.

Even when a custom's original purpose is lost in the mists of antiquity, we need not be left with a meaningless gesture, but may often find in such niceties profoundly ethical acts. That is to say, some forms of etiquette are not mere forms but are grounded in morality. Surrendering your seat on the bus to an elderly person is not just politeness, it is an act of kindness and generosity, a consideration for the needs of another person, and thus a moral act. Unless, of course, the robust granny who is the intended beneficiary of your act of kindness takes it as an affront to her vigor. Which is to say that the cultural meaning of an act changes as society changes, but its moral implications are no less present for that. The caustic comment of that bristling granny is itself a salutary moral lesson, reminding you that people are to be understood according to their actual circumstances, not seen as a stereotypical member of a group. And they are to be assisted according to their particular need, not just to satisfy your obligations to a perceived class. That is, offer your seat to any weary person, not just to the elderly. (New Yorkers may ignore this paragraph or ask an out-of-towner to explain it.)

This is not to overemphasize the moral import of manners. It is of little comfort to you if the person who steals your car sends a thank-you note. Unless the police can dust it for prints. (New York police officers can ignore this paragraph or chuckle good-naturedly over the idea that a car theft will be vigorously investigated.) In such a case etiquette is an empty shell, devoid of moral content. While such behavior may have originated in ethical necessity, it persists as mere social convention, etiquette without ethics.

But even here, Johnson would not be quick to forsake such amenities, however artificial they may seem.

When once the forms of civility are violated, there remains little hope of return to kindness or decency.

JOHNSON: *RAMBLER* #55 (SEPTEMBER 25, 1750)

Johnson saw the value of mutually comprehensible social customs. It would be exhausting if each of us had to create our own codes of behavior. It is, perhaps, the social equivalent of standardization. Just as it is useful that the plug on every lamp fits each electrical socket, so it promotes the general happiness when we are provided with standardized social codes whose meaning is clear to all. To Johnson, the opposite of such standardization is not freedom or informality, it is selfishness and hurt feelings.

As sickness shows us the value of ease, a little familiarity with those who were never taught to endeavour the gratification of others, but regulate their behaviour merely by their own will, will soon evince the necessity of established modes and formalities to the happiness and quiet of common life.

JOHNSON: *RAMBLER* #98 (FEBRUARY 23, 1751)

Thus, in many cases, the particulars of the social code hardly matter, as long as they are widely understood and practiced. For instance, some religions demand that one remove his hat when entering a house of worship; others demand that one cover his head. The specific disposition of the hat—hat on, hat off, hat tossed across the altar like a Frisbee—has no particular moral significance. Its ethical implications come through its understood social meaning, a demonstration of respect. This is rather different from, say, shooting or not shooting a guy, where the moral significance resides very much in the act itself.

And so, etiquette has at least two functions: to ease one's passage through society and to provide an ethical code for ephemeral social encounters. Etiquette also has another, more dubious, function—to identify and reinforce one's place in the social order. Gift giving, for example, is a river of beneficence that runs downstream, from the more to the less powerful. (Gifts can also be exchanged between equals, of course, but in unequal relationships it is a one-way transaction: Gifts flow from above to below, like water down a drain.) The king bestows bounty upon his subjects. Money that moves in the other direction is not a gift, it is a tax, not a voluntary offering of good will but an obligation. This goes for compliments, too. They are a verbal gift from the more to the less powerful: teacher to student, boss to employee. While a science teacher may compliment her pupil on an experiment well done, it would be impertinent of the student to say "Nice teaching!" The etiquette governing such exchanges not only announces but reinforces the social positions of those involved.

This use of etiquette is immediately apparent in the military, where rank is overtly announced by title and insignia. One salutes a superior officer; one stands when he enters the room. A noncom addresses an officer as "sir." In civilian life, rank is more ambiguous, influenced by race, class, and gender, of course, but also by professional accomplishment, physical beauty, and other subtler factors. Here, one is never certain who ought to toss a crisp salute to whom, and whom one ought to address as "Cappy." Probably no one.

But even here, the signs of respect can conceal a darker meaning. A couple of generations ago, men were taught to open a door for a woman. But this deference to women endowed them with a pseudostatus, awarding them the courtesy but not the actual power that went with their supposedly superior rank. It was deference as a form of social dominance. Here we see etiquette as antiethics, as perpetrating a kind of cultural falsehood.

Even these pointed courtesies met with Dr. Johnson's approval. He was a great defender of a hierarchy, of what was called "subjugation." Indeed, he found such a social order essential to the happiness of all. Dr. Johnson would argue, in his more reactionary and less appealing phase, that "knowing your place" is a profound and moral act, necessary for human happiness. That's probably why he doesn't get invited out so much lately. Well, that and being dead.

Ethics Pop Quiz

Below are four hypothetical questions for you the reader to answer.

Replies can be submitted to theethicistbook.com or e-mailed to theethicist@randomhouse.com.

Selected responses will appear in the paperback edition of the book.

I'm about to marry a man I don't love because he offers my only chance for a home and children. My best friend, Elizabeth Bennet, disapproves. She thinks him a ridiculous figure and me something of a coward even to consider such a union. But what choice do I have? My society offers few options for an unmarried woman. Am I right or is Miss Bennet? —CHARLOTTE LUCAS, RURAL ENGLAND

I've been seeing a woman for nearly a year now and, while I'm not in love, I quite enjoy our time together. I am frank about my feelings, and she wants to continue our relationship, but I can see it saddens her that I don't feel for her what she does for me. Surely she is an adult entitled to make her own decisions. But am I not exploiting her feelings? Knowing she's unhappy, am I obliged to take unilateral action and end our affair?

Everyone regards me as wicked, and it's really getting me down. I am typically associated with truly bad company— Gluttony, Pride, Sloth, Greed, Anger, and Envy—and I certainly see why they're considered a deadly crowd. But I think of myself as a force for life: I get people together; I increase the supply of human happiness. Sure, I can be misused, but if properly applied, I contribute to life's joy. Am I really so bad? —LUST

> I live in a city under military occupation where I've gotten myself in hot water and need to get away. Fortunately, I've acquired two letters of transit which would make that possible. But here's where it gets tricky. An ex-lover showed up in town with her new husband, a noble man, a real freedom fighter. I think my ex would come away with me if I asked her, but maybe I ought to give the letters to her and her husband so they can escape instead. What should I do?
>
> —RICK, CASABLANCA

Q & A

Dating and Dining

MAKING A PASS AT MARCUS

I have become obsessed with a man I presume to be heterosexual and I am by nature a very direct and forward person. Should gay men make romantic advances toward men they think might be straight? Lacking conclusive information either way, how should I express my romantic desire for "Marcus"?

—R.B., PALO ALTO, CALIFORNIA

You should not express your romantic desire for Marcus. Unless you believe your feelings are reciprocated, you should not make a pass at anyone. Gay or straight doesn't really come into it.

Romance may demand a bold gesture, but only where it is welcome. That is the difference between a hot embrace and a mugging. It is the lover's duty to know which is which—knowledge gained in small steps, in gesture and response, with time and conversation.

You are certainly free to display such tactfully escalating attention toward the appealing Marcus. If he is straight and he is offended by even these signs of interest from a gay man, that's his problem, not yours.

While you remain as unsure as you seem to be of Marcus's interest in you, however, you don't know him well enough for grand passionate advances. But the flowering of desire is often unpredictable. And one should never underestimate the power of expensive presents, cheap music, and freely flowing wine.

AMAZING GRACE

I had a dinner at the home of one of my neighbors, and he said Grace in a way that seemed appallingly sexist. Should I have voiced my dissent or kept quiet and allowed for the possibility that he feels differently than I do?

—ANONYMOUS, LOS ANGELES

Silently bowing your head is not a declaration of belief; after all, if a Christian dances at a Jewish wedding, no one assumes he's converted.

When one travels up the Amazon, he joins in tribal customs, not to endorse them but to learn. And sometimes the most alien culture of all is that of the house next door. If your host's devotions included stoning an infidel or sacrificing a particularly cute animal, you'd have been obliged to intervene to prevent harm. But as no one was being hurt, you were right to sit quietly and marvel at the variegated, and sometimes idiotic, beliefs of humanity. There is no obligation to inform your host of your spiritual views between the cocktails and the cognac.

However, there is also no obligation to remain silent. If you could raise the matter tactfully, particularly when all were mellowed by that cognac, that would have been even better. And besides, a lively conversation helps settle the stomach.

Just as I was about to leave my girlfriend, she learned that her father had a severe illness. Figuring it would be unnecessarily cruel to saddle her with a breakup, I kept my feelings to myself. The problem is, her dad remains ill, and I can't figure out when it would be right for me to leave. I have enough affection for her that I want to be honest, but what is my ethical obligation here?

—T.C., LOS ANGELES

In dozens of movies starring Academy Award–winner Bette Davis, just as her married lover is finally ready to leave his virago wife she has a horrible riding accident and is confined to a wheelchair. She's faking, but it's a clever fake, because no man worthy of Bette's love would desert an ailing wife.

You have a similar obligation not to abandon an intimate friend in a crisis. Of course, breaking up need not mean breaking off all contact. If she will accept your support despite this change in your relationship, you can act more quickly, but if a breakup means she'll spurn your help and suffer in isolation, you should wait. You'll have to judge when she is back on her feet, but as for being honest with her, if your romance has foundered, believe me, she knows.

Those in a hurry to split up often seek justification from another Academy Award winner, William Shakespeare: "If it were done, when 'tis done, then 'twere well it were done quickly," but the line was spoken by MacBeth; Shakespeare did not intend it as a dating tip. As you know, MacBeth's breakup with Duncan did not go well.

A male friend of mine occasionally goes to ethics society meetings where high-minded topics are discussed. He also has an ulterior motive: He wants to meet women, which he can do at the informal receptions afterward. He appears to be chasing skirts in a chaste setting. Is this ethical?

—F.K., WASHINGTON, D.C.

This behavior is not merely acceptable; it is admirable. Love and its neighbor, desire, are hardly unethical; they're two of life's pleasures. Your friend seems to be trying to increase the sum of human happiness.

People have multiple reasons for everything they do. For example, attending church has been not just a spiritual but also a courtship opportunity for hundreds of years (and nearly as many Trollope novels). As long as your friend isn't disrupting the discussion or pestering anyone with unwanted advances, I applaud his efforts. In fact, if I were establishing an ethics society, our slogan would be "You'll come for the high-minded discourse, but you'll stay for the pulse-quickening romance."

DINE WITH THE DEVIL

My wife and I are invited to a job-related dinner party, but she refuses to attend because one of the other guests is, she believes, a truly evil man. While he isn't Nero, he's certainly done some horrible things. Is my wife being a prig? Should I urge her to go? Should I go alone?

Certainly there are invitations one must decline: pancakes with Pol Pot, a cookout in hell with Roy Cohn. But when this sanction is promiscuously applied—such as when members of Congress snubbed President Clinton's State of the Union address—it becomes more posturing than principle.

Shunning everyone with whom you disagree limits your options not only for dining but for self-expression. Eartha Kitt shocked observers when she accepted an invitation to the White House in 1968 and used the occasion to criticize Lyndon Johnson for his Vietnam policy. But she was seizing the chance to practice democracy, and at some risk to herself exposing the President to ideas he seldom heard from those close to him.

Your wife might enjoy such an opportunity, but how can you get her to the dinner? James Boswell faced a similar predicament in 1776 when he and Samuel Johnson were invited to dine alongside a man Johnson detested. "If I had come upon him with a direct proposal, 'Sir, will you dine in company with Jack Wilkes?' he would have flown into a passion," Boswell wrote. Instead he mentioned an invitation, adding that Johnson might not approve of the company. Johnson replied, "Do you think I am so ignorant of the world, as to imagine that I am to prescribe to a gentleman what company he is to have at his table? I am sorry to be angry with you; but really it is treating me strangely to talk to me as if I could not meet any company whatever, occasionally." Only then did Boswell warn, "I should not be surprised to find Jack Wilkes there." Having made a show of his worldliness, Johnson was trapped. "And if Jack Wilkes should be there," he muttered, "what is that to me, sir?" That evening Johnson was affable, witty, and unambiguous in his opinions—a delight to all the guests, including Wilkes.

Is attending the dinner an endorsement of another guest? The answer is that it depends on what you do when you get there. A successful dinner party requires lively conversation, not artificial consensus. So go, but speak your mind. And don't be seduced by the Wilkes seated beside you, and don't make a habit of associating with bad company. Note that Johnson said "occasionally."

ON-LINE LIES

As a joke, my roommate started to correspond with her ex-boyfriend through an on-line dating service. She made up outrageous lies about her name, age, looks, and profession. Although I am not friends with the ex-boyfriend, I can't help but feel he is being deceived in a cruel way. What do you recommend?

—B.E., SAN FRANCISCO

This is not an ethical crisis; it is the premise for a romantic comedy. I'd keep quiet. Except, talk to Meg Ryan's people.

Obligations of Friendship

FRIEND'S NAKED BABY

Our friends in Manhattan are big on letting their 4-year-old boy play naked when they visit us in the country. We're all for "free and easy," but we've got a 9-year-old boy who's starting to cringe. Are we obliged to just wait and hope, or is it okay to tell them to cover the kid?

Backseat parenting is a hazardous act; people can be so prickly. However, if your friends are sensitive and considerate, you can indeed tell them. Of course, if they were sensitive and considerate, you wouldn't have to tell them; they'd have noticed your son's discomfort. And I gather from your letter that direct discourse would be perilous. So you might try something more oblique.

Do you have a particularly hideous relative who enjoys cavorting naked? (If you don't, I can provide you the names of several of mine who love country weekends.) Drop remarks like "When in Rome, do as the modest and toga-clad Romans do." Casually mention that "This time of year, the lawn is crawling with ticks as big as golf balls." Sprinkle your conversation and your garden with "nettles" and "thorns."

And in the end, when hints and humiliation are unavailing, employ the seasonal solution: Invite them to visit only between the first frost and the spring thaw.

FRIEND'S STUFF IN ATTIC

Years ago, I allowed a friend (known as a user of friends) to store some belongings in my attic. Recently, we came upon his things. I had completely forgotten about them, and obviously so had he. I ceased contact with him following an unpleasant incident several years ago, and I do not want to contact him. Yet I question whether I am entitled to keep the money if I sell these items. What is your opinion?

—M.Q., FREEPORT, NEW YORK

Alas, his being an unpleasant fellow does not justify your being a thief. Too bad, I admit. We would all feel better if we had to behave honorably only to people we liked. But there you are. Hold your nose and dial his number, which is surprisingly easy, even on a rotary phone. And comfort yourself by knowing this is the last time you'll have to see the guy.

About a year ago a friend borrowed $10,000 from another friend of mine. Not only has the borrower not returned the money, he shows no inclination of ever doing so. By remaining friends with the welcher without so much as a comment, am I condoning his reprehensible behavior? Am I wrong to remain his friend?

—LAWRENCE TOFFLER, LOS ANGELES

If every time two friends quarreled all their mutual friends had to choose sides, none of us would have many friends left. Fortunately, you are not obliged to cut off all ties to the deadbeat, but you should not ignore his bad behavior. Use your continued association to remind the defaulting friend of his obligation, gently, but persistently, and make it clear that you do not condone his lapse.

Your situation will become more difficult if the injured party demands that you break off with the deadbeat. Then you may have to take a side. But while there are indeed transgressions grave enough to sink a friendship, for now at least this isn't one of them. Still, I wouldn't lend him any money. Or a cup of sugar. Or a cup.

I have a vacation house in a dangerous area in Costa Rica. My friend Robert was reluctant to keep his CDs there—nearly 1,500 of them—but I urged him to so we all could listen to them. One evening before going out, he reminded me to close the window. I forgot, and the house was robbed via that window. We all lost big, but he claims I am responsible for replacing his CDs. I say we are each responsible for our own belongings. Who's right?

—GAVIN MCINNES, NEW YORK

There is something almost quaint about someone stealing actual CDs. We modern Americans, with our Space Age computer technology, can swipe other people's music right in our own homes, no heavy lifting. Maybe someday we will share the benefits of this digital wizardry with all the nations of the world, even the poor ones where we buy our vacation houses.

In the meantime, three people contributed to the loss of the CDs: you, Robert, and the robber; you each bear partial responsibility for their replacement (although I wouldn't wait around for the robber to kick in his share).

Knowing it was a dangerous area, Robert might have kept his collection elsewhere or taken out an insurance policy. But it was you who actively encouraged him to bring them over, enjoyed their use, and left the window open, in effect hanging out a big "Burglars Welcome" sign.

You should weigh these factors and determine just how much you contributed to the loss. Twenty-five percent? Fifty percent? Honorable people might differ as to the precise amount, but you are partly—mostly—to blame, and should pay part of the replacement cost.

SWEATSHIRT ETHICS

I bought a $70 sweatshirt on sale for $30. It was very fashionable, and one of the most comfortable articles of clothing I wore. I lent it to a friend of mine, and the next day she claimed it disappeared. How much money should I ask her for, $30 or $70?

—M. PAVLOVSKY, BROOKLYN, NEW YORK

I'm a replacement-cost kind of guy, myself. But I add this qualification: If your friend wants to replace the actual sweatshirt, she's free to get one however inexpensively she can. If you intend to replace it, she should give you enough money to do so. But if you've had your fun with it and do not intend to replace it, then she should give you only the $30 you were out of pocket. Any of these approaches will restore you to your original preloss state. I can't help but ask, though: Seventy dollars?! For a sweatshirt?!

A dear friend wants me to father her baby, which would be raised by her and her girlfriend. I would sign over all parental rights, though the baby would know that I was its father. My girlfriend is aghast at the prospect, as are the few friends I've told. Are they right to be so?

—ANONYMOUS

In three seconds (oh, okay, maybe half an hour) you go from good friend to bad father. People's reactions to a biological link are unpredictable, and by people I mean parents and children. If you're not prepared to be a real father, let your friend use a sperm bank.

A friend purchased what he thought was a stolen fine watch, at a discount. I can see from the way it has worn that it is not authentic. Should I tell him? I don't want to shatter his love for it or insult him. But I also don't want him to remain misled or make this mistake again.

—M.R., NEW YORK CITY

If I understand correctly, what was thought merely to be a case of receiving stolen goods turned out instead to be a swindle involving counterfeit products, and it's unclear to you if continued deception on your part is the honorable way to treat a friend and his bauble. I'm just relieved that no one got killed. And now I've got to go lie down and put a cold compress on my forehead.

Recreational Activities

My fun-loving friend Frank is celebrating his birthday next week, and he wants the festivities to include a tour of New Jersey's topless (and bottomless) bars. It sounds like a lot of fun (more for anthropological than prurient reasons—no, seriously), and I'm determined to go, but what do I tell my girlfriend? How do I convince her that I'm doing it for a friend?

—ANONYMOUS, NEW JERSEY

Convince *her*? You haven't convinced *me*. In any case, does doing it for a friend alter the essential act? Is the phrase "bottomless bar in New Jersey" already so far beyond the pale that there's little more to say? And might there not be a more evocative way to describe Frank than "fun-loving"?

Were your objections merely aesthetic, you should of course accommodate your jaunty pal. But if instead you or your girlfriend are discomforted by the moral implications of the festivities, then taking along some buddies is a feeble justification. Nor am I persuaded that there's a meaningful distinction between "anthropological" and "condescending."

So there's no point in convincing your girlfriend that you're going for Frank's sake. If you're comfortable with the plan, your task is to convince her that it's okay to go at all, at least once. Perhaps this will help. Invited by the Marquis de Sade to a second orgy, Voltaire declined, although he'd quite enjoyed the first. "Once is philosophy," he said. "Twice is perversion."

WEDDING PICTURES

After the big wedding that my mother-in-law threw for my husband's sister, the bartender found a canister of spent film. Mom's impulse was to have it developed to identify the photographer. I'm concerned that the owner may perhaps have used that film elsewhere in a compromising situation. What should the bride's mother do?

—LAUREN KOZLEN, SILVER SPRING, MARYLAND

Rather than rush that film to the photo shop, your mother-in-law should try gentler methods of finding its owner. She could simply wait a while and see if the mystery photographer calls. She could talk to some of her guests or add a note to the thank-you cards.

But even if the film remains unclaimed, she should hesitate before developing it; she might not like what she sees. In a classic French sex farce, the photographs would show the groom kissing a bridesmaid; in a modern American sex farce, they'd show the groom kissing the best man. And in a Hitchcock movie, there would be spy stuff on that film, hurling your mother-in-law into a nest of vipers.

The one person who will not be on the film is the photographer: He's behind the camera. So given the small chance of identifying him, and the real risk of invading his privacy, your mother-in-law should let the film, and her curiosity, remain undeveloped.

FRIEND'S KID BREAKS LAMP

While engaging in horseplay in my house, a friend of my 10-year-old son accidentally broke an antique lamp. I did not ask his parents to pay for it and would have declined if they'd offered, but it irks me that they didn't even make the gesture. May I surreptitiously break something in their house to settle the score?

—ANONYMOUS, HIGHLAND PARK, NEW JERSEY

If you smash something surreptitiously, those parents will have no way of connecting their loss to yours, so what will they learn? Better to proclaim in a stentorian voice, "I smash this vase to settle the score between us and to restore the honor of my shattered lamp!" Then smack it with a big stick. They ought to find that edifying.

Or better still, why not burn their house down? Then they'll *really* learn a lesson.

Sorry. Sarcasm is a temptation that those in my line of work ought to resist. Of course you shouldn't smash anything at their house. You would run afoul of that ancient precept "Two wrongs don't make a broken antique lamp whole again."

However, you need not persist in your high-minded but simmering silence. Your vivid revenge fantasies suggest that you have unfinished business with those other parents. You're likelier to mend your friendship by talking this over with them than by continuing to imagine the euphonious tinkling of breaking glass.

PARTY CRASHER

A friend eats, drinks, and makes merry four and five times a week by crashing New York publicity parties celebrating books, new restaurants, or other openings. He justifies freeloading on the basis of being a "good guest"—and populating places that depend on getting "a good crowd." Is this justifiable?

—M.F.S., NEW YORK CITY

If your friend is, as I surmise, a young journalist (how else would he know about all these parties?), he enjoys a privilege ratified by custom if not doctrine—that junior editors may wheedle their way into PR events. Much good derives from this practice for both host and guest. The editors lend youthful vitality to the proceedings, make their publication aware of whatever nonsense the event is touting, meet their more senior colleagues, and, as compensation for their meager wages, sustain themselves on shrimp puffs and ramaki, without which many a promising journalist would surely starve.

It is worrying that your friend's nights out necessarily begin with a lie. However, while one may question his ethics, one must appreciate his sense of irony. To habitually lie to publicists, those professional manipulators of the press, is almost poetry. So give your pal the benefit of the doubt but keep an eye on him: Voluntarily attending five publicity parties a week is surely a cry for help.

Arguing with The Ethicist

I'm a white male, straight, and I'm attracted to Asian women. It's a simple question of the sort of look that I find physically attractive. Recently, an Asian friend of mine (male) confided that he found my dating patterns offensive. Am I being racist, or does he have some issues of his own?

—ANONYMOUS

Here's what this is not: a simple question about looks. Here's what it is: racism, albeit not a malicious form. Here's how you can tell: Imagine the reaction of a new date when you take her hand, gaze into her eyes, and whisper, "What drew me to you was you're just so wonderfully Asian."

That you have ideas about Asians as a group is not surprising. How could you not? Racial definitions permeate our culture. But putatively positive stereotypes (e.g., the roles offered to Sidney Poitier throughout the first half of his career) are as reductive as more obviously negative stereotypes. Even positive images deny a person's individuality, defining him by a set of spurious racial characteristics. The good Negro; the gun-toting, drug-dealing boyz in the 'hood: Both are debilitating; both are false.

Your ethical responsibility is not to forswear your desires (even if that were possible) but you are obliged to understand them. Race is a cultural construct, a set of ideas. Before you try to date Michelle Yeoh, or Margaret Cho, or Madame Chiang Kai-shek, think a little harder about what those ideas are, about what you mean by "Asian."

H. S. LEWIS REFUTES:
Isn't it, in fact, possible to have preferences on sheer aesthetic grounds that do not involve deeper issues of racism? Ever?

I REPLY:

In short, no. Many things go into what you call "sheer aesthetic grounds," and it gets even more complex and subtle when we talk about what draws one person to another. It would be presumptuous of me to have the least objection to that letter writer's choices about love, but much more understanding is possible than what he dismissed as just happening to like Asians. I don't see his desire as malign, and it is certainly not willed. But when one notices a category of people to whom he is drawn, a category defined by race, i.e., Asian, then racial ideas seem a good place to begin if you want a little deeper self-knowledge.

SUSAN MIHO NUNES COUNTERS:

Your use of "racism" to describe a white man's attraction to Asian women was entirely inappropriate and does not bode well for your column or our country. Okay, so race is a "cultural construct," a "set of ideas." So what? Was my Portuguese father a racist for being attracted to my petite, almond-eyed Japanese mother? Was she a racist because she liked tall, dark men? Was her Japanese brother a racist for being attracted ONLY to Japanese women? Is my Caucasian husband a racist because he was attracted to someone who didn't look like she was born in his hometown in Ohio? As for my sisters' attractions, one of my brothers-in-law is African American, the other Iranian. If being attracted (initially, anyway) to "type" is racist, then we're all racists, I guess.

I REPLY:

Oh dear—the column and the country. I'm afraid you give me credit for more bad influence than I'm capable of. Yes, we are all racists, if what we mean by that is being influenced by that construct called race, and that includes your Japanese uncle who is attracted only to Japanese women as well as my Jewish uncle who is attracted only to anything but Jewish women. Both of them—all of us—have grown up in cultures permeated with ideas about race. We won't transcend these ideas by denying they exist but by understanding them. And that seemed what the letter writer was reluctant to do. What's key here is not that he was drawn to a particular woman who happened to be Asian; he was attracted to Asians who then turned out to be particular women.

Three years ago I met a forty-five-year-old woman in China. I arranged for her to come to New York. We were married within two weeks. Since that time she has refused to disrobe in front of me or to have sexual intercourse. We do not sleep in the same room. She refuses to visit a Chinese-speaking woman therapist. If I divorce her, she will lose her immigration status and be forced to return to China. Would it be unethical to divorce her?

—R.S., FLUSHING, NEW YORK

A whirlwind courtship, a quick trip to the altar, a romance gone sour . . . You know the old saying: Marry in haste, repent in China. But that is a harsh stricture to impose on a woman with whom you've lived for three years and for whom you seem to have some feeling. If the facts are as you describe, you are right to seek a solution to your intimate problems that does not involve a deportation hearing. Your first step should be to get some legal advice so she can learn her options for remaining in the country and so neither of you ends up on the wrong side of the immigration law.

Even if divorce would not lead to deportation, you should make every effort to understand and improve your marriage. This cannot be done if you see your unhappy circumstances as only your wife's fault. It is not just she who should talk to a therapist; resolving this conflict is something you must undertake together. If she married you simply to get to the United States, or if you married her as a kind of mail-order bride, the origins of your union are less significant than what you've made of it.

If these efforts fail, you might consider an accommodation that allows you to seek sexual satisfaction elsewhere while staying married; that is, without having your wife put on a plane to China. While her eagerness to remain in America does not trump your desire for marital happiness and a fulfilling erotic life, you should seek a solution that does not provide for one person's felicity at the expense of the other's.

It is possible that your wife will neither disrobe nor have sexual intercourse because love is absent or because of her sexual orientation. There is also an odder possibility to consider, a subject that is explored with great tact in *M. Butterfly.*

BARBARA STEWART DISAGREES:

Where do you suggest the husband find this alternative sexual satisfaction? Patronizing hookers? Lying to single women? If he dates a married woman, he would wind up breaking up the marriage and causing emotional damage to the woman he is seeing, her husband, and her children. All for a wife who, from the way it sounds, cares about her husband only because he provides a means of living in a rich country.

Here's a suggestion: Find out what the problem is with this wife, and either solve it or divorce her. And/or seek alternative sexual satisfaction alone.

I REPLY:

There are many ways this man might have an erotic life without prostitution or deceit. First, he must be honest with his wife, letting her know that while he accepts her refusal to have sex with him, that needn't mean that he forgoes sex altogether. If he does cultivate a relationship with a single woman, he must of course be honest with her about his situation. My observations of the world suggest that people have quite a variety of attitudes about their sex lives and that it is not at all unlikely that this man could find someone who wants to sleep with him even under these odd circumstances. Similarly, other people's marriages operate in a variety of ways; some couples demand monogamy and others do not. This man has more options than you allow.

We do agree that his first step should be to try to fix his marriage. But if he cannot do that, and if divorce means deportation, I believe he ought to find another solution, one that does not inflict such a harsh penalty on his wife.

DAVID SWANGER RAISES A MATTER OF FACT:

Why do you mention *Madama Butterfly* at the end of your first answer? Wasn't Pinkerton an imperialist who abandoned his Japanese wife and their child, and, further, married a second, British, wife? To what sensitive treatment are you referring? To us, the situations appear very different from each other.

I REPLY:

Not *Madama Butterfly*—*M. Butterfly,* a wonderful play by David Henry Hwang (later a movie with Jeremy Irons) based on the true story of a French diplomat carrying on an affair with a singer in the Beijing Opera who he thinks—or pretends to think—is a Chinese woman but is in fact a Chinese man. Its theme is the willful self-deception that is a part of all love. I was suggesting that the reason our inquisitor's wife will not undress or make love may be because his wife is a man.

DO YOU TELL?

Out of town on business, in the hotel bar, I saw a good friend's husband entwined with another woman. If I tell, my friend will be devastated, and she might hate me for it. If I don't, I'm joining her rotten husband in conspiring to deceive her. Should I tell?

—S.B., NEW YORK CITY

This is the question most often asked of The Ethicist, and opinions about it vary enormously. It is difficult to know from your brief glimpse, or your short note, if you witnessed long-term infidelity or anomalous indiscretion. Or what rules—spoken and unspoken—govern your friend's marriage. Some couples demand full disclosure and absolute fidelity; others allow a wider range of behavior.

And while it is clear that the overwhelming majority of married people forbid extramarital romance, not all of them necessarily want to know about it when it occurs. Even those who might say they do want to know often behave in ways that suggest that they really do not, going to elaborate lengths to ignore evidence that has long been apparent to their friends. So what do you do?

The utopian solution lies in prior notification, a sort of living will of the heart. The wishes of the patient, i.e., the wronged spouse, must be paramount, but you can't wait until she is too ill or too furious at her betrayal to convey them. Ideally, she would register her desire years in advance, on her driver's license, just below the organ donor form. Check one: I want to know/I want to remain in the dark.

If she hasn't registered that preference, you could try to deduce it by raising the question in an abstract way. But that's not easy to do without arousing her suspicions. And confronting the husband ("If you don't tell her, I will") might let the couple work things out on their own terms, but it might also force a showdown your friend does not want.

The practical solution usually demands that you guess your friend's wishes. Indeed, you must guess whether or not she already knows what her husband is up to. If she doesn't want to know, respect that desire. If she does want to know, you owe it to your friend to tell her. But if you don't know her well enough to be confident of her desire, then you don't know her well enough to intrude, so keep your suspicions to yourself.

DR. SANFORD ARANOFF ARGUES:

Jewish tradition has a different approach. It is forbidden to say anything bad about another person, except in certain cases (legal testimony or to prevent harm). The answer, in Judaism, is simple. She should not tell.

I REPLY:

Judaism also has a reverence for the truth—a curious paradox in this case, when your advice is to help a husband to deceive his wife. And of course the heart of the question is, which best prevents harm, telling or not telling?

SHERMAN MERLE DISAGREES:

A former psychotherapist for thirty-five years, in my experience with married couples I learned to have a very profound respect for the unspoken, often unconscious, "arrangements" they had established in many sensitive areas of their relationship, and particularly, in situations such as you described by the wife's friend. At some level the wife or husband "knew" what the rules of "the game" were, even if they were in "denial." Friends bringing infidelity to the spouse's attention do not help.

I REPLY:

A strong case, but troubling. Would you still not tell even if your friend had insisted—in the calm of happier days—that she absolutely wants to know? Do you not feel uneasy about, in effect, conspiring with the husband in his deception of your friend? And what do you say when she asks you a direct question? I believe there is a point at which you must honor your friend's clearly stated wish to know.

Guest Ethicist

Ordinarily, the guest ethicist responds to a new question rather than to one included in "Arguing with The Ethicist." But Dan Savage was eager to take up the question "Do You Tell?" And why not? He is the author of "Savage Love," a syndicated sex advice column that runs in over fifty weekly papers in the U.S., Canada, and Asia. His next book, a defense of sin, will be published this year. Here is his response:

There's a difference between conspiring to deceive a friend and keeping your big yap shut. Thanks primarily to Oprah, whom I blame for most of what's wrong in this country, keeping one's yap shut, like letter writing or butter churning, is something of a dying art.

Consider this: Open relationships are more common than most people would like to think, as so few people in open relationships (besides gay men) are willing to say so on the record. For all you or I know—or, for that matter, for all that woman wrapped around your friend's husband in that bar knows—your good friend and her husband may have an "agreement," something Clinton-esque, that allows them to remain married without having to swear off the occasional, life-affirming erotic encounter with another person. A lot of nonmonogamous couples keep up the appearance of an exclusive, monogamous relationship in front of friends and family, which can lead to confusion when they're spotted romping around in public with someone who isn't their spouse.

Of course, it's just as likely (okay, way more likely) that your friend's husband was cheating on her. But still, why not keep your yap shut? A lot of people who were cheated on and found out about it will tell you, post divorce, that they would prefer never to have found out and gone on living in ignorant bliss. If you must say something to someone, tell your friend's husband what you witnessed. In as low-key and nonconfrontational a manner as possible say, "I'm telling you what I saw, but if I ever see you doing something like that again, I will have to tell your wife." Perhaps the realization that he came this close—thumb and index finger held an inch apart—will bring your friend's husband to his senses, and he'll refrain from wrapping himself around other women in public places.

Postscript

WHERE THERE'S SMOKE

I have a dear 79-year-old friend on a fixed income. A heavy smoker, she is down to one lung and professes no desire to quit. She has no car, so once a month I drive her to the military commissary (her late husband was a veteran) in the Presidio to buy cheap cigarettes, for which I often pay. Should I continue to support her deadly habit or cut her off and force her to suffer the withdrawal she says she cannot endure?

—DAVE SWANSON, SAN FRANCISCO

If your friend is on her deathbed, you may honorably supply her with anything she desires. Given her increasing years and decreasing number of lungs, it would seem priggish to deny her any pleasure. Were she twenty-nine and amenable to reform, I might feel differently. At seventy-nine, she has surpassed the life expectancy of her contemporaries, and so it may be hard to persuade her that she does herself real harm by smoking or that she has much chance of quitting. If you believe she cannot change her behavior, it is not unethical for you to buy those cigarettes. Indeed, it would take a colder heart than mine to deny her this small joy.

Of course, the trouble with death is that it's so unreliable. How often does it happen to any of us? Once, tops. And its timing is so unpredictable. You can neither count on her imminent demise nor, it seems, stop worrying that you may hasten it. But while those who love her may—should—try to influence her behavior (without hectoring), as long as she's not harming anyone else, your friend—like all of us—has the right to make her own foolish, misguided, self-destructive decisions.

However, this is not just a question of her self-determination, but of your remorse about aiding and abetting. In deciding what to do, you should certainly consult your own feelings. So, while you may buy her cigarettes, you are not required to. You might instead offer her patches, trips to a smoking-cessation program, or a steady supply of gum to help distract her from the rigors of breaking the habit. She can always decline your offer and appeal to another friend to supply her with cigarettes.

DAVE SWANSON FOLLOWS UP:
You said I must follow my heart. That was the correct answer because even if you said it was unethical for me to buy her the tobacco, I would have done so anyway. My heart says she is a dear friend at the end of her life and I want her to enjoy her final years as much as possible.

One reason I wrote you was to assuage my remorse for abetting her in that disgusting habit. Sadly enough, however, I have not been able to tell my friend of the whole incident.

Taking her shopping was originally an excuse just to make sure we saw each other. According to PX rules, only people with proper military identification are allowed to make purchases. So I would have her pick me up a few items while she was in the store and pay her back. Like so many of us, she has a hole in her pocket and so preferred me to pay her back by check. As the years progressed and her living standards declined, I found myself making the checks out for a little more than I really owed, until it got to the point where it was obvious that she couldn't afford the cigarettes without a major contribution on my part.

As this was all unspoken, I wouldn't know how to broach the subject without destroying her pride. Being old, alone, and poor are bad enough, but to lose one's dignity is too much to suffer.

In conclusion, I'm still buying her cigarettes, which makes her happy. I got to see my name in print (spelled correctly, thank you) and you did take my guilt away, so I'm happy.

Family Life

*It is . . . at home that every man must be known by those who
would make a just estimate either of his virtue or felicity; for smiles
and embroidery are alike occasional, and the mind is often for show
in painted honour and fictitious benevolence.*

JOHNSON: *RAMBLER* #68 (NOVEMBER 10, 1750)

The obligation of each family member to the others is not merely to be
good but to be kind. To be a part of a family benignly entangles one in
a network of relationships defined not by duty but by love, transcending
anything as narrow as ethical necessity, and aspiring to true generosity
and a profound concern for the well-being of the other family members
that obviates moral obligation.

Of course, there's still time for bickering.

As in every aspect of life, daily reality frequently falls short of cherished ideals. And so families still have their obligations and their rules
through which those obligations are articulated and enforced. These duties can be all the more difficult to honor because, as Johnson observes,
at home they know who you are. It is one thing to adhere to one's principles when dealing with strangers; it is more difficult to be fair to those
with whom one's life has been entwined for years—relationships that inevitably include resentment, jealousy, the memory of past slights and
hurt feelings, that vast emotional thicket that is domestic bliss.

Family life has been portrayed variously as a microcosm of the
larger society and as a refuge from it. But even in a country that prizes
democracy, there's little of that in family life. There has been some
progress from the most authoritarian model of father-as-autocrat. Be-

tween the parents, power is now distributed a bit more equitably, at least along gender lines, with mother and father sharing the leadership (a change that paralleled women's increased economic power). But even in the most liberal households, the children function as a kind of constituent assembly with the power to consult but not to legislate, rather along the lines of certain moderate Persian Gulf states, if you see Kuwait as moderate.

Such regard for age is thoroughly consistent with the values of the larger society, where childhood confers a distinct status, and age is thought to be a reasonable consideration in assigning rights and responsibilities. For instance, in many locales one may drive at sixteen, vote at eighteen, and drink at twenty-one (although one is discouraged from driving to the liquor store and then voting drunk at any age, despite the understandable desire one may feel to do so after perusing the names on the ballot). Even in Texas, one may not be executed until the age of five, if I correctly remember local custom, which I assuredly do not. Youth has its privileges.

Beyond the ties of love, family life is indeed based on a set of ethical obligations, and the rules governing family life comprise a kind of legal system. It is a set of laws drafted by those in power, i.e., the adults, to govern the behavior of the powerless, i.e., the children. These rules naturally serve the interests of those who wrote them, as do all legal systems, but there is more to it than that. The rules regulating family life are also meant to promote the best interests of the children, even if, like all legal codes, they are imperfect in achieving these ends, and necessarily include all manner of prejudices, misconceptions, and simple wrongheadedness. That is, parents really do love their children and so try to devise rules that ensure their safety and cultivate their development as decent human beings. And keep them from stuffing a peanut butter sandwich into the VCR. At two in the morning. While screaming at the top of their lungs.

It is interesting to see how those who are held in check by a set of laws are sometimes able to use those same laws as a force in their own liberation. Consider, for example, that the civil rights movement of the 1960s made much progress in the federal courts, using law as a way to find relief from the oppression of law. Children employ a similar approach, using family rules to improve their lot. It is in their insistence on "fairness," by which they mean consistency of application, that children attempt to use the law as an instrument of self-defense. Not without some success. Indeed, the cry of "That's not fair!" is the central legal argument of childhood, and a leading cause of headaches in adults.

If parents reject this appeal to consistency, they teach children that the law is a lie; it is simply parental power disguised as justice. It has no ethical legitimacy. ("If I can't interrupt, neither can you!" "If I have to respect your privacy, you have to respect mine." They're all little lawyers.) Thus, parents would undermine the very rule of law and its claims to be humane, equitable, and predictable. Parents who are not evenhanded in the application of family rule, even when applying it to themselves, forsake all moral authority. Still, they have more money than their kids do and the keys to the car, but the resulting lawlessness can be most unpleasant.

Ethics Pop Quiz

Below are four hypothetical questions for you the reader to answer.

Replies can be submitted to theethicistbook.com or e-mailed to theethicist@randomhouse.com.

Selected responses will appear in the paperback edition of the book.

While I yearn for romance and rapture, I find myself with a husband who is dull and stifling; he is a doctor much older than I am. Recently, visiting Rouen to go to the theater, I met an old friend who offers the passion I crave. Would it be so wrong to have an affair? —EMMA BOVARY, YONVILLE, FRANCE

I recently learned (from a ghost! Scary!) that my uncle murdered my father and married my mother. I know that this isn't ethical; that's not my question. I am seriously considering some kind of revenge, but I can't make up my mind. Would that be right? (Please remember that I live in a different time with different values and that I'm fictional.)

—PRINCE HAMLET, DENMARK

Although I'm happy in my current job, having recently received a promotion (I'm the new Thane of Cawdor), that's not enough for my wife, who is eager for me to get ahead. I'm not saying I lack ambition, but I am reluctant to do what it takes to climb higher—the long hours, the bloody murders. And yet, don't I have a special obligation to consider my wife's desires? We are, after all, a family.

—MACBETH, SCOTLAND

Shortly after my husband was killed in an automobile accident, I learned I was pregnant (despite our persistent use of contraception). I have two wonderful children, but in my circumstances I feel I could not be a good mother to a third. Besides the grief of losing someone we love, my family now faces serious financial hardships, so I plan to terminate this pregnancy. I am familiar with the anti-abortion arguments, but believe I am making the right choice. Do you agree?

Q & A

Parents

We are writing a will and want to leave all our money to our two children. One is very rich and the other lives almost hand-to-mouth. Do we divide equally or give the poorer one a greater proportion?

—H.S. AND S.S., NEW YORK CITY

Why give the money to either of them? It's yours to enjoy as you choose; it is not their fortune to be held in trust. You're free to bequeath it to a home for incorrigible cats or squander it in riotous living. Parents are not obliged to enrich their adult children.

Perhaps the most ethical approach is to ask how the money will do the most good, a question that leads some people to donate their savings to a cause they believe in rather than keep it in the family. Indeed, this might be asked throughout one's life, not just when drawing up a will. And it is a question Donald Trump and Dorothy Day would answer quite differently.

If you still wish to give your savings to your children, it may reassure you to know that no matter how you divide it, you will be wrong. Distribute it evenly, and the poorer child will be hurt that you gave money he badly needed to his richer sibling out of some abstract sense of fairness—what vanity! Give more to the poorer kid, and the wealthier one will resent you for rewarding his sibling's fecklessness, proof that you loved him more—what cruelty!

There are other ways to employ a legacy. In Thackeray's *Vanity Fair*, that rollicking tyrant Miss Crawley used her will to bully her dreadful relatives, and they all sucked up nicely. She intended to divide her fortune neither evenly nor proportional to need, but to ensure her own entertainment, bequeathing the bulk of it to her scapegrace nephew, Rawdon Crawley, who had few virtues but much vitality: He amused her.

While not unethical—her crime here was merely putting temptation in the path of the greedy—it turned out to be ineffectual. Her relatives loathed her, and not even the prospect of her thousands could keep Rawdon in line. He disappointed her eventually, and she cut him out of the will.

Whatever you decide, the money should be a gift you wish to bestow, not an obligation you must discharge. And if you have a child living from hand-to-mouth, you might want to give him a gift right now.

WILLFUL BEHAVIOR

A single man dies without a will. His sister is the beneficiary of all of his retirement/insurance policies but one. On that one, quite old, a previous lover is the beneficiary. It is "assumed" that my friend never thought to change the beneficiary and "assumed" that his sister would have been the beneficiary if he had realized that the old lover was on it. The sister gets in touch with the old lover and asks him to give her the money he'd be receiving. What do you think?

—P.D., CALIFORNIA

There is certainly a lot of assuming going on. I've found it to be incredibly difficult to read another person's mind, doubly so when that person is no longer living. So I'd take him at his word. Who knows how much happiness your friend received in this romance? Who can say why he wants to remember a former lover? Your friend made his wishes clear; respect them. Although I must say, I'm amazed that the sister had the nerve to make such a request. Why not just say to the guy, "Hey, nice car. Can I have it?"

IS CHRIST REAL?

Should Christ get a longer free ride than Santa Claus? I told my daughter (age 7) that Santa is a wonderful character invented by

adults. She took it pretty well, and then she asked, "Is Jesus just a character, too?" Should I really saddle her with my doubt on a subject that big?

—ANONYMOUS

Contrary to the warning flashed before certain TV shows, all themes are suitable to a younger viewer: love and death, blood and terror, treachery and betrayal—hence the enduring appeal of Grimm's fairy tales. But younger children not only accept a brief and general explanation, they prefer it.

Start by telling her what others think. Some believe Jesus was a man who became a legend. Others believe the New Testament offers an authentic account of the life of the son of God. And some believe he is a fictional character. Tell her what you think, doubts and all.

Children live in a moral universe, and their questions deserve answers. When my Younger Viewer asked if it was the Tooth Fairy who slipped that money under her pillow, I asked her what she thought. She ventured that she suspected it was her parents. "Do you really want me to tell you?" I asked, giving her a chance to continue the fantasy. But when she demanded an answer, I gave it to her: The money comes from Barney, the friendly purple dinosaur; I won it from him in a poker game with the Teletubbies, who cheated all night long. Eventually, she stopped crying.

WEB PORN PROTECTION

I am the father of two early-adolescent boys, who are both active Web surfers. I am not a prude, but I think that exposure to extreme sexual images available on-line is not a good thing at their ages. I could retain a secret list of the Web sites they visit. But is that ethical? Is it equivalent to putting a hidden TV camera in their room (which I would consider a violation of their privacy), or is it an acceptable way for a parent to keep informed and be able to initiate discussion of this tricky topic?

—WILLIAM S. KESSLER, SEATTLE

Your admirable concern for your sons' development necessitates neither that you cast them adrift in a sea of disturbing porn, nor that you fill your house with hidden cameras, tiny microphones, and cagey men in dark glasses who'd make everyone uneasy at the dinner table.

There's nothing wrong with being involved with what your kids see on-line; it's deception that's unsettling. Just as you wouldn't sneak a look at their diaries to learn what they're writing, you shouldn't surreptitiously tap their computer to find out what they're reading. If you intend to retain a list of the sites they visit, tell them. That way you can discuss those sites with them, just as you might discuss a book that you saw them reading around the house.

But especially at this age, your boys may find parental scrutiny—even of the most innocuous activities—embarrassing. The problem is balancing their right to free inquiry with your duty to shield them from truly disturbing images. And here the solution is not a technological fix but the more difficult task of teaching your kids a system of values. Part of that system reserves certain activities (drinking, driving, perusing pornography) for adults.

In any case, just as the boys can hide an ugly and upsetting magazine under the bed, they can browse on-line porn with a friend's computer. But by creating a situation at home where conversation is encouraged and privacy is respected, you have a better chance of helping them deal with the rough stuff.

DO YOU TELL?: DRUGS

I'm surprised you haven't been inundated by some variation of this theme: My teenage daughter mentioned that a classmate at her elite private school asked if she could obtain illegal drugs. This classmate's mother is an old family friend who a year ago confided that her child had recently completed a recovery program for an addiction to an illegal substance. Should I alert her classmate's mother? She is divorced and apparently now estranged from her child, who lives with the father. And complicating matters, my kid will never forgive me if I tell.

—ANONYMOUS, NEW YORK CITY

I have, as you suspect, received many forms of this question. Indeed, what I'm most often asked is one or another version of "Do you tell?"—about the infidelity of someone's best friend's spouse, about wicked behavior in the office. . . . Most involve, as does your question, problems of divided loyalties.

The first thing you might try is to ask your daughter to release you from your vow of silence by persuading her that doing so is the best way to help her friend. If that fails, there are a couple of things to bear in mind. As you note, the mother knows that her child has a drug problem. Further, because the mother is estranged from the child, there seems to me little that the mother can do with your information.

Thus, the good you might do is not worth the harm of betraying your daughter's trust. However, that doesn't leave you without recourse. Surely you can express a general concern for your friend's child and draw out the mother (or the father, since surely he has a stake in this) about how the child is doing following rehab, pointing out that this is a long-term process where backsliding is not unknown.

BABY-SITTER STEALS

Last week at the mall, I saw the teenage girl who baby-sits for my young children steal a sweater. I feel like I should either tell her I saw her and make it clear to her that I don't want her passing her habit on to my kids, or else just fire her. The thing is, she's a great baby-sitter in all other ways. But is it wrong to leave my children in the care of someone who might be teaching them to steal, or worse?

—ANONYMOUS

Can you fire someone for what they do off the job? Everyone is entitled to a private life, even an imperfect one. If the offense is not job related, it is none of the boss's business. An arrest at a political demonstration, say, or for tax fraud, needn't affect the job performance of a lathe operator or a cardiac surgeon.

But caring for children is different. A sitter does more than protect them from physical danger. The children in her charge learn from her example. And while it is a wonderful thing for kids to master real-world skills, you might not be so eager for them to pick up shoplifting.

If after talking to her, you're convinced that this was a one-time crime not to be repeated, then give her another chance, although you should insist that she return the purloined sweater, not just as a token of good faith, but because it is the right thing to do. If, however, you believe she'll be playing Fagin to your kids' Oliver Twist, fire her. Your obligation to your children supersedes your obligation to her.

Kids

R&J DATE

I am a sophomore in high school. I'd like to ask a girl out but her parents do not want her to date yet. My friends have told me she would go out with me anyway, but that means she would be disobeying her parents because of me, and I'm not sure I should put her in that situation. I don't know what to do—be Romeo and Juliet, or just call the whole thing off.

—A.K., NEW JERSEY

If you preemptively decline to ask her out, you assume a kind of power over her that is not yours to take.

Her obedience is a matter between her parents and her, not between them and you. You should neither demand that she obey them nor pressure her to defy them. ("Virtue itself turns vice, being misapplied.") She must decide, and you must respect her choice. So ask her out, and see what she says. ("And vice sometime's by action dignified.")

Look on the bright side; you could be misreading the situation. Her parents might not be implacably opposed to dating, and she might not be so eager to go out with you. Either way, problem solved. (*Romeo and Juliet,* Act II, Scene iii, line 21.)

I'm a 21-year-old college student from the Great Plains. My friends are under the legal age to buy beer, so that task falls to me. On a $10 purchase, I charge $5. A buddy of mine says this is wrong. But I figure it's okay since here it's a felony, and I provide door-to-door service, even bringing booze into the dorm where it is prohibited. Is it fair to take a small cut off the top?

—N.H., SOUTH DAKOTA

One does not charge for a favor. That is: Friends don't let friends drive drunk with a 50 percent markup. But if you do decide to flout the law, violate campus rules, and exploit your pals, consider this Space Age technology: illegalLiquorDelivery.com. If the judge lets you keep your laptop, you'll be able to run the business from your cell.

FORGED PIZZA CHECK

My parents were out of the house when my brother and I decided to order takeout. The trouble was, we didn't have any money because our parents had forgotten to give us our allowance for weeks. So we paid with one of my parents' checks, which I signed with my mother's name. Had our parents paid us on time, we would have had the money. What do you think?

—EVAN, NEW JERSEY

I refer you to the ancient doctrine—how does that go again?—oh, yes: Two wrongs don't make a right. Just because someone owes you money doesn't give you the right to break into his house and beat him senseless until he pays up (as I'm constantly reminding my bookie and my hypothetical cousin Leo) nor does it give you the right to forge checks. You'll have to find a more direct way to remind your parents about your allowance.

Guest Ethicist

My mom, a recent widow in her mid-70s, wants to start driving again. She hasn't driven in years, had many accidents when she did, is hard of hearing and arthritic, and has a history of alcoholism. While we (her children) object, her therapist has told her that she should make her own decision and has encouraged us to be supportive. What's the right thing to do?

—ANONYMOUS

Since taking up the ethics column, I've come to think that systems of ethics are used more as a means of understanding and articulating one's beliefs than in creating them. Personal values seem to precede any ethical system that describes and justifies them. I believe that these values are learned from the culture in which one lives, and most important, from one's parents. And that is why I'm eager to include as a guest ethicist, my mother, Irma Cohen. She replies:

What? Hard of hearing? Accidents and alcoholism? For the therapist to want your mom to drive again is unacceptable. It would be impossible to support a plan that could have so negative an impact on your mom's safety and on everything in her path.

But there are a lot of options you can explore that will make it possible for her to go places without doing the actual driving. In an excellent article in the *New York Times* by Jane Brody, Linda Blake, a specialist in transportation planning for the New York Department of Aging, said that any community with mass transit must also have an alternative door-to-door service for people with disabilities. In New York, it is Access-a-Ride, with 58,000 people now registered to use it. Information is available through Eldercare Locator, 1-800-677-1116 or through an area's agency on aging. The Bureau of Aging is a great information source.

Near where I live, to help people get out of their houses to socialize, a Pennsylvania community center program offers $60 worth of taxi coupons for $15. Many local bus companies offer seniors special door-to-door service to malls, doctor appointments, cultural events, and more. You might even decide to hire a driver occasionally. And while you are considering your many new possibilities, I would encourage you to help Mom find a new therapist.

My own response to this question is, unsurprisingly, not so different from my mother's. It is, also unsurprisingly I regret to say, not nearly as generously filled with practical suggestions.

Before you make any decisions, have your mother take you out for a drive, not on the freeway at rush hour, but in a parking lot after hours, when she won't imperil others. Perhaps she drives better than you recall, or would with a few lessons. On the other hand, if she meanders menacingly across the blacktop, she may realize that she is the hazard you suspect she is. Either way, much conflict can be avoided when family members rely on firsthand information rather than on memories and opinions.

If your mother does indeed pose a threat to herself and others, she absolutely must not drive. She might find this precept easier to accept if it comes not from her own child but from an authority outside the family; for instance, her doctor. Or your state may require older folks to be tested, so your mom may not even be able to renew her license.

But if the awkward task of stopping her falls to you, you must not shirk it. Persuading aging parents to change their behavior is never easy. If your mother was endangering only herself—by, say, not eating properly or not taking necessary medication—it would be a thornier problem. You would have to rely not on a rule of ethics but on the messier necessities of love, always peculiar to each person and situation. Thus you may feel compelled to take forceful action that buffets your relationship. Sometimes it will be worthwhile, sometimes not.

To deal practically with this problem, you might look for other ways for her to get around: in some towns, organizations for seniors help arrange rides. To deal impractically with it, you should make your mom move to any big city where public transportation frees the very old and very young from the sad dilemma of dependency on a car vs. immobility.

Incidentally, your question brings up another important concern: keeping tabs on the medical advice a parent is getting. Her supportive and encouraging therapist may pose a greater danger to society than your mother's driving a burning Buick full of firecrackers and pit bulls on the Hollywood Freeway while blindfolded.

Families

NOVEL SOLUTION

I have a really crazy family. Dysfunction R Us! I've been reading all these memoirs about people's screwed-up childhoods, and even though I'm not a great writer or famous or anything, I thought I might try my hand at writing one. Do you think it's ethical to write a tell-all about one's own family while the people in question are still living?

—M.W., NEW YORK CITY

I see what you're getting at, but I can't in good conscience encourage you to murder your family.

Your problem would be easily solved if you would simply write an immortal work of genius. Critics might carp that you embarrassed a cousin or betrayed some old uncle, but if you produce a book so teeming with life, so profound in its understanding, so elegant in its prose that it enriches all humanity, you can endure their sneers. This is the Samuel Pepys solution. So brilliantly does he depict the turbulent world of seventeenth-century London that readers not only forgive but cherish his appalling indiscretions.

If you cannot be certain of writing an immortal work of genius, your situation is knottier. Fortunately, there is a wonderful literary form called fiction, in which the ideas and experiences of a lifetime are transmuted into art. Perhaps through effort and imagination and ability you could transform your family life into a novel. There is also a tactic called waiting. Write now; publish later. What's your hurry?

Autobiography is not a crime. You are entitled to have your own life and tell your own story. But you are not entitled to purchase a literary career at someone else's expense. So how do you balance their pain against your gain? It depends whom you plan to mortify. When it comes to voluntary associations—a spouse, a pal—they knew you were a writer when they met you; they must take their chances. But neither your parents nor your children have any choice in the matter; they're stuck with you. You must respect their right to privacy. You may not ignore the effect your work will have on those closest to you. Rather than make them suffer, you should write discreetly or write fiction or write later.

RETURN OF THE VANISHING BIODAD

A year ago, I got pregnant. The guy in question acknowledged his financial responsibility but clearly wasn't ready to be a parent. I told him it was a choice I was making on my own, and I quite willingly relieved him of any obligation. Since then I've entered a committed relationship with another guy, who loves and cares for my baby daughter. Now her biological father has decided he made a bad mistake and wants a part of her life, too. He's a decent guy, but I barely know him, and if it'd been up to him she would never even have been born. What do I owe him?

—ANONYMOUS

In many ways, the biological dad is analogous to any parent who gives up a child to adoption. He must be allowed a reasonable amount of time to reflect on so consequential a decision, but eventually he must let you get on with your life. A year later, he has no ethical claim upon you. Nor does he have much of a legal claim, explains Elizabeth Bartholet, a professor of law at Harvard, and the author of *Family Bonds: Adoption and the Politics of Parenting*.

"While federal law protects an unwed father's interests in his chil-

THE GOOD, THE BAD

dren," she says, "his situation is somewhat iffy because for so long he's not sought out active fatherhood. If he's stayed away voluntarily, federal law offers him little protection, although he might have more under state law."

However, the most pertinent question is not what you owe him but what you both owe your daughter. Her well-being is paramount. She may eventually become curious about her background and eager to meet her biological father. Many children do. What will you say when, a dozen years from now, your adolescent daughter protests: "My real father wanted to be with me but you wouldn't let him!"

Her biological dad is already a part of her life; it is up to you to determine what that part will be. There may be a place for him that neither makes him a forbidden and mysterious figure, nor lets him impinge upon your family life as a kind of third parent. If he's the decent guy you say he is, his occasional visits may be a good thing for the person to whom you both have an ethical obligation, your daughter.

MEDICAREFUL

My mother has Alzheimer's disease, and has been cared for at home by a hired aide with my help and supervision for the past several years. Recently her condition has deteriorated and her doctor has warned me that she soon will need to be placed in a nursing home. Several years ago her lawyer advised me to transfer her assets to my name so that when she enters a nursing home she will qualify for Medicaid and when she dies I will inherit her money. This is perfectly legal, and according to other people in the same situation I've spoken to, it is widely done. But is it ethical?

—ANONYMOUS, NEW JERSEY

Perhaps it is calling this "transfer her assets" that gives it a sinister tone; if you think of it as a mother offering her child a gift, albeit one you enact on her behalf, it couldn't be more ordinary or more benign. Indeed, federal law allows her to give $650,000 over her lifetime free of federal taxes. Furthermore, for your mother to do so deprives no one else of health care. Federal and state governments fund Medicaid for all who are eligible.

I believe that we ought to provide a basic level of services to all—schools, parks, roads, libraries, health care, etc.—and if you want more, you must pay for it yourself. Nearly every other Western nation is able to do that without requiring older people to lose the savings of a lifetime to get health care; I see no reason why America can't do the same. Many laws have unintended consequences, and the response to Medicaid and the tax code suggests that many Americans would like to make Medicaid available to many more people, including themselves. Indeed, the law encourages that idea by allowing a parent to give away his money, even to a child who will then use it for that parent's care. If the result is a more humane system of health care that eases the lives of the elderly, I cannot see this as unethical.

Some people will condemn you for shifting the cost of her care to the state, i.e., your fellow citizens, so that you might someday inherit her money. However, just as you are required to pay your taxes but not to toss in a bonus payment, your obligation here is to obey the law, including the laws governing gifts and power of attorney, and to use your mother's money in her best interest, and it is this last issue that must be your prime concern. You have a profound obligation to see to your mother's care. You have no ethical obligation to drive her into poverty. There is nothing unethical about wise financial planning.

With long-term nursing home care running to $8,000 a month, a cost not borne by Medicare, many older people quickly run through their life savings. Others avoid destitution by giving some of their money to their children. There are other solutions. You might consider—or, more accurately, ought to have considered—long-term care insurance, which can allow your mother to preserve her savings without burdening your fellow citizens; self-reliance is indeed a virtue. Or you might emigrate. Canada, for example, has found a way to provide for their elderly citizens without making them paupers. Or you could encourage Congress to emigrate to Canada until they can design a more humane health care system.

But if you decide to stay here, don't wait until the last minute to make your plans. "The government can look back over a three-year period, and any money transferred can still be counted toward Medicaid eligibility," says Jeffrey Abrandt, a partner in Goldfarb and Abrandt, a law firm active in elder law and health care law. "The legal obligations are complicated and changeable. It's certainly an area where you should consult a lawyer."

BROTHER IN PRISON WITH AIDS

My brother is in prison for a nonviolent offense, and I could help him gain early release. However, he is HIV positive and has infected his most recent girlfriend and 2 or 3 others, a result of broken condoms, he claims. I don't want him to die in jail, but there is no doubt in my mind that lives will be saved if he stays in. Should I place the needs of society over those of my own flesh and blood?

—C.F., NEW YORK

Balancing your brother's well-being against the harm he might do if released is an agonizing calculation, but it is not the choice you face. Your brother is a danger to others right now. High-risk behavior—unprotected sex and IV drug use—is common in prison. Your question, then, becomes this: Where will he do the least harm to others and to himself? The answer is not prison.

While prison officials are likely to know your brother's condition (HIV screening is common in many prisons), they are unlikely to do much to protect his fellow inmates. A few facilities, including New York's Riker's Island and some Philadelphia jails, distribute condoms, but most do not, arguing that this would encourage illegal behavior. And few prisons isolate inmates with HIV, except when the very ill are eventually moved to the hospital ward. But if your brother were that ill on the outside, he would also be hospitalized, thus posing no danger to others. And he would be receiving far better medical care.

Indeed, the longer someone with HIV is imprisoned, the shorter his life expectancy, says Catherine Hanssens, Director of the AIDS Project at the Lambda Legal Defense and Education Fund: "He'll have a worse diet, less access to health care, less exercise, and much more stress. And he's at a much higher risk of contracting TB or, more lethally, hepatitis C."

Further, his time in prison will not make him less of a threat when he is released. Little that happens to him in prison will encourage him to treat others with kindness, compassion, and empathy.

What prisoners do have in vast supply is boredom, and this may incline your brother at least to listen. You can use this time to try to persuade him to act more responsibly. And, says Ms. Hanssens, there are peer counselors and other groups who've had success working with inmates in this way. Your goal here is to make your brother agree that, if you help get him out, he will not imperil other people.

Because he'll be less dangerous on the outside, to himself and to others, you should facilitate your brother's release. And remember, no matter what you do, eventually he will be getting out. The quicker this happens, the better for everyone.

GRANDPARENTS' RIGHTS

I work with a woman who is not permitted to see her grandchildren. She has been a driving force for legislation in Pennsylvania to enable grandparents to petition for visitation rights; the legislation is currently on hold in the Senate judiciary committee pending the U.S. Supreme Court's action on *Troxel v. Granville,* a Washington State case. Do grandparents have an ethical right to visit their bloodline grandchildren?

—GEORGE BEEZER, PENNSYLVANIA

The mutual affection between grandparent and grandchild should be respected not as a right, and certainly not because of the blood ties you invoke, but because they love each other, sufficient justification in itself.

However, when a parent thwarts a grandparent's visits, all becomes murkier. Some advocates of grandparents' rights argue that one should always do what is in the best interest of the child. But while it may be great for a child to have an intimate and enduring involvement with, say, Britain's Queen Elizabeth II—attending concerts, addressing parliament, messing about with dogs and horses, dedicating new power stations—the beloved monarch has no right to demand such a connection, and neither does any grandmother.

For parents to raise a happy child (and by parents I mean a child's prime caretakers, without biology coming into it) they must be permitted to function without arbitrary challenges to their role. If they imperil the child, the state must intercede. But short of that, they should be left alone.

This is not to say an exiled granny must be silent. While the conflict continues, she should stay in touch with the grandchild by those means still available. She can make phone calls, write letters, send birthday presents, and hope that the situation will improve. But she should not drag the parents into court.

In *Bleak House* Dickens describes a place "which so exhausts finances, patience, courage, hope; so overthrows the brain and breaks the heart; that there is not an honourable man among its practitioners who would not give . . . the warning, 'Suffer any wrong that can be done you, rather than come here!' " He spoke of the Court of Chancery, but he might have meant any tribunal that would extend the crude mechanism of court-ordered visitation to proliferating relatives. A grandmother's relationship with her grandchild may be delightful and it may be profound, but it is not a right, and it ought not be enforced by the courts.

THE ODDS FATHER

My elderly father believes he is destined to win a sweepstakes, and he orders all sorts of magazines, books, and knickknacks to better his odds. Knowing he has no chance of winning, I threw away the dozen solicitations that arrived in his mail when I stayed at his house recently. My father is not mentally incompetent, but I feel he is being taken advantage of. Was I right to toss out his mail?

—STEPHEN SAWICKI, FAIRFIELD, CONNECTICUT

In the movie version of your life, you have just tossed away the letter announcing that your father had won a million dollars. And in the ordinary-life version, well, I'd have to say you were wrong here, too. All you gained was a brief lull in the flow of mail-order rubbish, bought at the price of your dad's trust. It hardly seems worth it. Instead, talk to your father about what you seem to fear could be a gambling problem. And be sure to mention that con artists are known to target the elderly with such sweepstakes schemes. (A call to your local precinct house will let you know what's been going on in your area.)

If that fails, you can always come around later, sneak into his house, and throw away all his mail and all his pens and pencils. Oh, all right, you can't. Your dad is an adult in possession of his wits, and while you can inform and encourage, persuade and cajole, you cannot force him to change his ways. Ultimately, the decision, even the foolish decision, is his.

DRIVEN TO PRAY

My elderly father-in-law has always been active in his synagogue, and he is also handicapped. The new rabbi, in an effort to more strictly interpret religious law regarding travel by vehicle on the Sabbath, has closed the handicapped parking area so worshippers will not drive. This prevents many disabled congregants from attending activities. How do you balance access for the handicapped with religious edicts?

—LINDA WATTS BROUN, WASHINGTON, D.C.

For the strictly Orthodox, it is better not to go to the synagogue at all than to ride on the Sabbath, and so your father-in-law seems stuck in an intractable situation. He may, however, have more options than you realize.

"Sometimes there are extenuating circumstances," says Rabbi Samuel Intrator of the Carlebach Schul, an Orthodox congregation. "He should discuss it with his rabbi and see if a dispensation could be found, respectful to the community and to his special needs. For instance, perhaps a non-Jew might drive him to the synagogue."

Your father-in-law's rabbi is obviously not trying to discriminate against the disabled. In addition, the synagogue is a voluntary association; no one is compelled to obey Jewish law. Your father-in-law chooses compliance, and in that sense is not a victim of injustice.

However, while the intent of the parking policy is not discriminatory, its effect is. And even when membership and obedience are voluntary, no group is exempt from ethical scrutiny. Some Boy Scouts object to their organization's exclusion of homosexual scoutmasters. Members of many religions criticize their faith's refusal to ordain women, i.e., to treat all congregants equally. A precept's being based on religious belief does not give it special ethical status.

Furthermore, one may embrace a body of beliefs but reject a particular edict. Such conflicts can lead people to reform an organization, secular or sacred. Religious practice is not immutable; all faiths have altered over the centuries. Rabbi David Lincoln of the Park Avenue Synagogue, a Conservative congregation, suggests that for some people "Conservative Judaism is the answer—a traditional service and plenty of parking."

However, your father-in-law does not seem inclined to leave his congregation. And you do not seem to have a principled objection based on rights for the disabled as much as a desire simply to get him to shul. I'd look for ways to do that.

COUSIN'S KID'S DENT

When my cousin's 12-year-old daughter got out of my car, she opened the door into a parked car, leaving a visible dent. I asked my cousin to leave a note. She said that if she did, she would have to pay for the repair. I said that was the point. She refused. We argued. I drove away feeling terrible. Should I have left a note myself with her name and number? With mine?

—J.C., NEW YORK

If that door ding was trivial, you need have done nothing. Tiny scrapes and scratches are an ordinary part of driving. If it was more serious, you should have left a note with your name on it. Your car, your dent. The driver of the car is not entirely analogous to the captain of a ship (you probably cannot perform backseat weddings) but while the car is under your control, you bear some responsibility for any damage it does.

How to apportion that responsibility between you and your cousin's daughter, I leave to you and the cousin to sort out. (This certainly has the makings of a lifelong family quarrel.) But one person who is not at all responsible is the guy whose car was damaged, and it's not right to leave him in the lurch when you were involved in putting him into that lurch.

I understand your reluctance to inform on a 12-year-old, but the ethical thing to do then is to take more—not less—responsibility on your own shoulders.

Arguing with The Ethicist

TAKE ME OUT TO THE CHEAP SEATS

My dad takes me to a lot of baseball games and always buys the cheapest tickets in the park. When the game starts, he moves to better, unoccupied seats, dragging me along. It embarrasses me. Is it okay for us to sit in seats we didn't pay for?

— GEORGE MURPHY (AGE 11), HOUSTON, TEXAS

Your dad's seat hopping is more than okay: It is a time-honored baseball tradition. He hurts no one, and it would be foolish to let good seats go unused when they can bring joy to fans who'd otherwise be way out in left field.

This is not how your Houston Astros see it. At Enron Field all seats are reserved; you may sit only in the one you paid for. "It's a customer service function," explains John Sorrentino, Vice President for Ticket Services. "Latecomers don't like asking people to move out of their seats. It makes them uncomfortable."

　　　　　　　THE GOOD, THE BAD

A feeble justification. At the theater and the opera here in New York, it is customary to move to a good unoccupied seat. If the ticket holder arrives, he politely asks you to move, and you courteously comply. Surely Texans can do the same.

But Sorrentino has another rationale. "There tend to be different people in different seating areas," he says. "If someone pays $200 for a seat, and people with $5 seats are sneaking down there, it distracts from their enjoyment." That is, uptown swells don't like to sit near bleacher riffraff. This view is contemptible. People from all walks of life sharing a common experience is one of the things that makes baseball our national pastime. The Astros' policy turns the amiable populism of the ballpark into a series of gated communities.

Sorrentino notes that attending an Astros' game is voluntary. If you choose to do so, you must follow the rules. True, but you and your dad had no say in devising those rules, and the Astros' monopoly in Houston means you have no other Major League alternatives. Civility urges us to follow the rules of the ballpark, mall, or movie theater, but the rules ought to be just. They should not sacrifice the happiness of the many to the social prejudices of the few. Placing a guard on an unused seat so it will remain vacant rather than allowing you and your dad to move down from the bleachers is not my idea of virtue.

Once the game begins and your dad moves, he adds no more cost to the team owner, nor does he prevent anyone else from buying a ticket. All he does is sit 100 feet closer to the field in a seat that would otherwise go unused (and indeed, may already be sold to someone who has simply not come to the game) if there is such a seat. If there's not, he happily sits in his original seat. (Well, maybe he's not so happy if the team loses, which the Astros often do, but perhaps that's outside the purview of our discussion.) The point is, it would help no one for the better seat to remain unused. I believe it is churlish of the team owner to prevent him from using it.

It is unfortunate that your dad's seat changing embarrasses you. But when you are 11, nearly everything your parents do is embarrassing. So as long as you're being mortified, you might as well endure it in good seats.

I was SHOCKED to read your response to the ballpark question. I write from the vantage point of a (former) Broadway theater manager (24 years of service). First thing I will say is that it is NOT customary in the theater or opera to move to unoccupied seats for very practical reasons (setting ethical ones aside for the moment), because moving out of those seats during a performance, when the legal ticket holder arrives, is very disturbing to the audience.

I REPLY:

I'd have thought that 24 years managing theaters would have left you unshockable. I'll bet you've seen some astonishing behavior even if you've never worked with Mickey Rooney, and I regret being the instrument of your upheaval, but I have to say that while I respect your experience, I'm unpersuaded by your argument.

I do agree that every audience member should try not to disturb his neighbors—by talking, eating, taking a cell phone call, or moving from his seat during a performance. But if the seat shifters act the moment the lights go down, as they often do, I see small harm in it. And certainly, when people take better seats for the second act, as you must admit is commonly done, they harm no one. Further, at the ballpark, there is much movement throughout the game, and folks seem to handle that just fine.

MR. LIEBERMAN FIRES BACK:

The ballpark/theater sells Red seats (sweaters) for price 100, Green seats (sweaters) for price 50, and Blue seats (sweaters) for price 25 (for instance). How is buying a Blue sweater for 25 and taking a Red sweater, priced at 100, much different?

I REPLY:

Your sweater analogy is inapt. The seat is not the product; the show or ballgame is the product. Were I to pay for a $25 sweater and take a $100 sweater, I'd be imposing a cost on the dealer in, say, better-quality wool or more elaborate stitching, but by moving my seat at the ballpark, I'm still seeing the same game and imposing no more costs on the team owner.

MICHAEL COLANGELO MOVES FROM WARM CLOTHING TO TROPICAL FRUIT:

Using your logic, I should steal bananas at the grocery store, knowing that a certain amount are sure to be thrown out at the end of the day. Taken to the extreme, no one would ever buy a banana, nor would anyone ever buy an expensive seat for a game that routinely fails to sell out.

I REPLY:

Your banana analogy is not an extreme example of my argument; it's not parallel at all (although it's really fun to say "banana analogy"). Once I eat my stolen banana, a legit customer can't ask me to return it. Well, he can, but it will be pretty revolting. Further, if I steal a banana, I deprive the shopkeeper of the money he'd make on it; when I move up in my seat, I deprive the team owner of nothing.

It's certainly true that some folks could decide not to buy a cheap seat and instead go for a bleacher seat in the hope that they'll get to move closer to the action, but there is no guarantee that they will be able to move, and no evidence that this in fact shapes people's seat-buying habits.

CARROLL ROBINSON WAVES THE RED FLAG:

WRONG! What kind of morality model are you peddling here? Why do you think there are varying prices for most things in our world? Duh! I suppose you would advocate moving from coach to an empty seat in first class? Come to think of it, why not take some of your neighbors' unused money, or drive his parked car? Gee, maybe we can start a society where everyone has equal property . . . what shall we call it? How about Cohen-mmunism?

I REPLY:

The reason there are varying prices for ballpark seats is because the owner has the power to charge them, not because it is a law of nature. It is not enough for you simply to assert the rights of property, even in capital letters with an exclamation point: You really do have to make an actual case that someone is injured when that kid and his dad move down a dozen rows to an unoccupied seat, as would be the case if you took your neighbor's money or used his car.

I would certainly extend my argument to your example of an airline seat. Once the plane is at 35,000 feet, and there is no possibility of any more passengers joining the flight, why shouldn't the airline allow someone in coach to move up to an unoccupied first-class seat? Who would be harmed by this? (Of course the lucky upgraded do not get to eat the meal: that would cost the airline more money.)

What a customer pays for in these cases is the game (or the flight). It costs the owners no more for him to enjoy it from a better seat that would otherwise go unused. It is petty of them to deny someone a chance for more happiness that comes at no cost to anyone.

CARROLL ROBINSON GOES ONE MORE AMIABLE ROUND:

Sorry about my offensive use of capital letters, just as I am sorry about your lack of sympathy for capital. One final caveat: Higher ticket prices for better seats are not the result of the owner's power, they are the result of supply and demand. Cheers.

"SUPPLY AND WHAT?" I ASK, FEIGNING CONFUSION AS A RHETORICAL DEVICE:

When a team has been granted a monopoly, ticket prices have only a marginal relationship to supply and demand. Here in New York, for example, Knicks games have been sold out for decades; that is, demand has not changed, but ticket prices have gone up about 400 percent. They're the only NBA game in town. Given the array of tax breaks, public money, and monopoly practices that underpin these circumstances, to ignore all these arrangements and suddenly invoke the free market's effects on ticket prices sounds disingenuous.

DAVE KHOURY DEFENDS THE POOR BALLCLUB OWNER:

I hope I'm not beating a dead horse, but I think it is ethically okay to run a business and try to make it profitable. In a baseball stadium or an airplane, this profitability is based on the more desirable seats being more expensive. If people are allowed to buy cheap seats and switch into more expensive ones, then why would anyone ever pay for the expensive seats?

I REPLY:

People will buy a good seat because that purchase *guarantees* you a good seat. You can attend the game with the confidence that your excellent seat is secure; you needn't take a chance on seat hopping. However, once the game hits the fifth inning or the plane hits 35,000 feet, those seats can no longer be sold. Further, our seat-hopping dad will never buy a $200 seat, and further still, the seat he hopped to has already been sold, but the corporate box holder never showed up. I too am for running a business at a profit, but that doesn't exempt you from ethical scrutiny.

MITCHELL GRUNAT MAKES A POINT:

Although I agree that the snobbery expressed by Sorrentino is contemptible, if the venue specifically has a policy prohibiting such aggrandizement, it must, ethically, be respected. And if the venue's policy is offensive, you are free not to attend.

I REPLY:

In general, I do encourage obeying the rules in the interests of civility (among other reasons), as I have written in this column. But the rules imposed by a baseball team owner have less moral force than those arrived at democratically, as I also have written. The rules must be just, and these rules are not. Further, "love it or leave it" is hardly ethics, and all the less so when there is a monopoly. There also exists an obligation to fairness, which is fallen well short of in this case. Thus, while our seat-hopping guy certainly breaks a ballpark rule, I don't see his behavior as unethical. And while the ballpark rules may be enforced, that doesn't make each one ethical.

VERN TROTTER APPEALS FOR MANNERS:

I have had Red Sox box seats for years and these people are nearly always loud, rude, and drunk. They create confusion in the aisles when they are forced to move, causing impaired vision for paying customers. In short, they just do not belong.

I REPLY:

The transgression you describe is bad manners not seat hopping. When I've asked people to move out of my (theater) seats, they've always complied promptly and courteously. Your problem is with loutishness, of which I am an implacable foe, lobbying for years for baseball to adopt a "No Spitting—At Least Not on the Other Patrons" rule. One can oppose excessive beer drinking, foul language, and fistfights, but still defend seat hopping. And I have it on good authority that the eleven-year-old kid rarely gets into a fight. (Perhaps it's because he can really hold his liquor.)

CHRISTIAN TALBOT PLAYS THE KANT CARD:

If enough people practiced this gentleman's policy of buying the cheap seats up solely to anticipate moving to expensive seats, it might eventually result in all of the cheap seats being bought up for a particular game. Then, if you or I were to want to buy a cheap seat to the same game, we might be unable to, because enough people thought that there was no need to pay full price since they'd surely be able to move later on.

I REPLY:

To ask what would happen if everyone did it is not entirely helpful. First, because everyone will not do it. Many fear the embarrassment of getting caught, others object on principle, and still others are content with their original seats. But beyond that, society seems to function quite well when 10 percent of the people break a rule. It's how we organize our traffic laws and presidential elections.

It doesn't always help to ask "What if everyone did as I do?" Such a question often leads you to reject perfectly benign activities. What if everyone went to the beach the day you do? It would be crowded and trash strewn, if, indeed, you could get there at all through the traffic. But the conclusion can't be that you ought not go to the beach.

There's a nice paradox here. If only a few people seat-hop, they and everyone else can count on getting a good seat. However, if seat hopping becomes widespread, the competition for good seats will be intense and not even the seat hoppers can count on getting one. Thus to be sure of getting one, all will be motivated to pay for one in advance. So, to my way of thinking, the Astros should encourage everyone to engage in this ad hoc upgrading. It'll pay off at the box office.

Postscripts

SCHOOL TIES

I volunteered to work on a directory of local private schools because it might give our 4-year-old daughter an edge when she applies to private school next fall. A friend argued that this was wrong: Most parents were denied this opportunity because they either didn't know about it or didn't have time to volunteer; in other words, it smacked of exclusion. Was she right?

—ANONYMOUS, CALIFORNIA

Unlike public schools, private schools make no promise of an even-handed admissions policy but are free to enroll whomever they choose. Some favor the siblings of existing students; some favor athletes—they'd be equally entitled to favor large tropical birds. It is not unknown for such institutions to rate the adults as much as the kids and to prefer parents who are rich or famous. Indeed, you might argue that offering an edge to parent volunteers levels the playing field for those who are not rich or famous or the mayor of a major East Coast city or the president of an important Western nation. So I'm more inclined to criticize a school for offering an unfair advantage than a parent for overreaching: Getting your child into a good school can be fraught with anxiety.

Although your volunteer work may be acceptable within the ethical system of private schools, it's fair to question that system. Is it really honorable to cultivate an admissions policy that is so decidedly unegalitarian? Given the many excellent public elementary schools in a place like New York City, for example, does any four-year-old there have a pedagogical need for private school? And does the establishment of a separate school system for wealthier families—for that is what we are talking about—contribute to the neglect of those children who are excluded?

The utopian—or at least longer-term—solution is to improve public education enough to obviate your question, but if you're committed to private school, then your volunteer work does not discredit you.

ANONYMOUS FOLLOWS UP:

I decided that the rumor of getting a "leg up" on other applicants was not necessarily a fact. The edge was vague enough to be real for those that thought it was okay and not real to those that thought it wasn't okay. So on one level we kinda took your advice as a stamp of approval and completed the project.

But that's not the end of the story. Our little play group had a huge fight over your reply. Two members of the play group stopped speaking to each other, and our play group has broken into two. (I am the only member of both groups.) I think the issue of privilege was just too much: The insider was willing to use it and the outsider was unable to accept unfair advantage on any level. The insider, by the way, is still deciding between public and private. The outsider is firmly committed to private school and to making the system as fair as possible. Me? I'm just a Midwestern, on-the-fence, golden mean, middle-of-the-roader. I finished the directory. I still think it gives one an edge, at least for some applicants, sometimes. And our child is going to public school, in part because of your opinion that elementary school is just the right place to be exposed to the diverse populations of American life.

School Life

To learn is the proper business of youth; and whether we increase our knowledge by books or by conversation, we are equally indebted to foreign assistance.

JOHNSON: RAMBLER #121 (MAY 14, 1751)

School life is the teacher's work life, of course, but it is also, in effect, the work life of the student (except for getting paid). Looked at this way, student life is governed by a kind of professional ethics, a code of conduct particular to a field of endeavor. But it is more complicated than that. Student life is governed by two sets of overlapping, and sometimes contradictory, rules. There are the overtly scholastic regulations—no cheating, for instance—but more important, and more Byzantine, are the codes governing student behavior outside the classroom.

Here, as in most societies, there is the official code and the more significant unofficial code of law and custom. And sometimes they clash. Some schools have a codified duty to report cheating that can conflict with the kid code of no ratting out another kid, not entirely unlike the code of dockworkers that confounded Marlon Brando in *On the Waterfront*. (Except for the brutal beatings. Actually, in some cases, including the brutal beatings.)

Another difference between the two codes is that the official rules are laid down by those in power. Adults set the rules for children; but the unofficial rules evolve in transactions between equals, students governing students. And further, the official rules comprise a formal written code; the unofficial an oral tradition. It is as if two cultures were overlaid—one of laws and one of traditions. The unofficial code is ambiguous and in flux. Although it is tough to pin down precisely, it is generally understood by all in the kid society, much as all in a village society know its mores. The official code is written; it is explicit. The law is stated openly for all to see. One consequence, the written code is in some ways more easily reformed. When a rule is clear-cut, a movement can be launched to change it. But customs, while always evolving, are more difficult to alter deliberately. For instance, a school's official dress code can be changed; a teenager's unofficial dress code is adamant. At least until Tommy Hilfiger hands down another edict from his fashion space lab orbiting high above the Earth.

At school, two societies and two codes of ethics are superimposed upon each other: the modern legalistic urban life of the teachers with its formalized rules of behavior, and a traditional custom-driven village life of the kids. Another word for that? Colonialism. The kids are the indigenous people with an oral tradition who must live under the rule of the far more powerful outsiders, the teachers. The teachers can punish. They have economic power. They live among the students but are not subjected to the petty restrictions that regulate the students. The teachers are often ignorant of the most powerful social forces surging through the corridors, and can neglect to consider their implications.

Like other colonial powers, the teachers offer the students a measure of self-government, but reserve the actual power themselves. And like other agents of colonial powers, the teachers have less money and less power than those who remain outside the colonial service—doctors, lawyers, brokers.

Or, if we need to find a still darker analogy, the prison parallel suggests itself. The warden (principal) and his guards (teachers) exercise genuine authority over the inmates (students), but there is another power structure and another set of rules laid down and enforced by the prisoners themselves. Or perhaps I'm thinking of *Blackboard Jungle* and ought to drink a glass of warm milk and calm down.

Both prison life and colonialism are, of course, extreme characterizations of school life (it is no doubt overstating things to suggest that, were the teachers removed from an elementary school, the resulting social order would resemble *Lord of the Flies*), but it is true that the school is a world with two distinct social classes, governed by two different moral codes, or at least two legal systems. (This is always pleasant to see in a country that prides itself on its classlessness.) There is an interesting tension along that border between the official and unofficial codes, the rules laid down by those with statutory authority (teachers) and the rules enforced more intimately by social equals (fellow students).

The synthesis of these two codes is indeed a kind of professional ethics, not just for teachers but for students. Such codes are prescriptive, of course, but they are also descriptive. They define what is acceptable standard practice in a particular area of life.

And much to my surprise, what is acceptable at school is cheating, at least to judge by my mail. A fascinating thing about writing an ethics column is that one is given a glimpse of the misdemeanors routinely engaged in around the country. This is not sociology of course, and one cannot assume that my correspondents are a scientific sample of the country—I receive so few letters from conscience-stricken burglars, for example (or Senators, for that matter)—but even anecdotal evidence ought not be dismissed out of hand. I receive a steady flow of letters asking not if it's okay to cheat but about the duty to report cheating when one observes it, which, apparently, kids do all the time. And, in researching the replies to such questions, my own conversations with teachers suggest that all manner of cheating—copying on tests, plagiarizing writing assignments—is commonplace in a way that it was not a generation ago.

Why should this be? It's a little outside my bailiwick to say. My brief is to think about the ethics of an action not determine its causes. And yet, simply as a matter of speculation, it's hard not to notice that kids born in the eighties are now of college age. They grew up under a president who emphasized self-interest at the expense of community, one who cultivated a goofy affection for cowboy fantasies of the autonomous individual who does not live among others, who denigrated public life as the machinations of wicked government. This is not a worldview apt to promote a sense of shared civic life with its concomitant sense of mutual moral responsibility. But, to be fair, it does promote capital gains cuts that benefit the wealthy, so things do balance out. Perhaps not in a freshman bio test, but maybe in some other sense.

Or maybe it's the hole in the ozone layer. I leave this sort of thing to the sociologists.

Ethics Pop Quiz

Below are four hypothetical questions for you the reader to answer.

Replies can be submitted to theethicistbook.com or e-mailed to theethicist@randomhouse.com.

Selected responses will appear in the paperback edition of the book.

I'm a new teacher at a middle school in Louisiana. Nearly all of my colleagues at one time or another keep discipline by spanking a disruptive child with a wooden paddle. At first I was offended by this, but now I'm not so sure. It certainly seems to work. But is it right?

Each year my university department accepts more students than can ever hope to find work in our field. When I interview applicants, if I am forthright about their eventual employment prospects, I'll scare many of them off, which ill serves the needs of the department that pays my salary. If I soft-pedal this sad fact, I betray the trust of the students. Where does my loyalty reside?

I am a dean at an Ivy League university located near Boston—you'd recognize the attitude—where some students are demanding that we pay our janitors a "living wage." On the one hand, we are probably the wealthiest university on Earth; we have a multi-billion-dollar endowment, and many of our graduates are among the country's most highly paid citizens. In addition, we try to teach our students humane values. On the other hand, I have a responsibility to protect our endowment (and the school's future) and so not overpay for anything. Am I right to let the free market determine the janitors' wages?

—PROF. CRIMSON, CAMBRIDGE, MASSACHUSETTS

> An impoverished student, I believe my sensitivity places me above moral law. I'm thinking of taking an ax to an old widowed pawnbroker—I might just murder her stepsister, too—and stealing her jewelry. Most people would say this is wrong, but what do you say?
>
> —RODION RASKOLNIKOV, ST. PETERSBURG

Q & A

Teachers

DEGRADING EXPERIENCE

In more than 25 years of teaching, I have never agreed with my students on what to do when one of them gets an answer wrong and I inadvertently mark it as correct. If the student lets me know, I praise him for his honesty, then take off the points I should have in the first place. Is this right, or should I let him keep the points because the mistake was mine?

> —SANDRA MARTIN, RAMSEY, NEW JERSEY

I can understand your students' disappointment. Having an 85 reduced to a 75 is more painful than receiving a 75 to begin with. But you're doing the right thing. One of the lessons that students should learn is that even a teacher can make a mistake.

At my daughter's middle school, some teachers take the contrary position, reasoning that their error raised a student's hopes; the extra points compensate him for his disappointment and reward him for his honesty.

That would be fine if he were the only kid in the class. However, if it is a typical New York middle-school class with 80 or 90 kids (or so it seems) that policy benefits one student at the expense of all the others. When this happened recently, the lucky student was widely resented, and the other kids beat the hell out of him in the exercise yard. No, wait, sorry: That thrashing happened in a prison movie I saw on TV (Cagney was wonderful!). But there was palpable indignation around the seventh grade.

The class resented not only the student who received an unearned credit but also the teacher who granted it. This policy undermines the sense of the classroom as a place where justice prevails. In addition, it teaches not the virtue of honesty but its utility. Speak up only when it's to your advantage.

It is worth reminding your students that a test is not merely a device for assigning a grade; it is a diagnostic tool meant to discover what the class knows and where it might improve. They should also remember, if they are ever sent to the big house, not to accept special favors from the warden; it will only diminish their social standing around the weight room.

TENURE DISCLOSURES

I am a professor at an Ivy League university. A close friend, with whom I went through graduate school, is up for tenure in my department. I think this is the wrong decision for my department, but by opposing it I feel like Judas. Am I?

—ANONYMOUS, MASSACHUSETTS

Were you employed in any other profession, the word "recuse" would be prominent in my response, wielded firmly but gently. But university life is different. It's a small small world, semiotics or sixteenth-century Belgian history. Many tenure decisions necessarily involve people who know one another.

Your first obligation is to tell the tenure committee about your connection to your former colleague. Your second is to make as fair and wise a decision as you can in your uneasy circumstances. But you do not owe your friend special favors. A shared history does not require a perpetual exchange of favors, unless, of course, you went through graduate school with anyone involved in Russian banking; then, apparently, you'd owe each other everything.

CONFIDENTIAL INFORMATION

I teach a high school seminar, and in one recent discussion about school violence, I was surprised by how many students sympathized with kids who have shot up their schools. One even admitted she'd entertained similar thoughts. Alarmed, I notified the principal. When the class found out what I'd done, most of them felt betrayed, though there was no promise of confidentiality. Was I wrong?

—ANONYMOUS

Yes, you were: You reported a thought crime. A principal's list of malcontents will neither deter crime nor help the students; it will only inhibit conversation. Students need to feel they can confide in teachers without being turned in. Surely there is an implicit pledge of confidentiality in a seminar such as yours.

You may want to consult with a lawyer to learn what legal obligations you have in this situation. And of course, if you had compelling evidence that a crime was about to be committed, you'd have to act. (Did the student have a plan? Arms? Were other people involved? Was she angry? What else was going on in her life?) But this doesn't seem to have come close to actual violence. If everyone who entertained murderous thoughts actually committed murder, we'd need a lot more cops and a lot fewer divorce lawyers.

REFERENCE WORK

I am a college professor, and one of my students has asked for a recommendation for a program sponsored by a group I find deeply offensive. I do not want to punish her for holding controversial political views, but I also do not want to support an education in what I consider hateful ideas. Must I write this letter?

—JOHN DRABINSKI, GRAND RAPIDS, MICHIGAN

You need not—and I suspect cannot—write this recommendation. Your disapproval of the sponsoring group would temper the passion you could bring to the task, and a lukewarm letter of reference is no reference at all. Tell this to your student and suggest she find someone else to write the letter.

Even if your conscience allowed you to write her recommendation, you would not be required to. She's asking you not simply to report on her work in your class (which you are obliged to do) but to tout the contributions she'd make to this group's endeavors, to elucidate how her personal qualities would aid their particular goals. To provide this endorsement is not a professional obligation; it is a favor you can grant or withhold.

You should not capriciously refuse to write such letters, of course. Do so only when high principles are involved. In other words, you should not decline if she wants you to recommend her to an employer you disapprove of but that otherwise falls within the range of choices our culture deems acceptable—for instance, work for *People* magazine rather than *The Nation*. You ought not hold her hostage to your ideology. But to demur in this case, involving what you consider a hate group, is not to control her career paternalistically, but to reasonably express your own deeply held values.

There are some letters that you must write. For instance, it is part of your job to evaluate a student's classroom performance. If she asks for a general letter of reference that she can send to various employers, you should provide it. But it is not part of your job to aid the personnel department of, say, the Augusto Pinochet Summer Workshop in Torture, Murder, and Dance.

A professor of sociology, I am editing an anthology with a colleague. I accepted, pending revisions, an essay from a young man who phoned to tell me how groundbreaking my own work was and in general to stroke my ego. I've since discovered that he reviewed a book of mine, calling it just plain bad. It seems dishonest of him to suck up to me while simultaneously destroying my book. May I cut his essay from the anthology, or should I refer the decision to my co-editor?

—L.E., BROOKLYN, NEW YORK

Having tentatively accepted his essay, you ought not reject it because the author is a deceiver who hurt your feelings. If editors rejected the work of every ill-mannered writer, our nation would face a serious literature shortage. (Not a problem for my editor, of course.) But once you've gone this far, you should take the high road and recuse yourself, leaving it to your co-editor to determine the revised essay's value or—with luck—lack thereof.

Were you starting anew, you'd have no obligation to accept this young cad's work. A book is not a public accommodation: It is your project and can be shaped by your personal preferences, however quirky—only brilliant writers, only stylishly dressed writers who know their way around a dance floor. But even then, your professional reputation would best be served were you to consider only the scholarly qualities of each essay, not the weaselly behavior of its writer. His insolence you could vividly describe, if not in the notes on contributors, then in your memoirs.

To revile you with one hand and suck up with the other (if that is anatomically possible) would be discreditable, but the putative hypocrite might see this differently. He may well admire your work in general while seeing flaws in your book. Such is the cut and thrust, the kick and kiss, of academic life.

I am an adjunct instructor at the City University of New York. Two of my Russian-born students told me that a few Russian immigrants are admitted to private and public universities and colleges throughout the city, although they have never graduated from high school. They warranted that it was easy to obtain a false high school diploma. Do I have some ethical accountability to alert the admission offices?

—D.H., BROOKLYN, NEW YORK

I think you should keep this to yourself. First of all, the information is entirely hearsay; you don't know if it is accurate. Second, although you may have given no explicit pledge of confidentiality, presumably your students would not have told you these things if they thought you'd run to the authorities. And third, why is it a bad thing that these immigrants are so eager to attend college that they'd engage in deception to do so? Their determination to pursue an education (although not, of course, their dishonesty) seems admirable. Why would you want to get them tossed out of school? Finally, the purpose of a college's requiring a high school diploma is to ensure that a student can do college work; if the students in question cannot, it will come to light soon enough. Certainly, those students ought not have acted dishonestly, but given their circumstances and yours, I would not encourage you to turn them in.

However, if all you intend to report is some general information about a rumor of wrongdoing, naming no particular student, then you are free to do so, although one suspects that if the admissions officers are any good at their job, they are already aware of such goings-on.

BUSINESS ED?

I teach business ethics for a local university. I wonder how you would respond to this classic moral dilemma: John walks into a village and finds Mary holding 15 people hostage. Mary says that she will kill

them all unless John takes a gun and kills one of the hostages. All of
the hostages are innocent people. What should John do?

—J. DE PAUW, ARLINGTON, VIRGINIA

What kind of business are you preparing these kids for? Microsoft?

Students

RECYCLED TERM PAPERS

Assigning a term paper for a history class, my professor said we were
not to use any papers we had written for other classes; he said this was
plagiarism. But is it plagiarism if the paper is my own work? Beyond
the legal discussion, is it ethical to hand in one paper for two classes?

—ANONYMOUS, ST. LOUIS, MISSOURI

You should not hand in a prewritten paper. Your professor's ban on this
practice is reason enough, but even absent his taboo, you should still forswear it. As unlikely as it may seem, a paper is not merely a dreary obligation to be discharged but a chance to learn, and that's what your prof
is trying to get you to do. Submitting a prewritten paper may not be plagiarism—it is no crime to copy from yourself—but it is no boon to your
intellectual growth either. And it certainly violates the spirit—and in this
case, the letter—of university life.

Similarly, even if your own lab work eventually makes it possible,
you ought not let a super-intelligent bioengineered dog take your exams
for you.

KID LIES TO POLLSTERS

In a poll on the health habits of high school students, a young friend
untruthfully "confessed" to multiple hazardous behaviors like taking
drugs. Unethical behavior or just youthful high jinks?

—M. DICKEY DRYSDALE, RANDOLPH, VERMONT

You may decline to answer a pollster's questions, but if you choose to participate, you ought not lie. That the poll is idiotic, the methodology questionable, the client dubious (new Beefalicious Cigarettes—dogs love 'em!), and the pollster calls during dinner don't obviate the virtue of honesty. The expectation that people speak truthfully to one another is essential to a civil society.

Full disclosure: I confess with some shame that I myself have slipped. Randomly chosen to be a Nielsen family, I lied flamboyantly when filling out the TV-viewing diary. I did not enter what I actually watched—movies and basketball, mostly—but instead logged shows I was eager to support for one reason or another: a friend worked there, a relative enjoyed it, I admired a cast member's lips. I sought to reward the good and punish the bad, a higher calling than helping the Tiffany Network set its ad rates. In fact, every Nielsen viewer I know behaved similarly: Each diary was a delightful fiction that portrayed a better TV world.

Of course, you should heed the wise advice and ignore the imperfect behavior of an ordinary mortal like me.

PARKING PROBLEM

My school's parking lot has only 47 spots for 100 driving students. I asked a school administrator where I could park off campus legally. I parked where he told me, but my car was ticketed and towed because the fire chief thought the many cars on that street caused a fire hazard. Who should pay for the impound and ticket? Who is at fault?

—JOSHUA FINK, ENGLEWOOD, NEW JERSEY

Bad advice offered in good faith is not bad ethics. If that administrator says it will be sunny tomorrow, you can't sue him if it rains. He is offering an opinion outside the authority of his office. The responsibility to wear a hat is yours.

If you parked in a legal spot, fight the ticket and ask the school official to help. If the spot was not legal, his opinion doesn't change that, so you're stuck. Tell him what happened so he'll know he is misinformed and stop giving bad advice. And who knows? He may offer to pay part of the ticket to compensate for his bad advice.

In New Orleans for Mardi Gras and drinking heavily, my friends and I got separated. When I returned to our hotel, I found my college roommate in bed with a girl from our school. Days later I learned he'd had sex with her while she was in a drug-and-alcohol–induced stupor. In my view, he is a rapist, but I don't know how to react, given my friendship with him and my sympathies for her.

—ANONYMOUS, VIRGINIA

This does sound like date rape, and the first thing you should consider are the wishes of the victim. How is she responding? Does she want to report this to the police? What help would she like from you? Her interests are paramount.

Your attitude toward the rapist should be shaped by his attitude toward his crime. If he is remorseful and has asked his victim's forgiveness and looked for a way to make amends and sought counseling, then you can continue your friendship. Remember, people make bad—even dreadful—choices. It is how they respond to their errors that is key. However, if he brushes off the entire matter, then you should have no more to do with him.

After all, how could you? Will you introduce him to your other women friends? Will you warn them to avoid him? It is difficult to see how you could ever again think of him in an amicable and unguarded way.

And you should say all this to him. Tell him that you value his friendship, but unless he takes this seriously and realizes he has a problem with drinking, or alcohol, or women, then you can no longer be his friend.

One other thing to bear in mind: Be sure of your facts before you take any action at all.

I am a 17-year-old who is half Hispanic and half Caucasian. I am in no way disadvantaged, but neither are many other blacks and Hispanics. Would it be unethical for me to list my race as Hispanic on college applications?

—ANONYMOUS, NEW YORK

Colleges ask about the ethnic backgrounds of their applicants not only because they want to compensate them for presumed disadvantages or the effects of past discrimination, but also out of a belief that it is in the school's interest to assemble a diverse group of students. Remember, the application asks a great deal about you—your address, your high school, your financial situation—so the admissions officers have a pretty good idea of what hardships you may or may not have overcome.

If you would like to be particularly scrupulous, you could write on the form what you've written here—half Hispanic, half Caucasian. (Indeed, you could write that Hispanic is not a "race." In fact, many scholars argue that there is no such thing as race, not in any biological sense; race is an idea, a social construct.) But given the particular use of the term on your application, if you are limited to marking a single box to denote your ethnic origins, you may check "Hispanic" with a clear conscience.

I'm contemplating applying to some master's programs in journalism that require an undergraduate GPA of 3.0. My current school provides only the grades of my individual courses, which I averaged out to 2.958. Should I just round that figure off, or is my falling short by .042 a detail I must disclose?

—NOELLE LESLIE DE LA CRUZ, PISCATAWAY, NEW JERSEY

Apply with a full heart. The way my sixth-grade math teacher taught me to round off to one decimal place would indeed make your average a

3.0. If they'd asked for a 3.00, then you'd have to express your grade as three digits, rounding it to 2.96. You'd be rejected from journalism school and have to find an honest job.

There are limits to the precision of any grading system, including variations from teacher to teacher and from school to school. Listing your average as a 3.0 honors both the letter and spirit of the requirement and would make my sixth-grade math teacher proud. And remember, the admissions office will have a chance to see your full transcript and decide if you qualify.

DATE YOUR PROF?

I am an attractive female, almost 30, attending college, and I like one of my professors. He is in my age range and is single, but says it is not ethical to date students. I understand that and have offered to drop his class. So what gives? Could this just be his way of saying, "Hey, I am not interested"?

J.W., FRESNO, CALIFORNIA

Many colleges have rules governing this situation. If you violate them, you can get the object of your affections into serious trouble, and there's nothing seductive about that. Such codes are designed to protect students from sexual harassment, always a risk when there is a power imbalance in a couple (for example, when one gives grades to the other). So, first learn what the rules are. If your school forbids relationships only between a professor and a current student, then wait until next semester to pursue this fellow. Consider him an investment in your sexual future.

Love is notorious for disregarding any rules that try to govern it, and it is true that more than one student-teacher intrigue has evolved into a happy (or not so happy) marriage. However, if Professor Dreamboat declines to date you, it doesn't matter if he's guided by his head or his heart (if those are the relevant body parts): You're out of luck either way.

Guest Ethicist

I am about to borrow a large sum to finance my education, on the pretext that it will provide me with the skills to earn back this money. I am using it, however, to get a Ph.D. in philosophy. Based on my looming inability to repay my most gracious lender, is it ethical to take the loan?

—A.T., SAN FRANCISCO

DAVE EGGERS IS THE AUTHOR OF _A HEARTBREAKING WORK OF STAG-GERING GENIUS_ AND THE EDITOR OF MCSWEENY'S. HE REPLIES:
First of all, we don't know who is lending you this money. A parent? A friend? A financial institution? If it's the last, we don't have to worry much—it's their job to calculate and assume the risk, and then keep track of you for the two or so decades it'll take you to repay the loan. But let's say it's a wealthy friend of the family; his name is Richard Steele, he has smooth silver hair and wears a fedora. He owns two homes, employs a staff of eight; he can afford to loan the money, but expects it back. So. Should you take it? Well, we still need more information. How old is Richard Steele? If he's very old, then you're off the hook: He will pass on, loan yet unpaid, content knowing he'd been of some assistance. The loan will be of little concern to him as he rises to the heavens. But let's say Richard Steele is not that old. Let's say he's sixty-seven, and he looks much younger. He looks great. However, his heart is not strong. No, scratch that, his heart is strong. Very strong. And he's Colombian. Of course he is. And his name is not Richard Steele, but Ricardo de la Manzana. Well, with a name like that, he sounds like a tough customer. He's not one of *those* de la Manzanas, is he? Jesus. Why didn't you say so? What if you can't repay this loan, a loan from this man of power and wealth, this suspected drug trafficker? You'd be in trouble for sure. Why didn't you just borrow the money from a bank? Man, oh man. Are you crazy? Why are you taking loans

from a man like this, anyway? Boy, you're in trouble. How did you get mixed up with Ricardo de la Manzana in the first place? This guy's a killer! A killer of judges and children and American nuns! I wouldn't want to be in your shoes. No way.

MY REPLY TO A.T.:

While your eventual destitution seems likely, sadly, it's not something you can count on. Carleton Fiorina, the recently named president and CEO of Hewlett-Packard, majored in medieval history and philosophy. Financial failure can be so elusive.

If you have not lied about your course of study, and if you've chosen it as a means to get an education, not to duck out on a loan, then you're in the clear. Despite our no-nonsense business culture, the study of the humanities is not yet absolutely forbidden. And maybe one day you can turn all that seemingly worthless Wittgenstein into philosopher.com.

Cheaters

AMBUSH THE CHEATER

I attend an Ivy League university where students are graded on a curve. During a midterm exam, the student next to me was copying answers from my paper. Because a higher score for her would mean a lower grade for me, I intentionally wrote some incorrect answers, waited until she handed in her test booklet, and then changed my answers to the correct ones. Was this wrong?

—BRENNA TINKEL, PHILADELPHIA

There is something disquieting about your deliberately harming another person, even a cheat. It is reasonable for you to thwart her deceit (telling her to cut it out, or covering your paper with your arm, for instance) but it is overreaching to punish her. Besides, if she doesn't know you've ambushed her, you will neither deter her future cheating nor reform her character. When she gets her grade, she'll conclude only that you're dimwitted, and next time she'll copy from a brighter student.

Incidentally, her cheating would have been wrong even at one of our fine state universities. At a savings of thousands of dollars a year.

A college student called last week to say his "friend" had visited my Web page, lifted something I wrote, and turned it in as her own work. Suspicious, her professor plans to search the Web; if he finds the paper was plagiarized, he'll recommend expulsion. The student implored me to take that paper off my site, lest his "friend's" academic career, and possibly her life, be ruined. What do I do?

—ANONYMOUS

Properly assigning credit is delicate business. If I sign Rembrandt's name to my work, it's forgery; if I sign my name to Rembrandt's work, it's plagiarism. There's just no pleasing some people. But what's astonishing here is not the expropriation; it's the request that you cover it up. Presumably, if this woman had stolen your stereo, she'd ask you for a lift to her fence.

When the penalty is severe enough, however, a wrongdoer's appeals for mercy are not entirely ludicrous. It would be hard not to relent if, say, the Taliban threatened to topple a wall onto her (though if she survived, I believe she'd automatically ace the semester).

Expulsion from college is not such a case. Even if she receives the worst possible punishment—by no means a certainty—it's unlikely to wreck her life. A young woman with this low level of moral inhibition and high level of chutzpah should flourish in modern America. She might be lucky enough to one day find herself in a nice federal minimum security prison, where she can make professional connections that will set her up forever. Or perhaps she'll get a job at Cliffs Notes, giving a new generation of kids a legitimate way to crib their way through college.

Even if your heart goes out to the young plagiarist, you're not at liberty to drop the charges, since you're not the victim of this crime. You can, however, call the professor and appeal for leniency. But destroying the evidence is definitely the wrong way to go. If you don't believe me, check out a 1976 movie called *All the President's Men*. I won't spoil it for you by giving away the ending.

A Web site that provides model research papers to college students offered me a position as a freelance writer. Although the site clearly states the papers are for reference only, I feel there is a lot of room for abuse. By working for this dot-com, am I inadvertently compromising academic standards?

—S.K. HANANY, FORDS, NEW JERSEY

If you believe this site sells papers that students hand in as their own work, you are not "inadvertently compromising academic standards," you are knowingly profiting from helping students cheat. The site's posting a sign that says "for reference only" doesn't change that, any more than would a gun shop's writing "for recreational hunting only" over their display of hand grenades.

My middle school's honor code requires us to report cheating. Is it fair [for the administration] to ask us to police each other? Would it be ethical to refuse to cooperate?

—AARON SCHEIN (AGE 12), LOS ANGELES

It is difficult to find fault with the first part of most honor codes: I will not lie, cheat, or steal. Nearly everyone would endorse those precepts, even liars, cheaters, and thieves. It is the second half of such codes, the obligation to tattle on violators, that is problematic. There is a paradox here. If students meet the code's demand of individual rectitude, there will be no transgressors to report. If the first half of the code is effective, the second half is superfluous.

While it is reasonable to ask students to regulate their own behavior, little good will come of compelling them to police the behavior of their schoolmates. For one thing, few will do so. Our society has real ambivalence about informants. To punish only the occasional kid for failing to inform is arbitrary and capricious, and it undermines the sense of the school as a just community. Calling such a dubious set of rules an "honor code" doesn't make it honorable any more than calling a husky guy "slim" makes him look great in a Spandex swimsuit. I believe George Orwell had a lot to say on this use of language. Or am I thinking of Ralph Lauren?

The happiest outcome would be for your school to abolish such dubious codes. There may well be times where one must make the painful choice between loyalty to a friend and loyalty to a code, but the school ought not multiply such occasions unnecessarily. You'd do nothing dishonorable were you to inform your teachers that you will neither cheat nor inform on those who do, although I suspect you will not like their response.

Here's another alternative: Warn your friends not to put you in untenable positions. You needn't—and shouldn't—report mere suspicion. And so at the first hint that a friend might be misbehaving, demand that he either stop doing so or keep his mischief to himself. It is a sad thing to seek recourse in ignorance, but it may be your best option.

In my school days, all too long ago, we had no honor codes and no cheaters. Or at least few enough that such transgressions were truly startling. This is, as I gather you realize, not at all the case today, when, by all accounts, cheating is rampant and honor codes never more common.

The real test of such codes is how well they teach honorable behavior. I see no evidence of their success. West Point, famous for its honor code, brought us the architects of the Vietnam War and, more recently, a history of cheating scandals, and a professional military that routinely covers up wrongdoing, relying on a code of silence.

I believe that there are other, better ways to establish honesty among students than by imposing such codes whose utility is questionable at best, and whose social harm is greater than any benefits they might bestow.

Arguing with The Ethicist

The mandatory meal plan at my college allows you to eat as much as you want but prohibits taking food out of the dining hall. However, I think it's okay to slip a sandwich into my backpack because I am only a little freshman, and the college needs to budget for lacrosse players. My sister, Shayna, believes this is tantamount to bringing an extra-large purse to a Holiday Inn buffet. What do you think?

—ERIN AND SHAYNA SILVERMAN, BOICEVILLE, NEW YORK

Under your meal plan, the small subsidize the large, and that's just not fair. In effect, you are compelled to pay more for your food than are your bulkier classmates. Thus you might make a case for slipping some food into your pocket. (Except, perhaps, for pudding. People look at you funny if you have a pocketful of pudding. People can be so cruel.) It's the same sandwich, eaten in the cafeteria or eaten in your room. Assuming you take away no more than you'd eat in the dining hall, you'd be breaking the rules, but you'd not be doing anything dishonorable. If there were something unethical about takeout, New York's Chinese restaurants would all be doomed.

Contrary to what your sister says, this is not akin to stuffing your purse at a restaurant buffet, because there, under our system of government, attendance is still optional. When you choose to patronize the buffet you agree to adhere to its rules. Similarly, were your meal plan voluntary, you'd have to forswear sandwich smuggling.

Your school would do better to charge students for what they actually eat. Another system: Weigh everyone when they enter and again when they leave. You pay by the pound for any increase whether in your backpack or on your thighs or on your mighty lacrosse-player neck.

STEVEN KRAMER DEMURS:

You REALLY blew it on Erin's MANDATORY meal plan! College, like the Holiday Inn buffet, is optional, not the rules once you enter.

I REPLY:

Your notion that having chosen to attend that college obliges her to obey every rule no matter how unjust strikes me as just a bit narrow, and certainly unlikely to promote reform. We can do better than "love it or leave it." Nobody obeys every campus rule. Would you really tell a kid to quit school if she'd had one beer or snuck her boyfriend into her dorm room? You're a tougher guy than I am.

DAVID MARTINDALE URGES PROTEST:

Societies and institutions benefit when unjust rules are successfully challenged. Does each of us have an obligation to endeavor in whatever small way we can to change society for the better? If we do, then does it not follow that we should, in situations like this, attempt to identify and organize like-minded others and openly voice opposition to rules that we perceive to be unfair, rather than quietly circumvent them?

I REPLY:

Your suggestion that this student work to reform the rules, while high-minded, seems unrealistic. In such situations, the student has little power; the institution has a great deal. And while I'd admire her more if she lobbied for change, in the meantime I'd not fault her for eating a sandwich (which she paid for) in her room.

STEVEN BURNS SAYS:

Many schools, such as my alma mater, a small Southern liberal arts college (Rhodes, in Memphis), have an honor code, which typically requires students not to lie, cheat, or steal. If the school's plan does not authorize her to take food from the cafeteria, then doing so is stealing—converting for her own consumption an object to which she has no right of possession. Honor code violations are typically grounds for at least a semester-long suspension.

I REPLY:

But of course she's not stealing. She paid for the sandwich. And it's the same sandwich in the dining hall as it is when she steps outside the door. That she violates a rule when she crosses the threshold, sandwich in hand, is certainly true. That it's unethical? I think not. And piling on an imaginary honor code that her school may or may not have only obfuscates the matter. Imposing a meta-rule that says "And you have to obey all our other rules" adds to the rule breaking but doesn't persuade me that she does anything unethical by transporting a sandwich without a passport.

MICHAEL STARR ARGUES:

There is nothing unfair about a one-price-for-all meal plan, even though some may not use it as much as another. Is the nonstudious college student entitled to steal books from the library, since his tuition dollar is subsidizing the bookworms who spend more time there? Is the college chemistry student who breaks no test tubes entitled to a rebate on the breakage portion of his lab fee or justified in taking something of equivalent value to break even?

I REPLY:

Your library example is interesting but unconvincing. While there is no way to predict how much a kid will use the library, it is entirely predictable that the large will outeat the small. However, it is certainly true that fee-for-service is not the only equitable system. However, in this case it would take a tiny effort to avoid having the slender subsidize the stout.

WILLIAM BIKALES RAISES A PRACTICAL CONSIDERATION:

Schools use buffets because they are vastly easier (and less costly) to administer, and because they allow a great deal of freedom and flexibility for all students. My impression was that they are quite popular.

I REPLY:

I've no doubt that all-you-can-eat is easier for the school; so is refusing to let grad students unionize; so would declining to pay the cafeteria staff. But just being advantageous for the school doesn't make the system a fair one. And I might add, all-you-can-eat systems have other unfortunate consequences, encouraging both overeating and waste. What's more, charging folks for what they actually eat does not seem an insurmountable task; nearly every restaurant does it nearly every day.

BUY THE BOOK

In my college poetry class, we used a book that was translated by my professor, and my Accounting 101 book was written by my professor. This has more than the appearance of a conflict of interest. Shouldn't colleges convey a higher sense of ethics?

—MARTIN LEVITT, ROCKAWAY, NEW JERSEY

There is a more apt paradigm here than conflict of interest: the greatest hits album. Many students select a class to get a particular professor's ideas on the subject, and they'd be disappointed were she to eschew her own books. It would be like going to hear Bruce Springsteen sing, and having him decline to perform "Born in the USA" because he wouldn't feel honorable pocketing the songwriter royalties. Instead: all Andrew Lloyd Webber.

However, a professor teaching a required or introductory course should err on the side of modesty and assign the standard work on the subject. Those who don't, says my pal Josh Freeman, an associate professor at Queens College, sometimes seek status more than cash: "Assigning one's own book, besides a way to make money—though in most cases trivial amounts—often is an effort to establish one's legitimacy and importance among students and colleagues."

In ambiguous cases, a professor should Xerox relevant portions of her books or put them on reserve in the library, making them available to her students at no cost, now and forever.

PROF. HOWARD SACHS ARGUES:
This column contains a mixture of misinformation, and poor and potentially illegal advice. First, college professors generally do not write textbooks in order to make money, nor would publishers issue books

that did not meet a need in the field. The real goal is to make a "contribution to the field," not one's bank account. In many cases, the author of the book has assigned the copyright of the book to the publisher. In such cases, the author may not copy the text without the express permission of the new copyright holder, i.e., the publisher. To do so, as suggested in the column, is to invite litigation for violation of the copyright laws. The best ethical solution I have heard from colleagues is to calculate the number of copies of the book used in their classes and pay the college an amount equal to the accrued royalties.

I REPLY:

I took it as understood by any reasonable reader that one ought not violate copyright laws; nor should you shoot anyone when demanding they read your book; I'm surprised you found that ambiguous. I quoted one professor, making the point that money was seldom the prime incentive for academic writing. I'm surprised you found that unclear. And surely the most cursory glance at the shelves in any bookstore would show you that publishers issue many books that meet no need of any kind. Your solution would indeed remove the financial incentive from this situation, but that is an incentive we both agree barely comes into play.

DR. JUSTIN STARREN SUMS UP THE OPPOSITION:

Your analysis contains an assumption that the professor's book is inferior to some other "standard" work. It is doubtful that anyone would go to the effort to write a book unless they believed that the new book was saying something of value. Professors who assign their own books often do so because they honestly believe that the book is the best presentation of the material.

I REPLY:

What made the student uneasy was that the people deciding on the best textbooks are the very people who write them rather than disinterested parties. Not a trivial complaint. I've since learned—I say with some embarrassment—that some universities demand that when a professor assigns his own book, the royalties go into a fund to be used for students. Not a complete solution, but not a bad start.

I'm a university professor, and I often get unsolicited copies of text-books from publishers in the hope that I'll adopt them for my course. They clutter up my shelves until book buyers come through, offering cash for old texts. Is it wrong for me to sell them and pocket the money? Should I donate them instead?

—ANONYMOUS, EVANSTON, ILLINOIS

The publishers sent the books hoping you'd find them worthy of inclusion in your class. They were not a bribe. They're yours to do with what you will. Not every perk is a transgression. (At a TV show where I worked, we received many T-shirts emblazoned with the names of Kevin Costner movies; I saw using them to clean up after the cat as a legitimate form of film criticism.) Unless university policy prohibits your selling these books, go to it.

If you still feel uneasy, note that some magazines give unsolicited books to the public library; others offer them to their unpaid interns. Consider following their examples or donating your book money to a student-aid organization.

STACEY BROWNE ARGUES:

I work for a textbook publisher. We develop the book. We work with the authors on the manuscript, editing and designing the finished manuscript. We produce the text and all ancillary materials (test banks, instructor's manuals, media components, etc.). We present the text to the professor and hope that he or she will find it pedagogically sound and helpful for his or her students. If so, the professor will adopt the book and order it through the bookstore. When a professor sells a review copy, he deprives us of our legitimate reward for these efforts.

I REPLY:

That the reselling of sample textbooks is unfortunate for publishers I have no doubt, but that does not make it unethical. If I receive unsolicited material, I have no obligation to return it. I needn't repack it; I needn't walk to the post office. I agreed to none of the terms you wish to impose on its resale. Once you give it to me, it's mine to do with what I choose.

One solution is for the publisher to send out promotional material and a book request card rather than the book itself. An interested professor can ask for a sample copy and, by signing the card, understand and agree to any limits on its use, e.g., no resale.

JEFF COREY SAYS:

One reason not to sell free textbooks is that this deprives authors of their due compensation.

I REPLY:

You're correct about writer's royalties, at least in the case of review copies of single-author books (for textbooks with multiple sources the royalties are negligible). One solution is for the publisher to pay the writer a royalty for every book that leaves the warehouse, including review copies. And further, the author has given his consent for free copies of his books to be sent out, willy-nilly, to professors across the country. If the author isn't happy with this arrangement, he or she should take it up with the publisher.

PROF. WILLIAM O'CONNELL ARGUES:

This resale market of examination copies raises the price of new textbooks, since the publisher must allocate the fixed costs over fewer volumes and it raises the price per book.

I REPLY:

My understanding of the marketplace is that publishers, like most businesses, raise their prices as high as the market will bear in order to maximize their profits. But even if selling review copies did raise prices, that would make reselling unfortunate but not unethical. However, if this whole market economics thing turns out to be true (an unsubstantiated claim, I grant you), shouldn't the presence of inexpensive textbooks lower prices?

While reselling the book no doubt costs the publisher some money, they are fully aware of the widespread practice we're discussing, and yet they continue to send out unsolicited textbooks. If this does not acquiesce to reselling, it certainly comes close. In fact, applying the principle of qui bono, I'd say the real beneficiary is the student, particularly the less well-off student more inclined to patronize the used-book stores. You might make a case that by selling the sample copy, you perform a real social good here.

Postscript

OUT MYSELF TO MY ROOMMATE?

I will be starting college in a few months and wonder if I am obligated to tell my dormmate that I'm a lesbian. Is it wrong to hide something that could be deemed significant, or may I keep my sexual orientation to myself? If I do tell her, can I at least wait until we know each other, so that she doesn't perceive it as my defining feature?

—ANONYMOUS, ORLANDO, FLORIDA

Sharing a room with someone does not mean relinquishing all claims to privacy. You have no ethical obligation to discuss your sexual orientation with your dormmate. And while it is certainly possible that someone may feel uneasy with a gay roommate or a Jewish roommate or a black roommate, that's his or her problem.

Of course, sharing a room with someone makes her comfort your problem, too, so your sense of tact is well placed. That is, if you decide to tell her, do it when you know each other well enough to feel at ease sharing so intimate a confidence. Unless you're planning to bring paramours back to the room your first week of school (this sounds awfully optimistic to me, but perhaps my own freshman experience is not a reliable guide here) there is no reason to hasten this conversation. And if you never feel like telling her, that's okay, too.

There is another practical matter to consider. Campus life is much like small-town life; you can anticipate much gossip and few secrets. So no matter what you decide to tell her, it is not impossible that your roommate will have an inkling about your sexuality. If her response to this information proves hostile, your life can become unpleasant. And if it is, you may be happier rooming with someone less ignorant and intolerant. That's the argument for talking to her sooner rather than later, one based not on ethical obligation but on self-preservation.

ANONYMOUS FOLLOWS UP:

I pretty much decided to dodge the question. I felt out my new roommates about the subject shortly after we moved in, which I think any gay person will tell you is standard operating procedure before coming out to anyone. They said stuff like, "I just feel sorry for gay people" and "They [gay people] shouldn't make such a big deal about it." One of their boyfriends made it clear that he is "disgusted" by "fags" and that "dykes just need to quit trying to be guys and find the right man." I know those quotes sound like they came straight from the what-not-to-say section of a sensitivity training booklet, but I swear that I heard them all in one ten-minute conversation with my roommates and their boyfriends.

So, anyway, I haven't said anything to any of them about my sexual orientation. Even so, I think that they might have some idea because I'm really bad at the pronoun game and I was kinda seeing a girl from down the hall for a while and I think they were suspicious that she came over so much.

Medical Life

Disease generally begins that equality which death completes; the distinctions which set one man so much above another are very little perceived in the gloom of a sick chamber, where it will be vain to expect entertainment from the gay, or instruction from the wise; where all human glory is obliterated, the wit is clouded, the reasoner perplexed, and the hero subdued; where the highest and brightest of mortal beings finds nothing left him but the consciousness of innocence.

SAMUEL JOHNSON, *RAMBLER* #48 (SEPTEMBER 1, 1750)

Johnson commented often on the effects of illness on the human spirit but wrote little about physicians themselves. And yet he certainly admired those who selflessly attended to the suffering of others, even sharing his household with a physician named Robert Levet, a rough, taciturn man with an extensive practice among the poor—"an obscure practiser in physick amongst the lower people," Boswell called him. Levet probably began his working life as a servant. Later, while a waiter in a Paris coffee house, he made the acquaintance of some French surgeons who arranged for him to attend lectures on anatomy and pharmacology. During the years he lived with Johnson, Levet rambled great distances across London to treat his patients for a small fee or whatever they could give him, often no more than a glass of gin. Johnson admired Levet for his modesty, his honesty, and for his steady, quiet usefulness to others. In a poem on Levet's death, Johnson described him as "Obscurely wise, and coarsely kind . . . The single talent well employ'd."

Levet's notion of medical ethics would likely have centered on just

THE GOOD, THE BAD

what Johnson so admired in him—doing one's best to help the patient. This duty to vigorously serve the client's interests accords with the advice Johnson frequently gave Boswell about his legal practice. In some ways, even today, the obligations of both fields are similar, although the codes of professional conduct for each have grown elaborate and specific.

This chapter, "Medical Life," is meant to illustrate how ethics plays out in a field regulated by such a professional code, where rules are enumerated by a guild of fellow practitioners to regulate particular professional behavior. These rules are meant to be more than a roster of common practice; they are intended to have a meaningful moral foundation. And while this chapter concerns itself with medicine, I might have chosen another field—law or engineering or, for that matter, interior design, any one of which would have a professional association and a formal code of ethics, without which, who knows what harm might have been done with the inappropriate use of red velvet sofas.

I receive many queries from physicians, a morally serious group—analytical, concerned with their patients, and quite able to see their profession in a larger social context, particularly in relation to managed care. I receive few queries from lawyers, although many write in to point out just how wrong I got it in my last column. I've received no queries and no complaints from politicians. No doubt they're far too busy either to carp or inquire. (But busy doing what?) I continue to hope for a letter that begins "I am the leader of a large Western nation who came to power through a series of maneuvers that were, at best, ethically dubious . . ." I watch my mailbox hopefully.

The most frequently asked medical questions concern other people's privacy, in this case the patient's. When must a doctor report a patient's dubious behavior to a spouse, to the cops, to an insurance company? (This may have less to do with my insight into this aspect of life than with my utter ignorance of surgical procedures. Physicians are wise enough to direct such questions to anyone but me.)

Confidentiality is a necessary condition for the practice not just of medicine but of other professions. Most of us would be reluctant to seek medical attention for, say, venereal disease, if an account of our infection were to run in the papers. No one would seek legal counsel if their lawyer were likely to rat them out to the police. There is a similar rationale for shield laws that protect a reporter from having to reveal a source: There can be no free press if people are too frightened of reprisals to talk to reporters.

In such fields, the benefits of the professional practice are deemed to outweigh any harm done by secrecy. But this confidentiality is not infinitely granted. There are many circumstances in which a doctor is obliged to report a patient's behavior to the authorities—in cases of suspected child abuse, for example. And a lawyer may not withhold knowledge that a client is about to engage in future wrongdoing. Furthermore, some professions are denied any legal right to confidentiality. New York State does not regard a patient's conversation with a psychiatrist as privileged information. A mechanic at a body shop has no explicit right to keep silent about the bullet holes riddling a sedan. Much as we Americans admire a well-kept car, it is—surprisingly—not our highest good.

While these codes of professional ethics are designed to protect the client from the misbehavior of the practitioner, they do little to thwart the greater risk to the infirm, the peril that comes not from a heinous physician but from the very system of medical care itself, a system of managed care and insurance companies that leaves more than 40 million Americans with little or no access to health care. Judging by the questions they send me, many physicians feel trapped between their duty to a patient and their obligation to follow the rules of an HMO. It is of little comfort to them when I argue that the only meaningful solution is to reform the system.

There is another sort of question of medical ethics, one that I am only occasionally asked: What is to be done about an inept physician? Does a doctor have a duty to report a colleague? And can a doctor ever really know what goes on in the privacy of someone else's consulting room? Looked at in a more general way, is incompetence synonymous with unethical? Not necessarily. There is certainly such a thing as an honest mistake. There are certainly limits to medical knowledge. It need not be the fault of the physician that the patient dies; we all do eventually. And yet, were an utterly unqualified goofball to wangle his way into the driver's seat of a New York taxi, his ineptitude would be not just unethical but criminal (not that such a thing could possibly happen). Here is where a professional code does seek to define conventional practice, and to demand that one adhere to those standards.

It can be distressing to nonpractitioners to note how infrequently even a dreadful physician is sanctioned, how rarely a maladroit lawyer is disbarred, and we needn't even discuss members of Congress. It may be some comfort to those readers to know that in other times and places, things worked, if not more ethically, at least in another way:

> Doctors faced a different sort of malpractice system in ancient Babylon under Hammurabi's code. A surgeon who operated with a bronze lancet on a man of standing and caused his death or opened up his eyesocket and caused blindness had his hand cut off. If the operation was successful, the doctor was paid ten shekels of silver. If the patient was a slave, the physician replaced a slave for the dead slave and for the loss of the slave's eye, paid the owner one-half the value of the slave. If the slave recovered, the physicians received two shekels of silver. [Ancient ethics, larue, 32, Singer's Companion to Ethics.]

Ethics Pop Quiz

Below are four hypothetical questions for you the reader to answer.

Replies can be submitted to theethicistbook.com or e-mailed to theethicist@randomhouse.com.

Selected responses will appear in the paperback edition of the book.

While there are dermatologists who do important medical work, helping burn victims, for example, I'm not such a physician. My practice mostly comprises cosmetic treatments for rich folks. Some say that in a world where so many poor people are desperate for medical care, my professional life is a shameful waste of my expensive training. I say the care of some kid in Senegal is a real problem, but it is not my problem. What do you say?

A 70-year-old man, I weigh 270 pounds, little of which is muscle. I don't exercise, I do smoke, I enjoy fried eggs for breakfast and a nice thick steak for dinner: And let me tell you, I love my life! Except for this—I'm on the waiting list for a heart transplant. Some doctors at the hospital don't want to give it to me. They say it would be a grotesque squandering of medical and financial resources, that the money and the skills would save a lot more lives if applied to, say, a neonatal clinic. I say they've got the heart and the talent; my insurance company will pay for it: Let's do it. Why should they play God? Thoughts?

I am an internist treating a patient with a painful and debilitating disease. Knowing there is no hope for recovery, my patient has asked me to provide her with drugs to end her life. Both she and I have discussed this with her family, who respect and support her desire. What should I do?

At my lab, we're on the brink of human cloning, but should we do it? Would it matter if we were financed by TV money and about to produce hundreds of identical Regis Philbins?

Q & A

Doctors' Dilemmas

A physician, I recently prescribed Viagra to a patient. Shortly after, his wife, also my patient, disclosed that they've not been intimate for months. On the one hand, his private affairs are none of my business. On the other, his wife is likely to feel betrayed if she discovers I've given him the means to satisfy his ends. What should I do?

—P.M., OHIO

Unless he is doing real physical damage, you must respect the husband's confidence. Few would seek medical care if a physician could take it on herself to violate a patient's privacy.

It would be a different matter if you were treating the wife for, say, a venereal disease contracted from the husband; then you'd have to speak up. (As nineteenth-century doctors often did not. Indeed, they frequently lied to the wife about what they were treating her for.)

As you've discovered, the interests of husband and wife do not always coincide. The best way for you to avoid such conflicts in the future is to see only one member of a family, a practice observed by many psychiatrists but few physicians. (Indeed, many proponents of family medicine believe they can better serve and better understand their patients when treating all members of a family.)

As things stand now, without violating anyone's privacy, you can still draw out either of these patients about their marital discontents or suggest counseling.

On the bright side, perhaps the husband is not unfaithful, but has found some other, socially beneficial, use for Viagra. Didn't I read about corn that grows straight and strong, fifty feet high? Isn't there a car that goes a thousand miles on a single tablet?

I believe everyone has the right to promote himself, but is it right for doctors to advertise? Does it compromise their ethics, or are they and the public protected by the 'truth in advertising' laws?

—R.S., ENGLEWOOD, NEW JERSEY

The American Medical Association's Code of Medical Ethics states: "There are no restrictions on advertising by physicians except those that can be specifically justified to protect the public from deceptive practices." But while this policy encourages innovations that may be great for business—Budweiser frogs that croak "bi-op-sy" or tireless robot bunnies that keep healing and healing and healing—it does not serve the interests of the patients.

Medical advertising risks a conflict of interest, making the doctor a salesman eager to persuade rather than a disinterested party eager to inform. This is especially perilous because most patients lack the sophistication to make complicated medical decisions. That is, while I may be qualified to select a laundry detergent and hence to evaluate a soap commercial, I'm not qualified to select a surgeon. And a thirty-second TV spot is unlikely to help me make so consequential a decision. ("With a name like Dr. Schattzbergg, he's got to be good.") I am, of course, similarly bewildered by ads for cars, computers, or even running shoes. A doctor, however, has taken an oath to serve his patients; I believe the oath at Nike involves only selling a lot of sneakers and delivering a dump truck full of cash to Michael Jordan.

There are better ways to meet the admirable goal of helping patients choose a physician. Doctors' medical techniques could be rated by a neutral party, much as the Barron's guides rate colleges. Or patients' opinions of bedside manner could be correlated into a kind of physician Zagat's. Neither puts the doctor in an ethically awkward position.

Advertising is always a dubious means of education, since it involves the testimony of interested parties. And while patients need information, that need will not be met by transforming the doctor-patient relationship into the McDonald's–burger-eater relationship.

As a physician, I treat patients and have instructed medical residents and medical students. But how can I justify using patients as a part of these students' training rather than having patients treated by the most experienced medical personnel available? Aren't people to be viewed as ends, not means?

—ANDREW MARCH, M.D.

While everyone wants first-rate medical care from sophisticated practitioners, nearly everyone understands that only well-trained doctors can provide such care. These two goals can be balanced, so long as doctors in training aren't clustered among a few unfortunate hospitals, and so long as they're properly supervised by more accomplished colleagues. Furthermore, a student's assignments must be appropriate to his skills: He may remove a splinter, but a more senior colleague should perform those experimental brain transplants. And finally, nothing is more important than informed consent, so make sure your patients know what's going on. Under these circumstances, they will respond with confidence when your receptionist announces, "Dr. March, one of your ends is here."

KNOWING THE BABY'S GENDER

What happens when a pregnant wife finds out the sex of the forthcoming baby but asks that the doctor tell no one, including her husband? If the husband wants to know, is the obstetrician ethically bound not to tell him at the order of his patient? Or does her husband have a right to know?

—SY PRESTEN, NEW YORK CITY

"It's not at all uncommon to have one parent want to know and one not," says Dr. Joshua A. Copel, Professor of Obstetrics and Gynecology at Yale. But, he emphasizes, "our medical relationship is with the woman." After the baby is born, the father and mother have an equal say in child rearing, but before that, the father's curiosity does not supersede the mother's right to privacy, an essential part of the doctor-patient relationship.

But your case, in which the mother already knows and does not want to tell the father, is unusual and perplexing. "I might worry a little," says Dr. Copel. "Does she not want him to know because he's said, 'If you don't give me a son, I'll wail the tar out of you?' Or, it could be something happier. Maybe she wants to preserve his surprise. I'd want to talk to her more about that."

There are times when a doctor is legally obligated to override a pregnant patient's wishes. "If the patient had a disease that might affect the husband—say tuberculosis or syphilis—the state requires us to report her illness and would step in to find and notify her contacts," says Dr. Copel.

Such troubling cases aside, there is much to be said for waiting. Discovering your baby's gender months before it is born is like pausing midway through a mystery novel and flipping ahead to the last page to find out who the killer is: You sacrifice an essential pleasure of the experience. Why deprive yourself of that classic delivery room denouement, the culmination of nine months of waiting, when you hear the obstetrician announce: "It's a monkey! A very attractive monkey!"

SLIPPING PSYCH

I am a psychiatrist, and I'm afraid a respected colleague is slipping dangerously. One of my patients mentioned that his wife's therapist (that's the colleague in question) has been forgetful, inattentive, and inappropriately angry. This could be the sign of a serious problem. Must I intervene on such unreliable information? Is it even possible without violating the rights of either my patient or my colleague?

—H.K., NEW JERSEY

"Unreliable information" is too generous a characterization. You've given me your version of the husband's version of his wife's version of her psychiatrist's behavior. If I wander into that swamp of complex motives, I'll never find my way out alive. The official line, as I'm sure you know, is that if your patient's wife has concerns about her therapist, you should encourage her to voice them to the therapist or to your profession's self-policing body. You should intervene directly only in extreme cases, such as immediate danger or obvious ethical transgressions. Of course, in extreme cases everyone knows how to act, and every system is self-regulating, as Lenin and Marie Antoinette can tell you.

Your situation, however, is more difficult to call. Psychiatry is a particularly cloistered discipline, since it's practiced in private (unlike, say, hospital medicine) and requires the strictest confidentiality. If you want to discover more about your questionable colleague and you want to do it tactfully, seek places where he works with others. Perhaps he supervises psychiatric residents or participates in academic life; if so, you could speak informally to his coworkers. Or you can talk to the husband in general terms about proper psychiatric demeanor; perhaps he'll motivate his wife to act. Or perhaps not. After all, there are good reasons why patients might not want to go down that road.

"When someone has invested years of her life, thousands of dollars, and enormous emotion," says Dr. Anna Fels, a psychiatrist affiliated with New York Presbyterian Hospital, "she has a vested interest in maintaining the relationship and her sense of the psychiatrist's capability."

Or, as perpetual analysand Woody Allen said (and I quote from unreliable memory), "I've been seeing a psychiatrist, a strict Freudian who's been dead for two years. But I can't quit seeing him because my analysis is at a delicate stage. And besides, he'd bill me for the sessions I'd miss."

E.R. COPS?

I am a physician in a trauma center that does not check accident victims for alcohol and drugs. If a driver were intoxicated, insurance would not cover medical costs. However, not knowing blood-alcohol levels may have adverse medical consequences. Should we check even if it means added financial burdens, suboptimal care, or exposure to criminal charges?

—ANONYMOUS, NEW YORK

A doctor is pledged to do what is in the patient's best interest medically. So check blood-alcohol levels, but do not disclose this information—neither to cops nor to insurance companies—without the patient's consent. The AMA's confidentiality policy is meant to protect individual patients, not to promote public health, aid law enforcement, or reduce insurance rates.

Of course, varying state statutes can create conflicts between what is legal and what is ethical, putting the doctor in an awkward position. Fortunately, even aggressive disclosure laws often allow some discretion. Some doctors, for example, regard a medical chart as a guideline for continued care: Anything not directly pertinent need not be recorded. From this perspective, a knowledge of a patient's blood-alcohol level that is vital for immediate treatment may not be germane to future care and can be omitted.

You should discuss these issues with your colleagues when reviewing E.R. policy, rather than leave them to the ad hoc decision of an individual doctor under pressure. And do this not when the patient is on the table but at the end of the working day. That is also the time to contact your representatives and rally your colleagues against laws that hinder patient care; this, too, is a doctor's ethical obligation.

UNCONSCIOUS BIAS

I am an anesthesiologist. Last week I had a young male patient on the table for an appendectomy. As I was pushing the drugs to put him to sleep, I noticed the Nazi flag tattoo enveloping his upper arm. Being Jewish and having a grandmother who lost her entire family to the Nazis, I was disturbed. What level of care must an ethical physician provide to an offensive patient?

—ANONYMOUS, ATLANTA, GEORGIA

You must give every patient proficient treatment. That is your sworn obligation. It is not for you to judge your patients' worth as people.

You may find the tattoo an obvious emblem for the man, but it's not. In fact, you know little about him except that at some point in his life he got a tattoo expressing odious ideas; you've no idea what he thinks now or what bad behavior, if any, he's ever engaged in. You do know, on the other hand, that your patient is probably too young to have been an active Nazi during World War II.

Still, it is true that we all treat different people differently. Plumbers, shopkeepers, and the late General Patton have been brusque with some people, solicitous with others. You, too, are entitled to human feelings. But you must always be thoroughly professional. If you can't do that, recuse yourself and let another anesthesiologist handle the patient.

JUNKET MEDICINE

A drug company invited me, a physician, to a weekend conference centered around one of their expensive new products. They flew my wife and me to a lovely resort where they fed and entertained us lavishly. I attended scientific meetings for a few hours; the rest of the time we were free to amuse ourselves. No quid pro quo was requested. To circumvent government regulations that limit such gifts, they made us doctors nominal "consultants" and paid us each $1,000. Everyone I spoke with felt a bit guilty about it (including me), but the inducements were too good to pass up. Do you see an ethical problem here?

—ANONYMOUS, KANSAS

I do see a problem, and so does the American Medical Association: It's called conflict of interest. To avoid it, the AMA's code of professional conduct says that an industry should not subsidize the cost of travel, lodging, or personal expenses of conference-attending physicians.

Accepting a drug company's largesse might bias you in its favor—if only subtly—when you're deciding what medication to prescribe to your patients or order for your hospital. You and your colleagues may fancy yourselves beyond such partiality, but if that were so, that would practically make you unique human beings. Certainly your susceptibility to influence is presumed by the pharmaceutical companies: that's why they ladle out the money for lavish dinners.

Signing on as a "consultant" heightens the ethical lapse. You yourself regard it as deceitful, and it is expressly forbidden by the AMA, which proscribes "token consulting" to justify the compensation of physicians by pharmaceutical companies.

What slightly ameliorates your experience is the extent to which it is shared by your colleagues, despite the AMA's code. One definition of ethics is to conform to the conduct of one's profession. By this standard, you've done nothing wrong. However, by this standard a bookie does no wrong when he breaks the legs of a guy who is tardy paying his gambling debts. We may, perhaps, make more rigorous ethical demands upon you.

If the conference was important, you should have bought your own ticket and attended with a clear conscience.

SINGLE INDEMNITY

As a doctor, should I shade the truth about a patient's condition in order to obtain their health plan's approval for medically appropriate care? Apparently, many doctors feel that their oath requires them to deceive the insurance company for the good of the patient even though they are taking a legal risk.

—D.H., NEW JERSEY

According to a recent article in *JAMA,* most physicians would overstate risk factors to qualify a patient for medical intervention for a serious condition; many fewer for a nose job, unsurprisingly. This does not seem unreasonable.

Your ethical obligation is, of course, to serve the medical needs of your patient, not to protect an insurance company's bottom line. My understanding is that there are vast gray areas, and my advice is that when navigating them, you will always err on the side of providing your patients with the best possible care. Often this is a matter of interpretation. However, it would indeed be unethical—and in many cases illegal—to lie to the insurance company.

Your situation is particularly frustrating because while many insurers acknowledge the value of preventative medicine, they refuse to pay for various tests without an immediate diagnosis. While this does not justify your lying to the insurer, it demands that you take other actions to change these policies—lobby your representatives, write your professional associations, phone the insurance company. Your ability to provide the best possible care to a patient is also shaped by what you do when the patient is not in your office.

To make an ethical choice in your situation means understanding the gross failure of our health care system to make decent coverage available to all. It is, as you know, extraordinarily difficult to behave honorably while operating in a dishonorable—or at least grotesquely inadequate—system.

Guest Ethicist

GIMPY CAT

How much is a cat worth? My affectionate and obedient Manx needs a procedure that will cost a few hundred dollars. My instinct, of course, is to pay for whatever she needs, but I can't help thinking it's wrong. Wouldn't the cash be better spent on sick humans?

—J.M., BOSTON

PETER SINGER'S BOOKS INCLUDE *ANIMAL LIBERATION*, *PRACTICAL ETHICS*, *RETHINKING LIFE AND DEATH*, AND, MOST RECENTLY, *WRITINGS ON AN ETHICAL LIFE*. HE IS CURRENTLY IRA W. DECAMP PROFESSOR OF BIOETHICS AT PRINCETON UNIVERSITY. THIS IS HIS RESPONSE:

Yes, it would be better to spend the cash on sick humans. Perhaps that's not the answer you expected to get from the author of *Animal Liberation,* a book sometimes credited with starting the modern animal rights movement, so let me explain why.

First, in the poorest parts of the world, where people lack the most basic health care or safe drinking water, $500 goes a long way. My colleague Peter Unger, of New York University, has conservatively estimated that $200, given to an agency like Oxfam America, is enough to save the life of a child who would otherwise not get through those dangerous years when child mortality is at its highest. So $500 can save between two and three human lives. Even if we were to put the same value on a cat and a human, there would be a case for saying that it is better to save two lives than one.

But second, it's not part of the philosophy of the animal movement, as I understand it, to say that all lives are of equal worth. While we should not discount the interests of beings just because they are not members of our species—that's speciesism—it is defensible to say that if a being is aware of its circumstances, and can see itself as having a past and—all being well—a future, then the death of that being is a greater tragedy than the death of a being without that capacity. That's not speciesism, because our differing judgments are not based on the species of the being, but on its nature. So we can reasonably judge it to be more important to save the life of a normal human being than to save the life of a cat. Though we don't know exactly what goes on in the mind of a cat, it is implausible to suppose that it has the same sharp awareness of itself and its future as a normal human being.

. Third, my guess is that a procedure that costs $500 is going to leave your Manx feeling fairly sick for some time. I don't know, because you haven't told me the details, but let's suppose that is the case. You can't explain to your Manx why she is going through this procedure. Since she has no future plans that her death will prevent her fulfilling, she does not have as much at stake as a normal human would, and it may be positively cruel to put her through a distressing treatment in order to save her life. If you decide to do it, it may be more for your benefit—because you love your Manx—than for hers.

So here's my final suggestion: Accept that your cat's time has come, and don't allow her to suffer anymore. Give $500 to Oxfam America or another equally efficient organization that helps the world's poorest people. Then go to the local shelter, and put your name down to adopt a cat who would otherwise have been killed. In that way you will have saved human lives and the life of a cat as well.

If you pose the question that way—cat care or human care?—most people (though not all people, and in any case very few cats) would say the
answer is easy. But this is a false equivalency. There's no reason, after all,
that the money you spend at the vet should reduce what you'd otherwise donate to helping sick people. It could just as easily come from your
vacation fund. It would be troubling if you ignored the needs of people
around you in order to treat your cat, but not if you merely sacrificed a
few days of Disneyfication.

It might help to think of the cat as a recreational device. Spending money
on it is no more profligate than purchasing a giant-screen TV or theater tickets or dinner at a fancy restaurant or . . . well, name your own sybaritic dis-
cretionary spending. There is, however, no getting around the fact that 43
million Americans lack health insurance, or indeed real access to decent medical care. So when you get back from the vet, write your Senator.

(NOTE: This column stimulated more reader response than any up until
that time. Many of these letters argued that, having agreed to take in an
animal, you are responsible for its medical care at any cost. Work a second job. Rob a liquor store. Whatever it takes.)

Non-Doctors' Dilemmas

HERBAL MEDICINE

I have HIV and use cannabis to alleviate nausea and lack of appetite.
A friend grows and provides it at no cost. I distribute the remaining cannabis to 15 or so other people who either have HIV or are
undergoing chemotherapy. We all know this is illegal but feel that
our lives come first. Are we not being ethical?

—ANONYMOUS, VIRGINIA

I'm with you: What you're doing is illegal but not unethical. Society ac-
knowledges a moral right to break the law in extreme circumstances.

Each time a sitcom cop pulls over some hapless guy for speeding and asks, "Okay, buddy, where's the fire?" the implication: If the driver really is racing to extinguish a blaze, exceeding the speed limit is acceptable. Similarly, medical necessity can trump marijuana laws. While there are sound arguments for law-abiding behavior even when a law is ludicrous, in this situation you harm no one while relieving the suffering of the gravely ill who have no alternative remedy—compelling reasons to violate the law.

And you needn't worry that you are implicated in the occasional gunplay of the marijuana trade; that violence is a consequence of prohibition, not pharmacology, and in any case, one would expect the not-for-profit, grow-your-own network of medical cannabis suppliers to be insulated from the excesses of the commercial trade.

A recent Supreme Court decision confirms marijuana's classification under federal law as an illegal Schedule I drug with "no currently accepted medical use." Although the ruling does not overturn state statutes—eight states have passed medical marijuana initiatives—it contradicts what many patients and doctors (including the California Medical Association) believe. Thus, for you to provide cannabis to the seriously ill is not just an act of compassion, but also an assertion of truth, albeit not one a Federal Drug Enforcement Agent would find persuasive.

I should add that clinical evidence of the efficacy of medical marijuana is sketchy and that some regard its successes as a consequence of the placebo effect. Thus, many choose to use it as a last resort after exhausting other remedies. And you should, of course, consult with your physician so he or she is aware of any potential interaction with other drugs you may be taking.

EMBRACESABLE YOU

My 11-year-old daughter has a lovely smile, but her dentist says her slightly crooked teeth could become a problem. He prescribes braces. She wants them, too. I can't help thinking that this has less to do with preventive medicine than with preying on kids' insecurity. Even without the several-thousand-dollar price tag, that seems pretty unethical. But can I hold my daughter to the same opinion?

Many a father who stoutly resists Rogaine for his own barren pate swiftly capitulates to braces for his beloved child, no matter how slight the need. Obviously there's no ethical dilemma if you're straightening her teeth to avoid actual dental distress now or years later. But what about the rest of the time? Such procedures have a troubling tendency to redefine the standards of attractiveness for everyone. As cosmetic medicine and dentistry become more available, all teeth are suddenly too crooked, all faces need lifting, all breasts are either too big or too small. Ordinary attractiveness becomes something achievable only by medical intervention. This is bad for the millions of people who end up judging themselves by those procrustean standards, but great for doctors, dentists, and *Cosmopolitan* magazine.

At a moment when growing numbers of people pay thousands of dollars to have the hair zapped off their legs by beauticians wielding surgical lasers, however, it can be tough to draw a sharp distinction between cosmetic surgery and all the other measures that people take to improve their appearance. But try this simple test: Does it require anesthesia? If a beauty treatment renders you unconscious, you might want to reconsider.

Happily, it is not just beauty but comfort that these new surgeries have redefined, and often for the better. People used to regard losing most of their teeth as a fact of life that only the fortunate few escaped. No longer. So err on the side of your daughter's happiness and get her the braces if you can afford them. (She won't even need local anesthesia.) By the time she's old enough to be bullied into a face-lift, she'll be mature enough, and confident enough, to make that decision for herself.

SPAY AND RESPAY

A few months after we had our cat, Minnie, spayed, she started behaving like a cat in heat. She went back to the vet, who billed us

$181 for the second surgery. My husband says we owe the vet nothing, since he just completed the job he was supposed to do originally. But the vet says the first surgery was performed to normal veterinary standards. The second operation was a major surgery, not a simple spaying. What's your view?

—J.F., STAMFORD, CONNECTICUT

I'm with your husband. You hired the vet to spay your cat, not merely to perform a narrowly defined medical procedure. He doesn't get paid twice for spaying once. If, however, before the first operation the vet explained what he intended to do and the risks of failure, then he's kept his side of the bargain, and you must pay for the second procedure.

It may also be that your cat was not actually in heat. "It is possible, though relatively rare, that an animal may have estrogenic tissue other than the ovaries, which may continue to cause apparent heat, even though the procedure was performed correctly," notes Paul Small, a doctor of veterinary medicine. "What I would tell clients with this problem is that we would see: If there was retained ovarian tissue, no charge; if it was otherwise, there would be a fee."

It is in everyone's interest to clarify these things in advance so such misunderstandings can be avoided. Had there been real informed consent, the vet would have given you the information you needed to make a decision, and your cat would have had a chance to try to talk you out of the entire business.

BLOOD SCREENING

When I went to donate blood, I found myself answering yes to several screening questions. Two examples: "Have you (a man) had sex with a man since 1979?" "Have you traveled to Britain since 1995?" I have a fair amount of medical training (I will receive my M.D. shortly), so I know the implications of these questions—and I also know that my donation would present no risk. Is it ethical to tell a few white lies for the greater good of contributing to the blood supply?

—D.S., PROVIDENCE, RHODE ISLAND

No, you must answer honestly. Remember, your blood alone is not the only issue here. The integrity of the screening process would be compromised were it known that donors lie whenever they feel confident about the safety of their blood or the excellence of their med-school learning.

In addition to securing the current blood supply, accurate information is necessary to develop future screening methods. Take the screen for the predominantly transfusion-borne hepatitis C, for example, which has been in place only since 1992. "Much of what was learned was gleaned from retrospective analysis of donor demographics," says Dr. Serena Yoon, an attending physician at Cayuga Medical Center and senior clinical instructor at the University of Rochester School of Medicine and Dentistry.

Incidentally, even if your blood is unacceptable for transfusion, it may still be valuable. Some agencies accept blood from people with certain risk factors and use it for research. So fill out the questionnaire accurately, and let the collection service decide how best to use your blood.

MEDICAL BILLS

My brother died owing about $20,000 in medical bills not covered by his insurance. Because the claim period has now expired, my lawyer says that, although the estate has enough money to cover these bills, I (as administrator of the estate) am not legally required to pay them. Do I have a moral obligation to pay those bills? May I consider the financial need of my mother and myself, who would inherit this money that would otherwise go to a huge for-profit hospital?

—M.P., NEW YORK CITY

I believe that you should pay the bills. That the money is owed to an unappealing creditor is beside the point. There are, of course, limits to your obligation. In many a Victorian novel, the children struggle for years to meet the debts incurred by their late parents. Spirits are crushed. Hair turns gray. You have no such obligation to pay your brother's debts from your own pocket, but insofar as his estate can make these payments, it should—his bills, his money, his responsibility.

There is also a legal aspect to your problem. As an administrator of the estate, you are obliged to consider the best interests of the heirs; you are in charge of what is now their money. So before taking the morally correct step, you may be legally required to persuade your mother and any other heirs that it is the right thing to do. You may want to consult a lawyer here.

ADMISSIONS LISTS

I work at a hospital that makes the admissions list available to those in charge of the foundation for raising money. If there is a donor on the list, they send a get well card or flowers. I have a problem with making the list "public." Isn't patient anonymity a right?

—ANONYMOUS

The hospital should not release its admissions list. This may be legal—state laws vary, and most concentrate on the privacy of medical records—but it violates the spirit of doctor-patient confidentiality and serves no purpose related to patient care. (Rules proposed by the Clinton administration would forbid hospitals to use patient lists for non-medical purposes like soliciting donations.)

In any case, this is certainly a morbid sort of fundraising: "Sorry you're ill, but are you still strong enough to lift your checkbook?"

FILE SHARING

While training as a psychoanalyst, my husband fails to protect his patient notes. I frequently find them next to the family computer or in any odd location around the house. I have complained that these notes should be kept away from my children and whoever might enter the house. He maintains that anyone who reads them has committed a boundary violation. With whom does the responsibility for confidentiality rest?

—ANONYMOUS, VIRGINIA

THE GOOD, THE BAD

Although it is unethical to rob a bank, Chase would open itself to criticism if it routinely strewed cash about the lobby, relying on the rectitude of potential safecrackers. Depositors—and analysands—can demand more prudence from the specialists they employ.

Thus, while you and your kids have a general ethical obligation to respect other people's privacy, even when you stumble upon a fascinating account of a neighbor's quirks, your husband has a greater responsibility, an explicit professional duty to ensure his patients' confidentiality. The American Psychoanalytic Association's "Principles of Ethics for Psychoanalysts" says: "Except as required by law, a psychoanalyst may not reveal the confidences entrusted to him/her in the course of his/her professional work."

Not only does your husband's insouciance violate a professional stricture, he also undermines the efficacy of his very work. Psychoanalysis requires self-revelation; to speak freely, a patient must be confident that these intimate matters will not be gossiped about by the analyst's kids over cookies and milk. (Nothing shakes a patient's confidence like seeing his records marked up with crayon.)

If you can't persuade your husband to be vigilant, you might press him to consult his colleagues, who, one hopes, are more scrupulous about the rules of the profession. You could urge the APA or your state's licensing agencies generally to remind all practitioners about the duties of confidentiality. Some hospitals, for example, post signs in the elevators reminding the staff to be discreet. And throughout World War II, government posters declared "Loose Lips Sink the Psychoanalytic Process," if I remember correctly, which I do not. I suppose any capable analyst could explain why. If I trusted him enough to speak freely.

THE SILENT TREATMENT

I'm a physical therapist, and my views about medical practice often clash with those of the chiropractors who own the multidisciplinary clinic where I work. One day they distributed pamphlets to our patients discouraging vaccination. I disagree with these ideas, but should I distribute material that contradicts my bosses? If I don't, patients may not get immunized; if I do, they'll end up confused. What to do?

—ANONYMOUS, NEW YORK CITY

Assuming you're not going to get yourself fired, let your counterleafleting commence. To provide people with the information they need to make an informed decision doesn't confuse, it educates. It can only help your patients to know that your bosses' views are, at best, idiosyncratic: Virtually all physicians favor vaccination. Your primary ethical obligation is not to support your bosses' dubious theories; it is to give your patients the best possible care, which, in this case, means to give them the best possible information. You can't effectively serve your patients if a gag rule is imposed—by you or by the chiropractors.

To contradict your bosses in this way may put you at risk of being fired, but perhaps the greater risk is that you won't get fired. Instead you'll continue to work for practitioners whose odd notions may lead them ever farther afield. Are you prepared to keep silent when they begin treating the patients by leeching or bloodletting? Maybe it's time to look for work at another clinic, preferably one conveniently located in the twenty-first century.

MAGAZINE THIEF

Occasionally while sitting in a doctor's waiting room, I get caught up in an article in a magazine that is several months old. Knowing that the magazine is no longer on the newsstands, I take it home with me. Is this stealing?

—K.B., BALDWIN, NEW YORK

It is stealing, although given the dusty and dated copies that languish in your doctor's waiting room, it could almost be classified as trash removal. But alas, it is not your trash. What strikes me about this pilferage is that it is so unnecessary. Why not just ask the receptionist to photocopy the article you're reading or to let you take the magazine home? You can promise to return it on your next visit, when it will be every bit as out of date as it is now.

Arguing with The Ethicist

DRUGSTORE COWBOY

A relative of mine is a physician whose "drug rep" gives him virtually unlimited samples of a drug I take daily, prescribed by another physician. Am I wrong to accept these samples rather than buy the drug?

—ANONYMOUS, EVANSTON, ILLINOIS

It is fine to accept a few samples to try out a new medication—that's why the drug company hands them out—but not to make them your regular source of supply. The problem is not your depriving a pharmaceutical company of its profits; it is that the company's lavish dispensing of free samples can skew a doctor's judgment about what to prescribe. Many doctors now learn about new medications not from unbiased journals but from drug-company reps who tend to accentuate the positive and eliminate the nausea, dizziness, and hair loss. Also, because companies tend to hand out samples of their newest, most expensive products instead of cheaper generics, and because doctors often stick with medications as long as they're working, prescription costs can become inflated.

Some doctors defend the current system as a source of free drugs for their uninsured patients and as a low-cost way to try out new treatments, but medical opinion seems to be running against them: Increasing numbers of hospitals and HMOs are also forbidding their doctors to accept such samples. And more germane to your situation, the American Medical Association recommends that doctors not accept gifts of substantial value or samples for personal use. No freebies for the family, in other words.

Thus your accepting these samples is wrong in itself, wrong for abetting your relative the doctor's dubious behavior, and wrong for reinforcing the questionable system created by the drug reps who last year passed out more than $7.2 billion worth of free samples.

In layman's terms, that means that each week a bazillion dump trucks filled with pills pulled up to doctors' doors and tipped their loads into the basement—hardly an inducement to prescribe inexpensive medications.

STEVE COTTON COUNTERS:

Your analysis of the doctor's and patient's situations didn't completely hold up. In the sense that drug companies are trying to get more patients to try the drug, they are foiled when a doctor gives the entire lot to a friend, relative, or needy patient, since this is limiting the number of patients who try the product.

I REPLY:

Your argument would be more persuasive if the drug company had a limited supply of a particular drug. Then, if the physician passed it on to a single patient (or in this case, nonpatient), he'd thwart the company's purpose. However, the companies seem to have endless rivers of the stuff. If you'll pay for it, they'll make more.

ERIC SAIDEL SAYS:

I'm not sure what dubious behavior the doctor is engaged in. She is not prescribing the drugs to her relative, and so is not influenced in doing so by getting the freebies. Perhaps because she gets the freebies she is more likely to prescribe them to her own patients, but the writer's continued use of the freebies has no effect on that.

I REPLY:

The doctor violates AMA conflict-of-interest guidelines by giving samples to a family member and participates in a system that grossly inflates prescription costs.

JONATHAN FREEDBERG ARGUES:

Doctors have always learned about new drugs from both medical journals and drug-company reps. This practice goes back as far as I can remember—my dad is a doctor and he received drug samples from reps forty years ago when I was just a kid. It never "skewed" his judgment.

I REPLY:

This situation has changed enormously in the forty years since your dad received a few samples; the influence of this practice on doctors is now pervasive. The thing about conflict of interest and biased sources is that it influences the judgments of all involved, not because they are bad people, but because it is not possible to be immune. The very nature of the scientific method relies on disinterested parties.

MR. FREEDBERG COUNTERS:

I can quite clearly see a direct financial benefit to HMOs and hospitals to stop doctors from handing out free drugs. Hospitals usually have in-house pharmacies and the ethics of HMOs are hardly of the standard I would imagine you would recommend.

I REPLY:

One undeniable effect of the current system is the increasing use of more expensive proprietary drugs in cases where less expensive generics would work fine. I think the HMOs are eager to reap those savings—and not unreasonably—rather than chance making a few bucks at their pharmacies.

Postscripts

As a Speech/Language Pathologist, I evaluate Medicare patients. A date of onset of their problem is required, and if that date is more than a few months old, Medicare might not reimburse the hospital. Therefore, my colleagues and I are encouraged to "fudge" the date. I fear that if I put down the correct date (which may be years in the past) and the hospital is not reimbursed, it will stop performing these evaluations, and the patient will suffer. What is the right thing to do?

—ANONYMOUS, NEW JERSEY

That the current system is always parsimonious, sometimes unfair, and frequently coldhearted does not justify falsifying records to secure a payment. If there were an immediate risk to the patient's health, the situation might be different; a doctor must of course act in the best interests of the patient. And that action should include insisting that the hospital perform all necessary medical tests.

Your question, however, is less about treatment than bookkeeping. You ought to be reluctant to perjure yourself merely to ensure that your hospital gets reimbursed. You'd not only be acting unethically, you may well be putting yourself in legal jeopardy. Neither your hospital nor Medicare is apt to have a sense of humor about the use of Wite-Out.

One other consideration: Are you absolutely certain that Medicare will reject the procedures you mention? The system does include an appeals process, and it is your responsibility to see that that process is vigorously employed on behalf of the patient.

ANONYMOUS FOLLOWS UP:

Since your column ran, I have been using actual onset dates on my Medicare paperwork. If the stroke was a few years ago, I question the nurses to see if there were any other medical changes since the stroke (e.g., pneumonia, mental status changes, onset of coughing while eating). If so, I use both dates and explain the details in the body of my report. If not, I just use the date from a few years ago. My next step is to talk to my supervisor and tell her that this is what I am doing. She is a reasonable person. While she will not be happy with this, I don't think it will cause major problems.

When you pointed out that not only is it unethical to falsify dates but that it could also put me in legal jeopardy (potentially causing me to lose my license, among other things), I realized that I really needed to change what I was doing.

STD DILEMMA

I am a female internist. A patient with a sexually transmitted disease asked that his wife—not my patient—be tested but not told about his extramarital affair. I worried that she might go untreated or be sent to a doctor unaware of her risk. I saw her, and she never asked about the source of her infection. As both patients are now entitled to confidentiality, I am apprehensive of conflicts of interest. Did I do right?

—ANONYMOUS

Your concern for both patients is admirable, but allowing the husband to limit your actions placed you in the wrong. The AMA's code of ethics demands that a doctor have her patient's informed consent in order to perform any treatment. This required you to tell her what you were treating her for and why, thus violating your pledge to the husband. Also, by not telling her the source of her infection, you deprived her of a chance to protect herself in the future.

The best solution is to avoid being in this position in the first place. Ethical behavior is meant as much to avert such situations as it is to extricate you from them. Ideally, you should have interrupted the husband as he made his request, saying that if his wife is worried about her health, you'd be happy to examine her.

Notwithstanding the wife's odd passivity, one thing you can do now is build a relationship of trust with her so that she is more able to participate in her own care. You could also refer her to a gynecologist who would be unfettered by any promise to the husband.

Despite your honorable intentions, it is difficult to see what the wife got from you that she wouldn't have received from a less scrupulous doctor selected by the husband. Further, it seems unlikely that, had you declined his terms, his wife would have gone without care. Surely the husband would be eager to have her treated, if only to protect himself from becoming reinfected. One lesson I draw from this: Husbands and wives should have different doctors. This, of course, contradicts one of the premises upon which family medicine is built, but it does avoid such painful conflicts of interest.

ANONYMOUS FOLLOWS UP:
The wife has since returned and continues to be my patient. She has become more communicative and has catalogued her unhappiness with her marriage. It does make me feel dishonest to withhold what her husband had said. However, I think I gave her better treatment than another doctor would have who followed your advice and refused to accept any information from her husband. I had a heads-up on what might be wrong with her, and so I tested her for things that might not have been included in a routine exam. I should add that the husband was surprised by my reluctance to go along with the charade.

Strictly speaking, she did not have an STD, although she had a cervicitis (a clinical diagnosis that has a variety of causes) and candidal vaginitis. The latter is really just an overgrowth of fungi that are normally present, and is a nonspecific indicator of perturbation of the vaginal microenvironment. Her husband appeared to have both nongonococcal urethritis and a candidal balanitis, the former almost always an STD, and the latter not. Her chlamydia test came back as negative, but his was positive; they both received prophylactic antibiotics (empirically) as well as antifungal medications.

There were a couple of social and cultural factors that I did not mention earlier. She is a recent immigrant who stays home to manage the household, the children, and her mother-in-law. He is a rather narcissistic and self-indulgent person, and she is quite passive and insecure.

Would the wife have received better care from another physician? It is the integral question and one that I really do not know the answer to. At the time I reasoned that another clinician would not have routinely ordered certain tests on an asymptomatic and unsuspecting patient, but who's to say the husband would not have taken that doctor aside, too?

I gather from your reply that I should have declined seeing the wife. This would certainly seem the easiest and most consistent route, yet by not treating her I would have felt that I had failed to do my duty as a physician. You state that I am ethically obliged not to accept any information about patients from sources other than themselves, but I know of no such code. I am not to solicit information, and I must use such sources with caution, but it would be fairly ludicrous to cut a family member off in mid-sentence, and I am frequently asked to intervene on behalf of concerned loved ones. Had I done so with my patient, it would have been tantamount to turning his wife away.

Regarding informed consent, you correctly point out that unless a person actively waives her right to know, it is incumbent upon me to fully disclose the work-up and treatment involved. In this case, I did so, however charily. I said, "I suspect you have an infection, and it is often sexually transmitted." She understood, but did not ask about her husband. I asked if she had any questions. She did not. The ethical gray zone is thus, how fully? Must I hit her over the head? If I have laid out my diagnosis, explained the necessary treatment, and invited her to ask questions, have I not obtained her informed consent? If she declines to ask, am I withholding information? Patients will rarely say "don't tell me any more," but will often give indications that they don't want to know.

One additional thought, lest you incur indignant letters from family practitioners everywhere: Advising married couples to see different doctors would seem to undermine the very philosophy that Family Medicine is built upon.

I Demand a Recant

The resentment which the discovery of a fault or folly produces must bear a certain proportion to our pride, and will regularly be more acrimonious as pride is more immediately the principle of action.

SAMUEL JOHNSON: *RAMBLER* #40 (AUGUST 4, 1750)

It is a disconcerting feature of my job that immediately upon my completing an appointed task, strangers let me know just how inadequately I performed. Very inadequately indeed, apparently. A few moments after my column is posted on the *New York Times* Web site, I inevitably receive e-mail that enumerates my shortcomings—not just rhetorical but personal—and often with astounding ferocity.

This is not the case for most airline pilots or regional sales managers. Indeed, most people do their work and, unless they foul up flamboyantly, they are not routinely denigrated. I don't mean to complain. It goes with the territory. And I remind myself that people are more inclined to write an angry letter than one filled with praise. I do receive a gratifying amount of those, too, and that is not a standard feature of most people's jobs, either pilots or sales managers.

While some of this mail is merely vituperative (and perhaps libelous, but then again, I'm not a lawyer, or a baby), much is earnest, informed, and elegantly reasoned. Such thoughtful correspondence has often led me to rethink my analysis of a question, refining and amending my response. For that, I am grateful. However, while I have revised many of my responses, seldom have I concluded that an answer was utterly erroneous. Seldom, but not never. Below are five questions I've come to think that I simply got wrong. I present each in all its original folly, and then give my new thinking along with the reason for the change. *Mea culpa. Mea maxima culpa.*

1. Let the Buyer Be There

My husband and I will soon put our house on the market. It is a beautiful house in a great neighborhood, but the builder cut some corners on the construction. After the closing, when my disclosure can't affect the sale, should I tell all? My husband says let the buyer's engineer determine what needs to be done, but I'm afraid he'll miss some things. What do you think?

—T.C., LONG ISLAND, NEW YORK

I'm with your husband. There is a built-in conflict of interest between seller and buyer: The former wants to get the highest price, the latter wants the lowest. The solution is for both parties to adhere to the standards of behavior customary in such transactions. That means you must honestly answer any question put to you, and you may not conceal any flaws, but the buyer should not rely on you to volunteer every defect in the house. It is the buyer's responsibility to have a good engineer check out the place. In short, *caveat emptor.*

The more important consideration is what you do before the sale, not after. If you spring a list of shortcomings on the buyers two minutes after the closing, they may not be as grateful as you anticipate. Even if unspoken, the word "sucker" might echo through the inadequately insulated bathroom beneath the leaky roof.

Alas, I was wrong on the law and lax on the ethics. Several lawyers wrote to tell me that while statutes vary from place to place, many jurisdictions impose an affirmative obligation to disclose the defects in a house, particularly the sort of problem that could not be discovered even by a capable inspection—for instance, a basement that looks dry to a house-hunter in July may flood each November.

Why did I miss this? As Dr. Johnson said when asked why in his great dictionary he defined *pastern* as the knee of a horse, "Ignorance, Madam, pure ignorance."

But even if the law did not require such positive actions, ethics does. While there is a distinction between passive silence and active deceit, to withhold important facts about the house is hardly honorable. In the buyer's place, surely you would want a candid account of the property. The seller should tell all and accept a fair price. And I should have set a higher ethical standard.

2. Motel Soap

THE ORIGINAL EXCHANGE:

When we stay at motels, I bring the unused, wrapped soaps and shampoos home to be passed on to a shelter for the homeless. My husband maintains I'm stealing. I consider the cost of these items built into the charge for the room, and that they are ours to do with what we wish. What is your opinion?

—R.S., SCHENECTADY, NEW YORK

What you're doing isn't exactly stealing, but it is taking advantage. While you're at the motel, you may wash yourself as lavishly as you like, but you may not back a truck up to the supply room or, for that matter, empty out the shelf above the sink. That the motel budgets for such things is neither here nor there; they budget for fire insurance, but you really ought not torch the place. If you want to donate to a homeless shelter, do so out of your pocket, not someone else's.

It is not the great issues of the day that generate the most mail, but the homely questions of ordinary life, like this one. Many people wrote to tell me what I've also come to believe: I was harsh with a well-intentioned woman and negligent in my research. There is a key question here that I failed to address: What does the motel owner want? It's his soap. And my response should have featured this advice: Ask the owner. If he's okay with it, no problem. As it happens, he may well be.

Natasha Gullett, a spokeswoman for Bass Hotels and Resorts, parent company of Holiday Inn, says: "Bass Hotels and Resorts has heard about guests at its hotels who are frequent business travelers taking the opportunity to donate unused toiletries to local charities. While BHR has no firsthand knowledge of such incidents, the toiletries are provided for our guests' use at their discretion. BHR is exploring programs that offer hotels the opportunity to make similar donations as a community affairs initiative coordinated by BHR."

So if you're staying at a Holiday Inn, your charitable impulse is not just ethical, it's inspirational. At other motels, opinions vary. There is no corporate policy at Best Western, whose motels are independently owned and operated, but there is a consensus view, according to Tiffany Collins, a spokeswoman. "The overwhelming majority of those polled (88 percent) said they build the cost of these items into the room price and it is assumed from a cost perspective that the guests will take them. Many consider it an additional form of take-home advertising. While the hoteliers expect the items to be taken, they don't always actively encourage the guests to take the items. The amenities have been placed there for the guests to use, if needed, but they wanted to remind guests that those items do cost money and the more items that are offered at a hotel (shampoo, soaps, breakfasts, newspapers, etc.), the more room prices may rise. So, in the end, they do not consider it stealing to take the personal toiletries."

3. Movie Food

I frequently carry a can of soda or a package of snacks into the movie theater. Does the theater have the right to insist on "No Outside Food"?

—MARGARET O'HORA, ALBANY, NEW YORK

Yes, it does. As transgressions go, yours is minor, but it is a transgression. The upright act is to obey the rules: Going to the movies is strictly voluntary, and from the theater's point of view, when you buy a ticket, you accept their strictures. By smuggling in food, you break your agreement and hence behave unethically. They also claim to price their tickets on the assumption that they'll be making some—indeed most—of their profits at the concession stand.

From the customer's point of view, however, there is no choice in the matter: Take it or leave it. (And stay home and watch TV.) Furthermore, even if Milk Duds profits run high, the movie theater isn't going to lower its prices. So the temptation to save money is understandable, but it ought to be resisted.

One thing I would add: If you come to the theater with popcorn stuffed inside your shirt, you should not offer any to your neighbors. A final thought: It is possible to go two hours without eating. Many people do it every week in church.

I believe I took too narrow a view of rules and following them. If all I had to do was write "Always follow the rules; never lie," my job would be easy (and I'd be more popular; most readers applaud such advice). A monkey could do the work. (Maybe not a little monkey, like a rhesus monkey. It would have to be one of those big, smart primates—an ape, or maybe a chimp who, being an ape, could probably handle the task.)

But I would not be urging ethical behavior; I would be demanding docility. And while civility requires that nearly all of us follow the rules nearly all of the time, it does not mean that we should not think critically for ourselves: There are unworthy rules that you may break without being dishonorable.

A valid ethical precept must work not just for one particular case but also for all similar situations. In the months after publishing my response, I received other questions about obeying the rules once you have chosen to put yourself in various situations—on an airplane, in a college dining hall, at Disneyland—and I came to see that participating in a voluntary pleasure (if airline travel can be considered a pleasure) does not mean that you have agreed to all of its rules. Nearly every pleasure in life is voluntary. Were one to forsake them, life would be bleak indeed, if it would be life at all. In this sense, pleasure is not as optional as it may at first appear.

The mandate for rule following exists in a world dominated by money. That is, we meet in the mall, not the town square. When commerce had not so totally colonized our lives, we engaged in such transactions only seldom, and might be said to participate voluntarily and hence be more obliged to follow the rules. Thomas Jefferson could go weeks on his autonomous farm without visiting the mall. But today, all is commerce. It is not possible to live in modern America without such transactions. Thus one has little choice in the matter. The notion that such participation is voluntary is, at best, vestigial. And while this idea may keep the wheels of commerce greased, it has little to do with true consent. This social arrangement did not happen by chance. Many people who profit from the current arrangement worked very hard for a very long time to make it so. It is they who bear the onus of reestablishing some kinds of democratic decision making if their rules are to have any moral weight.

For an agreement to be meaningful, it must be entered into freely by both parties, hardly the case when a theater owner stamps a list of rules on the back of a ticket. There is a difference between the rules imposed only through the authority of private property and the laws devised by a democratic society, which at least strive for the consent of the governed and are nominally under the control of their representatives. The latter have more legitimacy than the former.

It is no doubt true that theaters derive most of their profits from the concession stand. But because a system is profitable does not make it right. The theater would also increase its profits if it didn't have to pay that pesky minimum wage. Folks should patronize the concession stand not because the theater employs armed guards and candy-sniffing dogs to thwart snack smugglers but because they choose to, because it offers food they enjoy at prices they deem reasonable—in short, because they crave that gallon canister of cola. Commerce, too, should be freely entered into. And if fewer purchases at the concession stand means a theater has to raise ticket prices, so be it. Such adjustments are also a part of commerce.

I would set just this condition: You ought not contravene the ostensible function of a business: No smuggling liquor into a bar or cake into a pastry shop. It can be reasonably asserted that when you go to a restaurant, you agree to buy its food and drink; that is an agreement you did make. But you go to the movies for the movie, not for the $25 popcorn. In fact, the restaurant model might be worth adopting at the movies. Some restaurants permit patrons to bring their own wine, but charge them a corkage fee for the privilege. I'd cheerfully pay a $1 cornage fee to avoid eating anything fried in palm oil.

While I'm at it, let me add two other conditions. You shouldn't make a mess for the theater to clean up; that does add to their costs. And you shouldn't disturb others with pungent aromas, either from your food or from your person. But these two conditions apply no matter where you bought your Thai noodles—at the impressively well-stocked snack bar or outside restaurant.

4. Forms of Address

THE ORIGINAL EXCHANGE:

My full-time (but not live-in) baby-sitter hinted that she would like to use my address to enroll her daughter in my excellent local public elementary school; her neighborhood school is awful. The alternative is for her to send her daughter to private school, a financial burden but not an impossibility. Should I offer my address?

—L.A.B., BROOKLYN, NEW YORK

MY ORIGINAL RESPONSE:

You should not offer your address; it is not ethical to facilitate your baby-sitter's fraud. It is, of course, entirely admirable to help her get her daughter into a good school, but there are better ways to do so. Help her apply for a variance that allows her daughter to attend an out-of-district school. And, since that's an admittedly iffy proposition, together see if there are any good schools or special programs in her district.

That said, many districts, even here in New York, a city with some excellent public schools, offer sadly limited choices. As a consequence, while the deception your sitter proposes is improper, I don't have it in me to chastise a mother's deception in trying to get her daughter a decent education. The best way to eliminate these sort of address fiddles is not through calls for individual rectitude, but by providing good schools in all neighborhoods. Sometimes a personal ethical goal—a good education for your sitter's daughter—can be achieved only through political action. So beyond the immediate steps you take on her behalf, I hope you and she actively support efforts for better public schools.

If she does opt for private school, you might help her apply for a scholarship or even, if you can afford it, aid her financially yourself.

MY CURRENT THINKING:

While offering a false address ought not be done lightly, in this situation it could be considered. First, there is a technical point I ought to have included in my answer. Some cities permit using a parent's work address rather than a home address in applying to school. If that's the case here, problem solved. But there is a more fundamental point I ought to have considered. And looking at it now, my response seems sensible only in urging that using a false address should not be a first step, but it could certainly be a last resort.

Writing in *The New Yorker* of February 12, 2001, Louis Menand noted, as have others, that by most measures public schools today are less integrated than they were ten years ago. Here in New York, many schools are integrated only in the sense that an otherwise entirely black and Hispanic school includes a single program that is predominantly white. There is nothing honorable in demanding the baby sitter follow the rules of a segregated system.

Beyond race, there is a more pervasive form of segregation, by social class. The amount of money spent to educate children varies widely from town to town and even from neighborhood to neighborhood, and there is nothing ethical about that. Indeed, in a putatively egalitarian society, it is grotesque. Menand notes that "the sanctity of school-district lines" is a recent phenomenon; this demarcation was once little more than an administrative convenience. Today, such lines create two very different kinds of school.

This year, a state judge found New York's system of financing schools to be egregiously unfair, resulting in great disparities from throughout the state. Similar decisions have been made in many other states. One problem among many is that they rely on property taxes to fund education guarantees, so that kids in wealthy communities will have a very different education than those in poor communities. The system makes a mockery out of equality of opportunity.

In New York and other cities, many parents volunteer time and donate money to their children's school. As a consequence, the schools in middle-class neighborhoods, where the parents can afford to put in more hours, often are significantly better than those in poor neighborhoods. When a child is forbidden to attend any school in town simply because of geography, the result is a two-tiered system of education, with kids in poor neighborhoods sentenced to inferior schools. There is no ethical legitimacy in such a system, and no necessity for the baby-sitter to abide by its rules.

Given the current lamentable condition of public schools in New York, with the deck so stacked against this mother, her obligation to her child surpasses her obligation to tell the truth on an application form or to blindly adhere to school district border lines. That is, one does not have an ethical obligation to cooperate with an utterly unjust system. Thus I'd say you may offer your address to your sitter. While lying is always unfortunate, if it is the only way a hardworking mother can overcome injustice and get her child a good education, I do not have it in me to refuse her.

5. Fast Ad Man

"I'm an advertising copywriter who can complete a job in hours that my boss expects to take days. This allows me to close my office door and do what I love: write science fiction stories. If my boss knew, I'd be in trouble. He says he pays me for a full day's work. I say he pays me to do a particular task, and I shouldn't be penalized for doing it efficiently. So?"

—JIM O'GRADY, NEW YORK CITY

Reluctant as I am to say something that might augment the world's supply of science fiction, I agree with you. Unless you are paid by the hour, if you can complete your assigned task in eight minutes instead of eight hours, you should be rewarded, not punished. And that's what you must persuade your boss. While it is in his interest that you work swiftly and well, it is not honorable to deceive him. The two of you must come to an understanding about your job.

For him to delineate a reasonable workload is legitimate, but to demand your every waking thought is odious. People are not machines to be rented by the hour. Many years ago there was a system in America that required workers to be on constant call; I believe it was abolished by President Lincoln.

THE SCALES FALL FROM MY EYES:

Sometimes the obvious answer is the correct answer. I should not have encouraged Mr. O'Grady to perform personal tasks on company time. When he finishes his work, he should alert his boss, making sure that the boss realizes how swiftly and skillfully he's done his job, and implying that an efficient worker like him ought to be paid more than his stodgy colleagues, and perhaps given a fat bonus—a car, a boat, a vacation. Next he should ask the boss what task to undertake next. Then, if the boss gives him some downtime, he's free to write all the crazy moon-man stories he likes.

The Ten Toughest
Questions

Where there is no difficulty there is no praise.

SAMUEL JOHNSON, *LIVES OF THE POETS* (DRYDEN)

That the following questions were among the most difficult for me to answer may reflect more on the facility with which I swiftly sped to a faulty conclusion in answering others, than in the measured consideration I gave to those listed below. Some deal with the large issues much debated throughout the society, others with more homely issues. But all were particularly tough to answer.

Many readers write to tell me that before looking at my answer to a question, they devise their own, and some try to predict my response. To make this easier, here are the ten questions that were the toughest for me to consider, along with a reference to the page where I respond to each. (They are listed in no particular order.)

The question I receive most frequently is "Do You Tell?" in all its variants—about a spouse's infidelity, a coworker's petty pilferage, a fellow student's cheating. The duty to report is a tricky area, and no place more so than in this version:

& THE DIFFERENCE   273

1. Do You Tell? (page 166)

Out of town on business, in the hotel bar, I saw a good friend's husband entwined with another woman. If I tell, my friend will be devastated, and she might hate me for it. If I don't, I'm joining her rotten husband in conspiring to deceive her. Should I tell?

—S.B., NEW YORK CITY

Do you acquiesce in—even abet—a friend's behavior when it places the friend in jeopardy?

2. Where There's Smoke . . . (page 169)

I have a dear seventy-nine-year-old friend on a fixed income. A heavy smoker, she is down to one lung and professes no desire to quit. She has no car, so once a month I drive her to the military commissary (her late husband was a veteran) in the Presidio to buy cheap cigarettes, for which I often pay. Should I continue to support her deadly habit or cut her off and force her to suffer the withdrawal she says she cannot endure?

—DAVE SWANSON, SAN FRANCISCO

Here's a classic: Can the fruits of wicked deeds be put to good use?

3. Faith, Hope, and Clarity (page 126)

I am on the board of a health facility raising funds for a much needed extension. A local businessman with known ties to organized crime has offered a substantial donation. Should we take the money?

—S. WAGNER, STAMFORD, CONNECTICUT

Next, a particularly difficult question for parents:

4. Heir Unapparent—Leave $ to Kids? (page 176)

We are writing a will and want to leave all our money to our two children. One is very rich and the other lives almost hand-to-mouth. Do we divide equally or give the poorer one a greater proportion?

—H.S. AND S.S., NEW YORK CITY

The following question involves the clash between personal values and civic obligations:

5. Hung Juror (page 143)

Called for jury duty, I was asked if I would be able to impose a death sentence. I am an ardent foe of capital punishment, but if I answered no, I would have been left off the jury and replaced by a juror who believes in the death penalty. If I had lied and said yes, perhaps I could have saved the defendant's life. What should I have done?

—A.B., PHILADELPHIA

This question considers the duty to intercede in two very different circumstances:

6. A Slap in the Face (page 113)

I was on the subway when I saw a frustrated mother slap her child for crying. She didn't hit him hard enough to endanger his life, but the scene suggested something equally scary: an eternity of whacks, verbal abuse, and humiliation. I was afraid to say something, lest I make the mother even angrier at the child. Should I have?

If a doctor does not agree to withhold information from a patient, the patient may go untreated. What should the doctor do?

7. STD Dilemma (page 259)

I am a female internist. A patient with a sexually transmitted disease asked that his wife—not my patient—be tested but not told about his extramarital affair. I worried that she might go untreated or be sent to a doctor unaware of her risk. I saw her, and she never asked about the source of her infection. As both patients are now entitled to confidentiality, I am apprehensive of conflicts of interest. Did I do right?

—ANONYMOUS

Sometimes the right action seems to turn on the effect of the action even more than the motives for undertaking it.

8. Degrading Experience (page 207)

In more than 25 years of teaching, I have never agreed with my students on what to do when one of them gets an answer wrong and I inadvertently mark it as correct. If the student lets me know, I praise him for his honesty, then take off the points I should have in the first place. Is this right, or should I let him keep the points because the mistake was mine?

—SANDRA MARTIN, RAMSEY, NEW JERSEY

What does it mean to own an idea? This question challenged the nature of originality and of intellectual property.

9. Art of the Matter (page 100)

I am an artist, and I support my family by painting reproductions of the work of more famous artists, a common practice in the tradition of painting. However, some say this is akin to stealing the famous artists' work. Is it right for a wealthy client to commission a copy of a work available in the original? Is it wrong for an artist to accept the job?

—RAY ABEYTA, BROOKLYN, NEW YORK

When may one's obligations to the larger society—if, indeed, there are any—inhibit one's actions?

10. Hat in Hand (page 135)

I often ride my motorcycle without a helmet. Our state helmet law basically applies to motorcycle riders under 18. I figure I'm not putting anyone but myself at risk. My friends say that this is tantamount to suicide. But isn't it just one of many risks all of us take every day?

—KELLY KREBS, MINNEAPOLIS